SPANISH VERBPACK

JOHN BUTT

OXFORD
UNIVERSITY PRESS

OXFORD
UNIVERSITY PRESS

Great Clarendon Street, Oxford OX2 6DP

Oxford University Press is a department of the University of Oxford.
It furthers the University's objective of excellence in research, scholarship,
and education by publishing worldwide in

Oxford New York

Auckland Cape Town Dar es Salaam Hong Kong Karachi Kuala Lumpur
Madrid Melbourne Mexico City Nairobi New Delhi Shanghai
Taipei Toronto

With offices in

Argentina Austria Brazil Chile Czech Republic France Greece Guatemala
Hungary Italy Japan Poland Poland Portugal Singapore South Korea Switzerland
Thailand Turkey Ukraine Vietnam

Oxford is a registered trade mark of Oxford University Press
in the UK and in certain other countries

Published in the United States
by Oxford University Press Inc., New York

First published as *Spanish Verbs* 1997
First published as *Spanish Verbpack* 2000

British Library Cataloguing in Publication Data

Data available

Library of Congress Cataloging in Publication Data

Data available

ISBN-13: 978-0-19-860340-5

7

Printed in Great Britain by
Clays Ltd, Bungay, Suffolk

CONTENTS

HOW TO USE THIS BOOK

This book is designed as a pocket or handbag reference guide to the Spanish verb system.

It shows 92 common verbs, regular and irregular, fully conjugated in their most important tenses and moods. These verbs, shown on pp.185–276, represent the various patterns that all the other verbs in Spanish conform to. If one knows the rules for conjugating these model verbs, one can conjugate all the other verbs listed in the Verb Directory on pp.1–179.

Books like this one tend to discourage beginners: the number of forms for each verb and the number of verbs listed are initially dismaying. But the picture is in fact a good deal simpler than it seems, and the following notes are designed to make the task of learning Spanish verbs easier.

THE SPANISH VERB SYSTEM

What you need to know

For nearly all the verbs in the language the following forms are in everyday use:[1]

The Infinitive, e.g. **hablar** *to speak* (verb no. 41[2])

The Past Participle, e.g. **hablado** *spoken*

The Gerund, e.g. **hablando** *speaking*

Four Imperative forms, e.g.

habla (familiar singular) **hablad**[3] (familiar plural) *speak!*

hable (polite singular) **hablen** (polite plural in Spain, polite or familiar in Latin America)

Eight Indicative tenses:

The Present, e.g. **hablo** *I speak*

The Preterit,[4] e.g. **hablé** *I spoke*

The Imperfect, e.g. **hablaba** *I was speaking*

---

[1] The anterior preterit (**hube hablabo**, etc.) and the future subjunctive (**hablare, hablares**, etc.) are not now used in everyday Spanish and are not discussed in this book.

[2] The numbers in brackets refer to the position of the model in the tables on pp.185–276.

[3] Imperative forms ending in **-d** are not used in Latin America where they are replaced by the imperative forms ending in **-n**.

[4] The American spelling 'preterit' (British 'preterite') is used throughout this book.

The Perfect, e.g. **he hablado** *I have spoken/I spoke*

The Future, e.g. **hablaré** *I will speak*

The Conditional, e.g. **hablaría** *I would speak*

The Pluperfect, e.g. **había hablado** *I had spoken*

The Conditional Perfect, e.g. **habría** or **hubiera hablado** *I would have spoken*

Four Subjunctive tenses (no exact English translation):

The Present Subjunctive, e.g. **hable**

The Imperfect Subjunctive, e.g. **hablara** or **hablase**

The Perfect Subjunctive, e.g. **haya hablado**

The Pluperfect Subjunctive, e.g. **hubiera** or **hubiese hablado**.

All of the above (except the gerund, past participle and imperative) can also appear in the continuous form, e.g. **estar hablando** *to be speaking*, **estoy hablando** *I'm speaking*, **habría estado hablando** *I/he/she would have been speaking*, etc.

As far as regular verbs are concerned, one simply adds the correct endings of the forms listed to the stem left after removing the **-ar**, **-er**, or **-ir** of the infinitive. The simple spelling rules listed on p.xv must be applied if necessary. A few otherwise regular verbs have irregular past participles. These are mentioned in the Verb Directory.

These remarks also apply to most radical changing verbs (see below): only the present indicative, singular familiar imperative, and present subjunctive show irregularities.

In the case of irregular verbs (listed on p.xiv) and also radical changing verbs that are conjugated like **sentir** (no. 78), **pedir** (no. 54), **reír** (no. 68), and **dormir** (no. 34), one needs only to memorize the following forms since all the others can be predicted from them:

The Present Indicative

The Preterit

The Imperfect (but only three verbs are irregular)

The Present Subjunctive

The second-person singular Imperative (only a few verbs are irregular)

The Past Participle (in the case of a few verbs)

The Future (only a few verbs are irregular)

Regular verbs

Regular verbs are divided into three types of conjugations, according to whether their infinitive ends in **-ar**, **-er**, or **-ir**.

The great majority of Spanish verbs are regular **-ar** verbs (about 70% of the verbs listed in the Directory belong to this type), so one should begin by thoroughly learning the conjugation of **hablar** *to speak* (no. 41). The three regular verbs **pagar** (no. 52), **realizar** (no. 65), and **sacar** (no. 74) should be studied next. These conjugate in exactly the same way as **hablar**, but they are affected by the spelling changes listed on p. xv.

The forms of the regular -**er** and -**ir** verbs (exemplified by **comer**, no. 22, and **vivir**, no. 89) can be learned simultaneously, since they are almost identical.

Once these forms are thoroughly memorized, the regular verbs **proteger** (no. 62) and **vencer** (no. 86) should be studied: they are affected by the spelling changes listed on p. xv. However, most verbs ending in -**cer** are in fact slightly irregular and are conjugated like **parecer** (no. 53), and since this type includes a large number of verbs it should be memorized now (only the forms containing -**zc** are irregular).

Verbs like **tañer** (no. 81), **gruñir** (no. 39), and **bullir** (no. 15) should also be noted since they are affected by spelling changes, although this type is not particularly common.

When (and only when) the forms listed above have been thoroughly memorized, students should learn the irregular verbs and radical changing verbs.

Radical changing verbs

These are only partly irregular. Their endings are always regular and correspond to the -**ar**, -**er**, and -**ir** endings of regular verbs, according to the ending of the infinitive. However, there are certain changes that affect one of the vowels in the verb. The only forms affected are the **tú** and **usted/ustedes** imperative, the present indicative and present subjunctive, and, in the case of a few verbs, the preterit and the imperfect subjunctive (but the latter can always be deduced from the former).

The main types of radical changing verb are exemplified by the following model verbs, listed in order of frequency of occurrence in the Directory:

● **Type 1** (121 examples in the Verb Directory)
cerrar (no. 18) *to shut*
comenzar (no. 21, spelling changes) *to start*
negar (no. 49, spelling changes) *to deny*
errar (no. 36, spelling changes) *to wander*

● **Type 2** (71 examples)
contar (no. 24) *to tell, to count*
almorzar (no. 6, spelling changes) *to have lunch*
colgar (no. 20, spelling changes) *to hang up*

● **Type 3** (48 examples)
pedir (no. 54) *to ask for*

reír (no. 68, accents and no second consonant) *to laugh*

regir (no. 66, spelling changes) *to rule*

reñir (no. 69, spelling changes) *to scold*

seguir (no. 77, spelling changes) *to follow*

● **Type 4** (43 examples)

sentir (no. 78) *to feel*

erguir (no. 35, spelling changes) *to prick up (ears)*

● **Type 5** (27 examples)

perder (no. 55) *to lose*

● **Type 6** (22 examples)

mover (no. 48) *to move*

cocer (no. 19, spelling changes) *to cook*

● **Type 7** (4 examples, including **dormirse** and **morirse**)

dormir (no. 34) *to sleep*

● **Type 8** (4 examples)

discernir (no. 32) *to discern*

● **Type 9** (2 examples)

adquirir (no. 3) *to acquire*

● **Type 10** (1 example)

jugar (no. 44, spelling changes) *to play*

Irregular verbs

There are twenty-two common Spanish irregular verbs, although some of them form compound verbs, conjugated like their simple form, e.g. **componer** *to compose* is conjugated like **poner** (no. 58). These are:

andar (no. 7) *to walk*	**poner** (no. 58) *to put*
caber (no. 16) *to fit into*	**producir** (no. 60) *to produce*[5]
caer (no. 17) *to fall*	**querer** (no. 64) *to want*
dar (no. 27) *to give*	**saber** (no. 73) *to know*
decir (no. 28) *to say*	**salir** (no. 75) *to go out*
estar (no. 38) *to be*	**ser** (no. 79) *to be*
haber (no. 40) (aux.)	**tener** (no. 82) *to have*
hacer (no. 42) *to do*	**traer** (no. 83) *to bring*
ir (no. 43) *to go*	**valer** (no. 85) *to be worth*
oír (no. 50) *to hear*	**venir** (no. 87) *to come*
poder (no. 57) *to be able*	**ver** (no. 88) *to see*

As the meanings show, all these verbs are in frequent use, so they must be learned thoroughly.

For a detailed discussion of the uses of the Spanish tenses, see the *Oxford Minireference Spanish Grammar*.

---

[5] There are several verbs conjugated like **producir**. They are listed with **producir** (no. 60)

Spelling changes

Certain spelling changes affect all verbs, regular and irregular. The most common are:

- Infinitive ends in **-car**: **c** > **qu** before **e** or **i**. See **sacar** (no. 74).
- Infinitive ends in **-gar**: **g** > **gu** before **e** or **i**. See **pagar** (no. 52).
- Infinitive ends in **-zar**: **z** > **c** before **e** or **i**. See **realizar** (no. 65).
- Infinitive ends in **-ger** or **-gir**: **g** > **j** before **o** or **a**. See **proteger** (no. 62) and **rugir** (no. 72).
- Infinitive ends in **-guir**: the **u** disappears before **o** or **a**. See **distinguir** (no. 33).
- Infinitive ends in **-guar**: dieresis needed on **u** before **e**. See **averiguar** (no.13).
- Infinitive ends in **-cer**: a few verbs are conjugated like **vencer** (no. 86) i.e. **c** > **z** before **a** or **o**: these include **ejercer** *to exercise*, **convencer** *to convince*, **mecer** *to rock/sway* and a few others. **Escocer** *to sting* and **torcer** *to twist* are conjugated like **cocer** *to cook* (no. 19).   The rest, which are the vast majority, are conjugated like **parecer** (no. 53) and show a slight irregularity: **c** > **zc** before **a**, or **o**.
- Infinitive ends in vowel + **-er** or vowel + **-ir**: a *y* sound is written **y** between vowels. See

poseer (no. 59) and **construir** (no. 23) for examples.

- Infinitive ends in **-cir**. Check verb in list.
- Infinitive ends in **-ñer**, **-ñir**, or **-llir**: diphthong **ió** in preterit > **ó**; **ie** in imperfect subjunctive > **e**. See **tañer** (no. 81), **gruñir** (no. 39), and **bullir** (no. 15).
- Irregular verbs whose preterit stem ends in **-j**: in these verbs, e.g. **decir** (no. 28), **traer** (no. 83) and verbs like **producir** (no. 60) (but not in regular verbs like **tejer** to weave/(Lat. Am.) to knit) the third-person plural of the preterit ends in **-eron**, not **-ieron**, and the imperfect subjunctive endings begin with **-e**, not **-ie**, e.g. **dijeron**, **dijera**, **dijese**, etc.

Transitive and intransitive verbs

Spanish generally[6] distinguishes clearly between transitive and intransitive verbs, whereas English often does not. Transitive verbs can (and in Spanish usually must) have a direct object: **la vi** *I saw **her***, **escribieron una carta** *they wrote **a letter***. Intransitive verbs cannot have a direct object: **murió** *he/she died*, **me río** *I laugh*. One cannot die or laugh something or someone.

---

[6] But not always, cf. **aumentar**, which means *to increase* both in the sense of *to make larger* and *to get larger*, or **dormir**, which can mean either *to sleep* or *to put to sleep*.

It is important to keep the distinction clear in Spanish. The Spanish verb **casar** is transitive: it means *to marry* but only in the sense of *to marry someone off to someone else*: **casó a su hija con un abogado rico** *he married his daughter off to a rich lawyer.* **Casarse** is intransitive and must be used for the more normal meaning of the English *to marry*, i.e. *to get married.* If the forms are confused, incomprehensible Spanish will result: '**caso mañana**' means something like '*tomorrow I'm making someone marry*'; the correct form is **me caso mañana** *I'm getting married tomorrow.* For this reason, the words 'transitive' or 'intransitive' are included in the Directory whenever the English translation does not make the difference clear.

'Reflexive' (i.e. **pronominal**) verbs

Pronominal verbs are those whose infinitive is shown in the Verb Directory as ending in **-se**: **arrepentir*se*** *to repent*, **ir*se*** *to go away*, etc. These verbs are traditionally called 'reflexive' verbs, but this name is inaccurate and misleading.

These verbs are conjugated according to the pattern indicated by the model verb in brackets, but the following pronouns are required (present indicative of **ir*se*** *to go away*, no. 43 as an example):

me **voy**	*I'm going away*
te **vas**	*you're going away*
se **va**	*he's/she's going away*
	you (**usted**) *are going away*
nos **vamos**	*we're going away*
os **vais**	*you're going away*[7]
se **van**	*they're going away*
	you (**ustedes**) *are going away*

Such verbs are very common in Spanish and they have a number of different uses, some of which are rather difficult to classify. In most, but not all cases, the pronominal form shows that the verb is intransitive, cf. **acostar** *to put someone to bed* and **acostarse** *to go to bed*. But in some cases (e.g. **arrepentirse** *to repent*) the verb has no non-pronominal counterpart, and in the case of many verbs, especially common verbs of motion, the difference is one of nuance, cf. **salir** *to leave* and **salirse** which means *to walk out* or *to leak*. In a few cases, e.g. **morir** and **morirse** *to die*, no English translation can make the difference in meaning completely clear. For fuller details on this point and on the other uses of pronominal verbs, see the *Oxford Minireference Spanish Grammar*.

---

[7] Spain only.

VERB DIRECTORY

The Verb Directory shows in alphabetical order

- All irregular and radical changing verbs in current use
- Common regular verbs

You are given:

- the infinitive and its meaning
- the preposition used if the verb is usually followed by a preposition
- the most common translation(s) of the verb
- an indication of whether the verb is regular. If the word **Reg.** is missing, the verb is irregular in some way.
- in some cases, information as to whether the verb is transitive or intransitive
- the model verb on whose pattern the verb is conjugated
- the number of the model verb in the verb tables on pp. 185–276

Criteria for inclusion

The Directory contains the immense majority of verbs used in plain prose and ordinary conversation. Slang terms are omitted, as are many familiar or popular terms currently used in

Spain and Latin America. Forms used exclusively in Latin America are marked Lat. Am.

For the sake of completion a number of verbs appear that are usually confined to literary usage, and one or two archaic verbs are included (marked 'archaic'). In some cases two or more verbs exist with the same meaning, e.g. **balbucir** and **balbucear** *to stutter*: in such cases the reader is referred to the most commonly used form (in this case **balbucear**). When a form is very rare or literary the equals sign points to the verb of the same meaning that is most commonly used, e.g. **desposarse** = **casarse**.

abalanzar *to balance; to hurl* Reg.	realizar	65
abalanzarse sobre *to rush upon; to lunge at* Reg.	realizar	65
abanderar *to register (a ship); to champion (a cause)* Reg.	hablar	41
abandonar *to abandon* Reg.	hablar	41
abanicar *to fan* Reg.	sacar	74
abaniquear = **abanicar** Reg.	hablar	41
abaratar *to reduce the price of* Reg.	hablar	41
abarcar *to include, cover* Reg.	sacar	74
abarquillar *to wrinkle, curl* (transitive) Reg.	hablar	41
abarquillarse *to become curled, wrinkled* Reg.	hablar	41
abarrotar *to jam full; to overfill* Reg.	hablar	41
abastecer *to supply*	parecer	53
abatir *to knock down; to depress* Reg.	vivir	89
abatirse por *to get depressed about* Reg.	vivir	89
abdicar en *to abdicate in favour of* Reg.	sacar	74
abigarrar *to daub* Reg.	hablar	41
abismar *to spoil completely; to ruin* Reg.	hablar	41
abjurar de *to renounce; to recant* Reg.	hablar	41
ablandar *to make soft* Reg.	hablar	41
ablandarse *to grow soft* Reg.	hablar	41
abnegarse *to go without*	negar	49
abocarse hacia *to head towards* Reg.	sacar	74
abocetar *to sketch* Reg.	hablar	41
abochornar *to make embarrassed* Reg.	hablar	41
abochornarse *to feel embarrassed; to blush* Reg.	hablar	41
abofetear *to slap* Reg.	hablar	41
abogar por *to plead for* (i.e. *to defend*) Reg.	pagar	52
abolir *to abolish*	abolir	1
abollar *to dent; to knock hard* Reg.	hablar	41
abollarse *to become dented* Reg.	hablar	41

abominar de *to abominate* Reg.	hablar	41
abonar *to pay for; to vouch for; to deposit (money); to fertilize* Reg.	hablar	41
abonarse a *to subscribe to; to take out a season ticket for* Reg.	hablar	41
abordar *to approach; to deal with a problem; to accost* Reg.	hablar	41
aborrascarse *to get stormy* Reg.	sacar	74
aborrecer *to loathe*	parecer	53
abortar *to abort; to have a miscarriage* Reg.	hablar	41
abotagarse *to become bloated* Reg.	pagar	52
abotargarse = **abotagarse** Reg.	pagar	52
abotonar *to button* Reg.	hablar	41
abrasar *to burn, scorch* (transitive) Reg.	hablar	41
abrasarse *to burn, scorch* (intransitive) Reg.	hablar	41
abrazar *to hug; to embrace* Reg.	realizar	65
abrevar *to water (cattle)* Reg.	hablar	41
abreviar *to abbreviate* Reg.	hablar	41
abrigar *to shelter; to cherish (an idea, etc.)* Reg.	pagar	52
abrigarse de *to shelter from* Reg.	pagar	52
abrillantar *to polish; to make shiny* Reg.	hablar	41
abrir *to open; to unlock*	abrir	2
abrochar *to fasten* (e.g. *a belt*); *to button up* Reg.	hablar	41
abrogar *to abrogate; to repeal* Reg.	pagar	52
abrumar *to overwhelm; to oppress* Reg.	hablar	41
absolver *to absolve*	volver	90
absorber *to absorb; to take up (energies, time)* Reg.	comer	22
abstenerse de *to abstain from*	tener	82
abstraer *to abstract*	traer	83
abstraerse *to be lost in thought*	traer	83
abuchear *to boo* Reg.	hablar	41

abultar *to bulge; to inflate (figures)*
  Reg.   hablar   41
abundar en *to abound in* Reg.   hablar   41
aburguesarse *to become bourgeois/*
  middle-class Reg.   hablar   41
aburrir *to bore* Reg.   vivir   89
aburrirse de *to get bored with* Reg.   vivir   89
abusar *to misuse* Reg.   hablar   41
acabar *to end* (transitive and
  intransitive); **a. de** + infinitive *to*
  have just done something Reg.   hablar   41
acabarse *to come to an end; to run out*
  (supplies) Reg.   hablar   41
acaecer *to happen* (third person only) parecer   53
acalambrarse *to get cramp (muscles)*
  Reg.   hablar   41
acallar *to silence (criticisms, etc.)* Reg. hablar   41
acalorar *to make heated; to inflame*
  (passions) Reg.   hablar   41
acalorarse *to get worked up* Reg.   hablar   41
acampar *to camp* Reg.   hablar   41
acanalar *to groove* Reg.   hablar   41
acaparar *to stockpile, hoard; to take up*
  all of (time, interest, etc.) Reg.   hablar   41
acaramelar *to caramelize* Reg.   hablar   41
acardenalar *to make black and blue*
  Reg.   hablar   41
acardenalarse *to become black and blue*
  Reg.   realizar   65
acariciar *to caress* Reg.   hablar   41
acarrear *to give rise to (a problem,*
  difficulty); to lug, carry along Reg. hablar   41
acartonarse *to become wizened* Reg.   hablar   41
acatar *to comply with* Reg.   hablar   41
acatarrarse *to catch a cold* Reg.   hablar   41
acaudalar *to hoard (money)* Reg.   hablar   41

acaudillar *to lead (*i.e. *to be the leader
of)* Reg.   hablar   41
acceder a *to accede to; to gain
admission to* Reg.   comer   22
accidentarse *to have an accident* Reg.   hablar   41
accionar *to operate (a device)* Reg.   hablar   41
acechar *to lie in wait for; to spy on* Reg.   hablar   41
aceitar *to oil* Reg.   hablar   41
acelerar *to accelerate* Reg.   hablar   41
acendrar *to refine* Reg.   hablar   41
acensuar *to tax* (= **gravar**, **tasar**)   continuar   25
acentuar *to accentuate; to stress*   continuar   25
aceptar *to accept* Reg.   hablar   41
acercar *to bring near or nearer* Reg.   sacar   74
acercarse a *to approach* Reg.   sacar   74
acerrojar *to bolt (*i.e. *lock)* Reg.   hablar   41
acertar *to hit upon, guess right;* **acertar
con** *to get right;* **a. a** + infinitive *to
manage to*   cerrar   18
acezar *to gasp; to pant* (= **jadear**) Reg.   realizar   65
achacar a *to attribute to* Reg.   sacar   74
achaflanar *to bevel, chamfer* Reg.   hablar   41
achantar *to intimidate* Reg.   hablar   41
achantarse *to back down from (a
confrontation)* Reg.   hablar   41
achicar *to make smaller; to take away
one's confidence* Reg.   sacar   74
achicarse *to be intimidated; to lack
courage* Reg.   sacar   74
achicharrar *to crisp; to scorch*
(transitive) Reg.   hablar   41
achicharrarse *to be burnt to a cinder*
Reg.   hablar   41
achisparse *to get tipsy* Reg.   hablar   41
achocharse *to become 'gaga', senile*
Reg.   hablar   41
acholarse *to be abashed* Reg.   hablar   41

achuchar *to set (dogs, etc.) upon; to unleash (dogs)* Reg.   hablar   41

acibarar *to embitter* (= **amargar**) Reg.   hablar   41

acicalarse *to get dressed up; to smarten oneself up* Reg.   hablar   41

acidificar *to acidify* Reg.   sacar   74

aclamar *to acclaim* Reg.   hablar   41

aclarar *to brighten; to make clear; to clarify* Reg.   hablar   41

aclararse *to see the light; to sort one's ideas out* Reg.   hablar   41

aclimatar *to acclimatize* Reg.   hablar   41

aclimatarse *to become acclimatized* Reg.   hablar   41

acobardar *to intimidate* Reg.   hablar   41

acobardarse ante *to lose one's nerve at* Reg.   hablar   41

acocear *to kick (said of horses)* Reg.   hablar   41

acodar *to bend into an elbow* Reg.   hablar   41

acoger *to welcome; to take in (a guest, etc.)* Reg.   proteger   62

acogerse a *to have recourse to; to seek refuge in* Reg.   proteger   62

acogotar *to kill (an animal by breaking its neck)* Reg.   hablar   41

acolchar *to quilt* Reg.   hablar   41

acolchonar = **acolchar** Reg.   hablar   41

acometer *to attack* Reg.   comer   22

acomodar *to make someone comfortable;* **a. algo a algo** *to adapt something to something* Reg.   hablar   41

acomodarse *to make oneself comfortable; to settle in* Reg.   hablar   41

acompañar *to accompany* Reg.   hablar   41

acompasar *to keep time (rhythm); to keep step* Reg.   hablar   41

acomplejar *to give someone a complex*
Reg.   hablar   41
acomplejarse *to get a complex* Reg.   hablar   41
acomunarse *to join forces* Reg.   hablar   41
acondicionar *to condition* Reg.   hablar   41
acongojar *to distress; to grieve* Reg.   hablar   41
aconsejar *to advise* Reg.   hablar   41
aconsejarse de *to seek advice from* Reg.   hablar   41
acontecer *to happen* (3rd-person only)   parecer   53
acopiar *to gather together* (transitive)
Reg.   hablar   41
acoplar *to couple; to fit together*
(transitive) Reg.   hablar   41
acoplarse a *to adapt oneself to* Reg.   hablar   41
acoquinar *to intimidate* Reg.   hablar   41
acorazar *to armor/(Brit.) armour-plate*
Reg.   realizar   65
acorazarse *to protect oneself; to become*
hardened Reg.   realizar   65
acordar *to agree on*   contar   24
acordarse de *to remember*   contar   24
acordonar *to cordon off; to lace (shoes)*
Reg.   hablar   41
acorralar *to corner (= to force into a*
corner) Reg.   hablar   41
acornar *to butt; to gore*   contar   24
acornear = **acornar** Reg.   hablar   41
acortar *to cut short (meeting, etc.)* Reg.   hablar   41
acosar *to harass* Reg.   hablar   41
acostar *to put to bed*   contar   24
acostarse *to lie down; to go to bed*   contar   24
acostumbrar a *to accustom to;*
  acostumbra a hacerlo *he habitually*
  does it Reg.   hablar   41
acostumbrarse a *to get used to* Reg.   hablar   41
acotar *to mark off; to fence in; to*
annotate Reg.   hablar   41

acrecentar *to increase* (transitive)	cerrar	18
acrecentarse *to increase* (intransitive)	cerrar	18
acrecer *to increase* (transitive)	parecer	53
acreditar *to accredit; to authorize; to validate* Reg.	hablar	41
acreditarse *to prove one's value* Reg.	hablar	41
acribillar a *to riddle with (e.g. bullets)* Reg.	hablar	41
acriminar *to incriminate* Reg.	hablar	41
acriminarse *to be incriminated* Reg.	hablar	41
acriollarse *to acquire Latin-American ways* Reg.	hablar	41
acrisolar *to refine (a metal)* Reg.	hablar	41
acristalar *to glaze* Reg.	hablar	41
activar *to give an impetus to; to stimulate* Reg.	hablar	41
activarse *to go off (bells, alarms)* Reg.	hablar	41
actualizar *to bring up to date* Reg.	realizar	65
actualizarse *to get up to date* Reg.	realizar	65
actuar *to act (in all senses of the word)*	continuar	25
acuartelar *to quarter (troops); to billet* Reg.	hablar	41
acuatizar = **amarizar** Reg.	realizar	65
acuchillar *to knife* Reg.	hablar	41
acuchillear = **acuchillar** Reg.	hablar	41
acuciar *to plague (e.g. with problems)* Reg.	hablar	41
acuclillarse *to squat down* Reg.	hablar	41
acudir a *to come to (an appointment, etc.)* Reg.	vivir	89
acuitar *to afflict* Reg.	hablar	41
acular *to back up (said of horses)* Reg.	hablar	41
acumular *to accumulate* (transitive) Reg.	hablar	41
acumularse *to pile up* (intransitive) Reg.	hablar	41
acunar *to rock in a cradle* Reg.	hablar	41
acuñar *to coin (money, phrases)* Reg.	hablar	41

acurrucarse *to huddle up; to squat* Reg.	sacar	74
acusar *to accuse (of a crime);* **acusar recibo** *to acknowledge receipt* Reg.	hablar	41
acusarse de *to confess to* Reg.	hablar	41
adaptar *to adapt* (transitive) Reg.	hablar	41
adaptarse a *to adapt to* (intransitive) Reg.	hablar	41
adecentar *to make decent; to tidy up* Reg.	hablar	41
adecentarse *to make oneself tidy* Reg.	hablar	41
adecuar a *to adapt to* (transitive) Reg.	hablar	41
adecuarse a *to fit in with* Reg.	hablar	41
adelantar *to move forward; to advance; to overtake* (transitive) Reg.	hablar	41
adelantarse *to go forward; to gain (clocks); to get ahead* Reg.	hablar	41
adelgazar *to lose weight* Reg.	realizar	65
adentrarse en *to penetrate; to go deeper into* Reg.	hablar	41
aderezar *to season (food); to get ready* (transitive) Reg.	realizar	65
adestrar = **adiestrar**	cerrar	18
adeudar *to owe; to debit (an account)* Reg.	hablar	41
adherir a *to glue to* (transitive)	sentir	78
adherirse a *to adhere to; to stick by (things or principles)*	sentir	78
adiestrar *to train (an animal)* Reg.	hablar	41
adivinar *to guess* Reg.	hablar	41
adjudicar *to adjudicate* Reg.	sacar	74
adjudicarse *to win (trophy, etc.)* Reg.	sacar	74
adjuntar *to enclose (a note, document)* Reg.	hablar	41
administrar *to administrate; to administer (medicine, etc.)* Reg.	hablar	41
administrarse *to handle one's own affairs* Reg.	hablar	41

admirar *to admire; to surprise* Reg.	hablar	41
admirarse de *to be surprised at* Reg.	hablar	41
admitir *to admit (*i.e. *to accept); to confess* Reg.	vivir	89
adobar *to marinade; to pickle* Reg.	hablar	41
adoctrinar *to indoctrinate* Reg.	hablar	41
adolecer de *to suffer from (illness, defects)*	parecer	53
adoptar *to adopt* Reg.	hablar	41
adoquinar *to pave* Reg.	hablar	41
adorar *to adore* Reg.	hablar	41
adormecer *to make sleepy*	parecer	53
adormecerse *to get sleepy; to get numb*	parecer	53
adormilarse *to doze* Reg.	hablar	41
adormitarse = **adormilarse** Reg.	hablar	41
adornar *to decorate* Reg.	hablar	41
adosar algo a *to lean against* (transitive)*; to attach/secure to* Reg.	hablar	41
adquirir *to acquire*	adquirir	3
adscribir a *to assign (someone) to*	escribir	37
adscribirse a *to join (an organization)*	escribir	37
aducir *to adduce; to supply (arguments, evidence)*	producir	60
adueñarse de *to take possession of; to overwhelm* Reg.	hablar	41
adujar *to coil* Reg.	hablar	41
adular *to flatter* Reg.	hablar	41
adulterar *to adulterate* Reg.	hablar	41
advertir *to notice;* **advertir de** *to warn of*	sentir	78
afamar *to make famous* Reg.	hablar	41
afanarse en/por *to strive hard to* Reg.	hablar	41
afear *to make ugly* Reg.	hablar	41
afearse *to lose one's looks* Reg.	hablar	41
afectar *to affect;* + infinitive *to pretend to* Reg.	hablar	41
afeitar *to shave* (transitive) Reg.	hablar	41
afeitarse *to shave* (intransitive) Reg.	hablar	41

afeminarse *to grow effeminate* Reg.	hablar	41
aferrar *to weigh anchor* Reg.	hablar	41
aferrarse a *to cling to* Reg.	hablar	41
afianzar *to make firm/solid; to underwrite* Reg.	realizar	65
afianzarse *to become established* Reg.	realizar	65
aficionar a *to make someone like* Reg.	hablar	41
aficionarse a *to become fond of; to get interested in* Reg.	hablar	41
afilar *to sharpen* Reg.	hablar	41
afiliar a *to sign up* (transitive) Reg.	hablar	41
or	liar	45
afiliarse a *to sign up for* (intransitive) Reg.	hablar	41
or	liar	45
afinar *to tune (motors, instruments); to sing or play in tune* Reg.	hablar	41
afinarse *to get thinner* Reg.	hablar	41
afirmar *to declare; to affirm; to strengthen (a statement)* Reg.	hablar	41
afirmarse *to assert oneself* Reg.	hablar	41
afligir *to afflict*	rugir	72
afligirse *to grieve*	rugir	72
aflojar *to slacken* (transitive) Reg.	hablar	41
aflojarse *to slacken* (intransitive) Reg.	hablar	41
aflorar *to come to the surface (water, minerals, etc.)* Reg.	hablar	41
afluir *to flow (rivers, etc.); to flock (people, crowds)*	construir	23
afrancesarse *to grow Frenchified* Reg.	hablar	41
afrentar *to affront; to insult* Reg.	hablar	41
afrontar *to confront* Reg.	hablar	41
agachar *to bow (the head)* Reg.	hablar	41
agacharse *to crouch; to squat* Reg.	hablar	41
agarrar *to grasp; to grab* Reg.	hablar	41
agarrarse *to stick (e.g. food to a saucepan);* **a. a** *to grab hold of* Reg.	hablar	41

agarrochar *to goad* Reg.	hablar	41
agarrotar *to make stiff (muscles); to garrotte* Reg.	hablar	41
agarrotarse *to grow stiff (muscles, etc.)* Reg.	hablar	41
agasajar *to shower attentions on* Reg.	hablar	41
agazaparse *to crouch down* Reg.	hablar	41
agenciar *to manage to; to manage by 'fiddling'* Reg.	hablar	41
agenciarse *to get hold of (by 'fiddling')* Reg.	hablar	41
agigantar *to make huge* Reg.	hablar	41
agigantarse *to grow huge* Reg.	hablar	41
agilizar *to expedite (formalities, etc.)* Reg.	realizar	65
agitar *to agitate; to stir; to flap* (transitive) Reg.	hablar	41
agitarse *to flap, wave* (transitive) Reg.	hablar	41
aglomerar *to agglomerate* Reg.	hablar	41
aglomerarse *to pile up; to form a crowd* Reg.	hablar	41
aglutinar *to agglutinate; to bring together in one group* Reg.	hablar	41
aglutinarse *to form one group* (intransitive) Reg.	hablar	41
agobiar *to overwhelm; to overburden* Reg.	hablar	41
agobiarse *to be overwhelmed, overburdened* Reg.	hablar	41
agolparse *to throng, crowd (*e.g. *ideas in the mind)* Reg.	hablar	41
agonizar *to be in the throes of death* Reg.	realizar	65
agorar *to predict*	agorar	4
agostar *to parch* Reg.	hablar	41
agostarse *to become parched, withered* Reg.	hablar	41

agotar *to exhaust; to use up* Reg.	hablar	41
agotarse *to become exhausted* Reg.	hablar	41
agraciar *to grace* Reg.	hablar	41
agradar *to please* Reg.	hablar	41
agradecer *to thank for*	parecer	53
agrandar *to enlarge* Reg.	hablar	41
agrandarse *to get bigger* Reg.	hablar	41
agravar *to aggravate; to make worse* Reg.	hablar	41
agravarse *to grow worse* Reg.	hablar	41
agraviar *to offend* Reg.	hablar	41
agraviarse *to be offended* Reg.	hablar	41
agredir *to attack; to assault*	abolir	1
agregar a *to add to* Reg.	pagar	52
agregarse a *to join (a group, organization)* Reg.	pagar	52
agriarse *to turn sour* Reg.	hablar	41
or	liar	45
agrietarse *to crack* (intransitive) Reg.	hablar	41
agringarse *to become like a gringo* Reg.	hablar	41
agrumar *to clot* (intransitive)*; to get lumpy* Reg.	hablar	41
agrupar *to divide into groups* Reg.	hablar	41
agruparse *to form groups* (intransitive) Reg.	hablar	41
aguantar *to tolerate; to put up with* Reg.	hablar	41
aguantarse *to restrain oneself; to bear with* Reg.	hablar	41
aguar *to spoil (e.g. parties, atmosphere); to water down*	averiguar	13
aguardar *to wait for* Reg.	hablar	41
agudizar *to make more acute; to intensify* Reg.	realizar	65
agudizarse *to grow more intense (e.g. feelings, symptoms)* Reg.	realizar	65
aguerrir *to inure, toughen (persons)*	abolir	1
aguijar *to urge on; to goad* Reg.	hablar	41

aguijonear = **aguijar** Reg.	hablar	41
agujerear *to make a hole or holes in* Reg.	hablar	41
aguzar *to sharpen;* **a. el oído** *to prick up one's ears* Reg.	realizar	65
aherrumbrarse *to get rusty* Reg.	hablar	41
ahijar *to adopt (e.g. child)*	aislar	5
ahilar *to line up; to go single file*	aislar	5
ahincar *to urge; to press,* but see **aislar** (no. 5) for accents	sacar	74
ahitarse de *to gorge on*	aislar	5
ahogar *to drown* (transitive) Reg.	pagar	52
ahogarse *to drown* (intransitive) Reg.	pagar	52
ahondar *to make deeper;* **ahondar en** *to go deeper into (a subject)* Reg.	hablar	41
ahorcar *to hang (as in executions)* Reg.	sacar	74
ahorcarse *to hang oneself* Reg.	sacar	74
ahormar *to shape, mold/(Brit.) mould* Reg.	hablar	41
ahorrar *to save; to spare* Reg.	hablar	41
ahorrarse *to spare oneself (trouble, bother, etc.)* Reg.	hablar	41
ahoyar *to dig holes in* Reg.	hablar	41
ahuchar *to stash away (money)*	aullar	11
ahuecar *to hollow out* Reg.	sacar	74
ahumar *to smoke (e.g. meat, fish)*	aullar	11
ahumarse *to get blackened with soot, smoke*	aullar	11
ahusarse *to taper* (intransitive)	aullar	11
ahuyentar *to frighten away* Reg.	hablar	41
airar *to anger*	aislar	5
airarse *to get angry*	aislar	5
airear *to air; to ventilate* Reg.	hablar	41
airearse *to get some air* Reg.	hablar	41
aislar de *to isolate from*	aislar	5
aislarse de *to cut oneself off from*	aislar	5

ajar *to make something look worn or frayed* Reg. — hablar — 41

ajarse *to become worn, rough, or frayed* Reg. — hablar — 41

ajardinar *to landscape* Reg. — hablar — 41

ajetrearse *to rush around; to be very busy* Reg. — hablar — 41

ajuiciar *to bring to one's senses* Reg. — hablar — 41

ajustar *to tighten; to adjust* Reg. — hablar — 41

ajustarse a *to become adapted to; to obey (norms, rules)* Reg. — hablar — 41

ajusticiar *to execute (= to inflict death penalty)* Reg. — hablar — 41

alabar *to praise* Reg. — hablar — 41

alabarse *to boast* Reg. — hablar — 41

alabear *to warp something* Reg. — hablar — 41

alabearse *to become warped* Reg. — hablar — 41

alambicar *to distill/(Brit.) distil; to make flowery (e.g. style)* Reg. — sacar — 74

alambrar *to fence with wire* Reg. — hablar — 41

alardear de *to boast about* Reg. — hablar — 41

alargar *to lengthen; to stretch out (the hand)* Reg. — pagar — 52

alargarse *to get longer* Reg. — pagar — 52

alarmar *to alarm* Reg. — hablar — 41

alarmarse *to get alarmed* Reg. — hablar — 41

albergar *to accommodate (i.e. to house); to harbor/(Brit.) harbour (feeling, etc.)* Reg. — pagar — 52

albergarse *to take shelter* Reg. — pagar — 52

alborotar *to make a racket; to make excited, overworked* Reg. — hablar — 41

alborotarse *to get excited, overworked* Reg. — hablar — 41

alborozar *to fill with joy* Reg. — realizar — 65

alborozarse *to be overjoyed* Reg. — realizar — 65

alcanzar *to catch up with; to reach; to hit the target;* **a. a** *to manage to* Reg.   realizar   65

alcoholizarse *to become an alcoholic* Reg.   realizar   65

alear *to alloy* Reg.   hablar   41

aleccionar *to lecture (*i.e. *deliver a sermon to)* Reg.   hablar   41

alegar *to put forward (reasons, motives)* Reg.   pagar   52

alegrar *to gladden* Reg.   hablar   41

alegrarse *to be glad* Reg.   hablar   41

alejar de *to move away from* (transitive) Reg.   hablar   41

alejarse de *to move away from* (intransitive) Reg.   hablar   41

alelar *to stupefy* Reg.   hablar   41

alelarse *to become stupefied* Reg.   hablar   41

alentar *to encourage; to cheer on*   cerrar   18

alentarse *to get better; to take heart* Reg.   cerrar   18

alertar de *to alert to (danger, etc.)* Reg.   hablar   41

aletargar *to make lethargic* Reg.   pagar   52

aletargarse *to become lethargic* Reg.   pagar   52

aletear *to beat, flap (wings, fins)* (intransitive) Reg.   hablar   41

alfabetizar *to teach how to read and write* Reg.   realizar   65

alfilerar *to pin* Reg.   hablar   41

alfombrar *to carpet* Reg.   hablar   41

aliar *to ally*   liar   45

aliarse con *to become an ally of*   liar   45

alicatar *to tile* Reg.   hablar   41

alienar *to alienate* Reg.   hablar   41

alienarse *to become alienated* Reg.   hablar   41

aligerar *to lighten; to hasten (pace)* (transitive) Reg.   hablar   41

aligerarse de *to remove (cloak, etc.); to lighten* (intransitive) Reg. hablar 41

alijar *to smuggle ashore (drugs, contraband, etc.)* Reg. hablar 41

alimentar *to feed* (transitive) Reg. hablar 41

alimentarse de/con *to feed on* (intransitive) Reg. hablar 41

alindar *to mark off* Reg. hablar 41

alinear *to align* Reg. hablar 41

alinearse *to get into line* Reg. hablar 41

alisar *to smooth* Reg. hablar 41

alistarse *to enlist; to get ready* (transitive) Reg. hablar 41

aliviar *to alleviate* Reg. hablar 41

aliviarse *to ease (pain)* (intransitive) Reg. hablar 41

allanar *to raid (a house); to sweep away (problem)* Reg. hablar 41

allanarse a *to agree to accept* Reg. hablar 41

allegar *to gather together* (transitive) Reg. pagar 52

allegarse a *to approach; to take up (an opinion)* Reg. pagar 52

almacenar *to store (goods, data on disk)* Reg. hablar 41

almibarar *to preserve in syrup* Reg. hablar 41

almidonar *to starch* Reg. hablar 41

almohadillar *to pad; to cushion* Reg. hablar 41

almorzar *to eat lunch* almorzar 6

alojar *to accommodate (e.g. in hotel)* (transitive) Reg. hablar 41

alojarse *to stay, lodge (in a hotel, etc.)* Reg. hablar 41

alongar *to lengthen* (transitive) Reg. pagar 52

alquilar *to rent, hire* Reg. hablar 41

alquilarse *to be for hire* Reg. hablar 41

alquitranar *to tar* Reg. hablar 41

alterar *to alter, upset* (transitive) Reg.	hablar	41
alterarse *to get upset* Reg.	hablar	41
altercar *to argue* Reg.	sacar	74
alternar con *to alternate* (transitive); *to mix with the 'best' set (socially)* Reg.	hablar	41
alucinar *to delude; to astound;* also intransitive = *to hallucinate* Reg.	hablar	41
alucinarse *to hallucinate; to be astounded* Reg.	hablar	41
aludir a *to allude to* Reg.	vivir	89
alumbrar *to illuminate; to be bright* Reg.	hablar	41
alzar *to raise* Reg.	realizar	65
alzarse *to rise* Reg.	realizar	65
amaestrar *to train (an animal)* Reg.	hablar	41
amagar *to hint;* **a. con** + infinitive *to look as though one is going to...* Reg.	pagar	52
amainar *to shorten; to wane* Reg.	hablar	41
amalgamar *to amalgamate* Reg.	hablar	41
amamantar *to nurse (*i.e. *to breastfeed)* Reg.	hablar	41
amancebarse *to set up house together* Reg.	hablar	41
amancillar *to tarnish* Reg.	hablar	41
amanecer *to dawn;* **amanecí cansado** *I woke up tired*	parecer	53
amansar *to tame* Reg.	hablar	41
amar *to love (passionately)* Reg.	hablar	41
amarar = **amarizar** Reg.	hablar	41
amargar *to embitter* Reg.	pagar	52
amargarse *to become bitter (person)* Reg.	pagar	52
amarillear *to turn yellow* Reg.	hablar	41
amarillecer = **amarillear**	parecer	53
amarizar *to land on water (aircraft)* Reg.	realizar	65
amarrar *to moor; to tie up (boat)* Reg.	hablar	41

amartelar *to make jealous* Reg.	hablar	41
amartillar *to cock (a gun); to hammer* Reg.	hablar	41
amasar *to knead; to amass* Reg.	hablar	41
ambicionar *to earnestly desire to; to aspire to* Reg.	hablar	41
ambientar *to give atmosphere to; to set a film, story* Reg.	hablar	41
ambientarse *to adjust to one's surroundings* Reg.	hablar	41
ambular *to walk; to move about* Reg.	hablar	41
amedrentar *to frighten* Reg.	hablar	41
amedrentarse por *to get scared about* Reg.	hablar	41
amelgar *to plow/plough regularly* Reg.	pagar	52
amenazar de *to threaten with;* **a. con** + infinitive *to threaten to* Reg.	realizar	65
amenguar *to wane, diminish*	averiguar	13
amenizar *to make agreeable* Reg.	realizar	65
americanizar *to Americanize* Reg.	realizar	65
ametrallar *to machine-gun* Reg.	hablar	41
amigarse *to make friends* Reg.	pagar	52
amilanar *to intimidate* Reg.	hablar	41
amilanarse *to become intimidated* Reg.	hablar	41
aminorar *to diminish* Reg.	hablar	41
amistarse = **amigarse** Reg.	hablar	41
amnistiar *to grant amnesty*	liar	45
amoblar = **amueblar**	contar	24
amodorrar *to make drowsy* Reg.	hablar	41
amodorrarse *to become drowsy* Reg.	hablar	41
amodorrecer *to make drowsy*	parecer	53
amohecer *to mold/(Brit.) mould*	parecer	53
amohinar *to annoy*	aislar	5
amohinarse *to get annoyed, sulky*	aislar	5
amojonar *to mark off boundaries with posts* Reg.	hablar	41
amolar *to sharpen* (= **afilar**)	contar	24

amoldar *to mold/(Brit.) mould* Reg.	hablar	41
amoldarse a *to adapt to* Reg.	hablar	41
amonedar *to coin; to stamp (an imprint on)* Reg.	hablar	41
amonestar *to admonish* Reg.	hablar	41
amontonar *to pile up* (transitive) Reg.	hablar	41
amontonarse *to become piled up* Reg.	hablar	41
amoratar *to make black and blue* Reg.	hablar	41
amoratarse *to become black and blue* Reg.	hablar	41
amordazar *to muzzle; to gag* Reg.	realizar	65
amorrar *to hang one's head* Reg.	hablar	41
amorrarse *to sulk* Reg.	hablar	41
amortajar *to shroud* Reg.	hablar	41
amortecer *to tone down*	parecer	53
amortiguar *to cushion; to absorb shock*	averiguar	13
amortizar *to be write off (costs, debts)* Reg.	realizar	65
amoscarse *to become annoyed, huffy* Reg.	sacar	74
amotinar *to incite to riot or mutiny* Reg.	hablar	41
amotinarse *to rebel, riot* Reg.	hablar	41
amparar de *to protect from* Reg.	hablar	41
ampararse en *to seek protection in/with* Reg.	hablar	41
ampliar *to expand, extend*	liar	45
amplificar *to amplify (sound, etc.)* Reg.	sacar	74
ampollar *to make blistered* Reg.	hablar	41
ampollarse *to get blistered; to blister* Reg.	hablar	41
amputar *to amputate* Reg.	hablar	41
amueblar *to furnish* Reg.	hablar	41
amunicionar *to supply with ammunition* Reg.	hablar	41
amurallar *to wall* Reg.	hablar	41
amusgar *to throw back the ears (said of animals); to squint to see better* Reg.	pagar	52

anadear *to waddle like a duck* Reg.	hablar	41
analizar *to analyze* Reg.	realizar	65
analizarse *to undergo psychoanalysis, be analyzed* Reg.	realizar	65
anarquizar *to spread anarchy* Reg.	realizar	65
anarquizarse *to become anarchic* Reg.	realizar	65
anatematizar *to anathematize* Reg.	realizar	65
anatomizar *to anatomize* Reg.	realizar	65
anchar *to widen* Reg.	hablar	41
anclar *to anchor* Reg.	hablar	41
ancorar *to anchor* Reg.	hablar	41
andar *to walk; to go; to run (e.g. clocks, motors)*	andar	7
aneblarse *to cloud up, grow misty*	cerrar	18
anegar *to flood* Reg.	pagar	52
anegarse *to become flooded* Reg.	pagar	52
anestesiar *to anesthetize* Reg.	hablar	41
anexar *to annex* Reg.	hablar	41
anglicizar *to Anglicize* Reg.	realizar	65
angostar *to narrow* Reg.	hablar	41
angustiar *to distress* Reg.	hablar	41
angustiarse por *to get distressed about* Reg.	hablar	41
anhelar *to desire eagerly; to yearn for* Reg.	hablar	41
anidar *to nest* Reg.	hablar	41
anillar *to fit a ring on (animals, pistons)* Reg.	hablar	41
animar a *to encourage to* Reg.	hablar	41
animarse *to be encouraged; to cheer up; to become more lively* Reg.	hablar	41
aniquilar *to annihilate* Reg.	hablar	41
anochecer *to grow dark (day)*	parecer	53
anonadar *to overwhelm; to leave dumbfounded* Reg.	hablar	41
anotar *to note down; to enrol (e.g. for a course) (transitive)* Reg.	hablar	41

anquilosarse *to become stiff (joints, etc.)* Reg.	hablar	41
ansiar *to long for; to yearn to*	liar	45
anteceder *to precede* Reg.	comer	22
antedatar *to antedate; to backdate* Reg.	hablar	41
antedecir *to predict* (usu. **predecir**)	decir	28
antepagar *to pay in advance* Reg.	pagar	52
anteponer a *to put before; to prefer*	poner	58
anticipar *to bring something forward in time; to advance (information, etc.)* Reg.	hablar	41
anticiparse a *to act or happen before; to jump ahead of* Reg.	hablar	41
anticuar (often conjugated like **continuar**) *to antiquate* Reg.	hablar	41
anticuarse (often conjugated like **continuar**) *to become antiquated* Reg.	hablar	41
antiguarse *to attain seniority*	averiguar	13
antipatizar *to arouse a strong dislike* Reg.	realizar	65
antojarse : se me antoja... *I feel like...; it seems to me...* Reg.	hablar	41
anublar *to cloud; to obscure* Reg.	hablar	41
anublarse *to become cloudy* Reg.	hablar	41
anudar *to knot; to tie* Reg.	hablar	41
anular *to annul; to cancel* Reg.	hablar	41
anunciar *to announce; to advertise* Reg.	hablar	41
anunciarse *to promise to be (e.g. fruitful, problematic)* Reg.	hablar	41
añadir *to add* Reg.	vivir	89
añejar *to age (e.g. wine)* (transitive)	hablar	41
añilar *to use bluing (on clothes)* Reg.	hablar	41
añorar *to long for* Reg.	hablar	41
aojar *to cast the evil eye* Reg.	hablar	41
apabullar *to crush; to overwhelm* Reg.	hablar	41

apacentar *to pasture*	cerrar	18
apacentarse de *to feed on*	cerrar	18
apaciguar *to pacify*	averiguar	13
apaciguarse *to calm down*	averiguar	13
apachurrar *to crush* Reg.	hablar	41
apadrinar *to act as a godfather; to be best man; to back* Reg.	hablar	41
apagar *to put out; to extinguish; to turn off* Reg.	pagar	52
apagarse *to go out (lights, etc.); to fade away* Reg.	pagar	52
apalabrar *to speak for; to reserve* Reg.	hablar	41
apalabrarse para + infinitive *to agree to do* Reg.	hablar	41
apalancar *to jack; to lever up* Reg.	sacar	74
apalancarse en *to make oneself comfortable in* Reg.	sacar	74
apalear *to beat (with a stick)* Reg.	hablar	41
apandillarse *to band together* Reg.	hablar	41
apantanar *to make swampy* Reg.	hablar	41
apantanarse *to get swampy; to get stuck in the mud* Reg.	hablar	41
apañar *to rig (elections, etc.)* Reg.	hablar	41
apañarse con *to manage with, get by on; me las apaño I get by* Reg.	hablar	41
aparcar *to park* Reg.	sacar	74
aparear *to make even; to pair; to mate* (transitive) Reg.	hablar	41
aparearse *to mate* (intransitive) Reg.	hablar	41
aparecer *to appear*	parecer	53
aparecerse *to appear (ghosts, visions, etc.)*	parecer	53
aparejar *to prepare (e.g. boats); to harness* Reg.	hablar	41
aparentar *to look to be; to feign* Reg.	hablar	41
apartar *to separate* Reg.	hablar	41

apartarse *to move further away/to one side;* **a. de** *to drift off (the subject, etc.)* Reg.	hablar	41
apasionar *to arouse passion (in someone)* Reg.	hablar	41
apasionarse por *to become impassioned, wild about* Reg.	hablar	41
apayasarse *to clown around* Reg.	hablar	41
apear *to help someone alight (e.g. from a vehicle)* Reg.	hablar	41
apearse de *to get off; to get out of (vehicle)* Reg.	hablar	41
apechugar con *to put up with; to grin and bear it* Reg.	pagar	52
apedazar *to mend; to patch; to tear to pieces* Reg.	realizar	65
apedrear *to stone, pelt with stones* Reg.	hablar	41
apegarse a *to become attached to; to grow fond of* Reg.	pagar	52
apelar de or **contra** *to appeal against;* **a. a** *to have recourse to* Reg.	hablar	41
apellidar *to give someone a surname* Reg.	hablar	41
apellidarse : **se apellida González** *his surname's González* Reg.	hablar	41
apelmazarse *to squeeze together; to squeeze into one* Reg.	realizar	65
apelotonar *to bunch together; to pile up; to roll (something) into a ball* Reg.	hablar	41
apelotonarse *to roll (oneself) up into a ball; to crowd together* Reg.	hablar	41
apenar *to cause sorrow; to fill (someone) with grief* Reg.	hablar	41
apenarse de/por *to grieve over* Reg.	hablar	41
aperar *to repair* Reg.	hablar	41
apercibir *to warn* Reg.	vivir	89
apercibirse de *to notice* Reg.	hablar	41

apercollar *to grab by the neck* (archaic)	contar	24
apergaminarse *to become withered like parchment* Reg.	hablar	41
apersogar *to tether* Reg.	pagar	52
apersonarse *to appear in person; to show up (somewhere)* Reg.	hablar	41
aperturar *to open (*e.g. *exhibition, conference)* Reg.	hablar	41
apesadumbrar *to fill with grief; to make sad* Reg.	hablar	41
apesadumbrarse *to grieve* Reg.	hablar	41
apestar *to stink* Reg.	hablar	41
apetecer (usually third person only): **no me apetece** *I don't feel like it*	parecer	53
apiadar *to move to pity* Reg.	hablar	41
apiadarse de *to have pity on* Reg.	hablar	41
apicararse *to become a rascal; to turn into a ne'er-do-well* Reg.	hablar	41
apilar *to pile up, heap up* Reg.	hablar	41
apiñar *to squeeze together; to pack (things/people) together* Reg.	hablar	41
apiñarse *to be crowded together; to squeeze together* Reg.	hablar	41
apisonar *to roll with a roller; to flatten* Reg.	hablar	41
aplacar *to placate; to satisfy* Reg.	sacar	74
aplanar *to level, flatten; to astound* Reg.	hablar	41
aplanarse *to cave in; to become discouraged, give up* Reg.	hablar	41
aplastar *to smash, flatten; to leave (someone) speechless* Reg.	hablar	41
aplastarse *to flatten oneself (*e.g. *against a wall)* Reg.	hablar	41
aplaudir *to applaud, clap* Reg.	vivir	89
aplazar *to postpone* Reg.	realizar	65
aplicar a *to apply (match, flame) to; to assign to* Reg.	sacar	74

aplicarse a *to apply oneself to; to devote oneself to* Reg.	sacar	74
aplomar *to plumb; to make straight with a plumb-line* Reg.	hablar	41
aplomarse *to collapse* Reg.	hablar	41
apocar *to lessen; to humiliate; to humble* Reg.	sacar	74
apocarse *to feel humiliated; to feel small* Reg.	sacar	74
apocopar *to apocopate* Reg.	hablar	41
apodar *to nickname* Reg.	hablar	41
apoderar *to give legal powers to; to empower* Reg.	hablar	41
apoderarse de *to take possession of* Reg.	hablar	41
apolillarse *to become moth-eaten* Reg.	hablar	41
apologizar *to praise; to defend* Reg.	realizar	65
apoltronarse *to sprawl in a chair; to become lazy* Reg.	hablar	41
aporrear *to club (*i.e. *to hit with a club)* Reg.	hablar	41
aportar a *to contribute to* Reg.	hablar	41
aportillar *to break down; to breach (wall, etc.)* Reg.	hablar	41
aposentar *to lodge (someone)* Reg.	hablar	41
aposentarse *to take lodging* Reg.	hablar	41
aposesionarse de *to take possession of* Reg.	hablar	41
apostar *to bet*	contar	24
apostarse con *to compete with*	contar	24
apostar *to post a sentry* Reg.	hablar	41
apostarse *to position oneself (*e.g. *near the door, etc.)* Reg.	hablar	41
apostatar de *to apostatize from; to renounce (beliefs)* Reg.	hablar	41
apostillar *to annotate; to add a comment* Reg.	hablar	41

apoyar *to support;* **a. algo contra** *to lean something against* Reg.   hablar   41

apoyarse contra *to lean (oneself) against;* **a. en** *to rely on* Reg.   hablar   41

apreciar *to value; to evaluate; to appreciate* Reg.   hablar   41

aprehender *to apprehend; to confiscate (assets, etc.)* Reg.   comer   22

apremiar *to urge; to harass* Reg.   hablar   41

aprender *to learn* Reg.   comer   22

aprensar *to crush; to press (in a press or crusher); to oppress* Reg.   hablar   41

apresar *to seize; to capture; to grab* Reg.   hablar   41

aprestar *to make ready* Reg.   hablar   41

aprestarse a *to get ready to* Reg.   hablar   41

apresurar *to make someone/something go faster* Reg.   hablar   41

apresurarse *to hurry* (intransitive) Reg.   hablar   41

apretar *to press; to squeeze; to fit tightly*   cerrar   18

apretarse *to get narrower, tighter; to become squashed together*   cerrar   18

apretujar *to jam; to press hard* Reg.   hablar   41

aprisionar *to imprison; to shackle* Reg.   hablar   41

aprobar *to approve; to pass an examination*   contar   24

aprontar *to prepare quickly; to prepare without delay* Reg.   hablar   41

aprontarse *to get ready* Reg.   hablar   41

apropiar a = **adecuar** Reg.   hablar   41

apropiarse de *to appropriate something* Reg.   hablar   41

aprovechar *to make use of; to take advantage of.* **¡Que aproveche!** *bon appetit!* Reg.   hablar   41

aprovecharse de *to take advantage of*
Reg.   hablar   41
aprovisionar *to supply with provisions*
Reg.   hablar   41
aproximar *to bring near* Reg.   hablar   41
aproximarse a *to approach* Reg.   hablar   41
apuntalar *to prop up, shore up* Reg. hablar   41
apuntar *to note; to write down; to begin*
   to show; to sprout; **a. a** *to point at; to*
   point out; to aim at Reg.   hablar   41
apuntarse *to chalk up (point, victory);*
   to score (victory); to be in
   agreement; to sign up for (**para**)
   something Reg.   hablar   41
apuntillar *to kill off (an animal)* Reg. hablar 41
apuñalar *to stab* Reg.   hablar   41
apuñalear = **apuñalar** Reg.   hablar   41
apuñetear *to punch with the fist* Reg. hablar 41
apurar *to drain dry; to annoy; to press*
   (someone to do something) Reg.   hablar   41
apurarse *to fret;* (Lat. Am.) *to hurry*
Reg.   hablar   41
aquejar *to afflict; to distress* Reg. hablar 41
aquietar *to quieten; to calm down; to*
   allay (fears) Reg.   hablar   41
aquilatar *to assay (metal); to appraise;*
   to appreciate in value Reg.   hablar   41
aquistar *to gain in value* Reg.   hablar   41
arabizar *to make Arabic; to Arabize*
Reg.   realizar 65
arañar *to scratch* Reg.   hablar   41
arar *to plow/(Brit.) plough* Reg.   hablar   41
arbitrar *to referee; to arbitrate* Reg. hablar 41
arbolar *to raise (flag); to set upright (a*
   pole) Reg.   hablar   41
arbolarse *to rear up (horse)* Reg. hablar   41
arborizar *to plant with trees* Reg. realizar 65

arcaizar *to make archaic*	arcaizar	8
arcar *to arch; to beat (wool);* also = **arquear** Reg.	sacar	74
archivar *to file (= to store away in a file)* Reg.	hablar	41
arder *to burn* (intransitive) Reg.	hablar	41
arenar *to spread with sand; to sprinkle with sand* Reg.	hablar	41
arengar *to harangue* Reg.	pagar	52
argamasar *to mix (cement); to plaster a wall* Reg.	hablar	41
argentar *to silver* Reg.	hablar	41
argüir *to argue (a point)*	argüir	9
argumentar *to argue (a point)* Reg.	hablar	41
aridecerse *to become arid; to become dry*	parecer	53
armar *to arm; to assemble (a mechanism); to kick up (a fuss)* Reg.	hablar	41
armarse de *to arm oneself with; to equip oneself with* Reg.	hablar	41
armonizar *to harmonize* Reg.	realizar	65
arpar = **arañar** Reg.	hablar	41
arponear *to harpoon* Reg.	hablar	41
arquear = *to retch* Reg.	hablar	41
arquearse *to form a vault, arch, curve* Reg.	hablar	41
arracimarse *to cluster; to hang in bunches* Reg.	hablar	41
arraigar *to take root* Reg.	pagar	52
arraigarse *to become deeply settled* Reg.	pagar	52
arramblar con *to sweep away; to make off with; to push to one side* Reg.	hablar	41
arrancar *to pull out, up; to start up (motor)* Reg.	sacar	74
arrasar *to level; to raze to the ground; to sweep away (obstacles)* Reg.	hablar	41

arrasarse en *to become flooded with (tears)* Reg.	hablar	41
arrastrar *to drag* Reg.	hablar	41
arrastrarse *to crawl, creep* Reg.	hablar	41
arrear *to urge on (horses, etc.); to deliver (a blow)* Reg.	hablar	41
arrebañar *to scrape together; to scrape up (remains)* Reg.	hablar	41
arrebatar a *to snatch from* Reg.	hablar	41
arrebatarse por *to become ecstatic over; to get carried away by* Reg.	hablar	41
arrebolar *to redden* Reg.	hablar	41
arrebozar *to wrap up in a cloak* Reg.	realizar	65
arrebozarse *to muffle oneself; to wrap oneself up in a cloak* Reg.	realizar	65
arrebujar *to jumble together* Reg.	hablar	41
arrebujarse en *to snuggle into, wrap oneself in*	hablar	41
arreciar *to grow worse; to get more severe (weather, etc.)* Reg.	hablar	41
arreciarse = **arreciar** Reg.	hablar	41
arrecirse *to grow stiff with cold*	abolir	1
arredrar *to frighten off; to drive back (by intimidation)* Reg.	hablar	41
arredrarse *to be intimidated; to back off* Reg.	hablar	41
arregazar *to tuck up* Reg.	realizar	65
arreglar *to fix; to repair; to put right; to arrange* Reg.	hablar	41
arreglarse con *to come to an agreement with;* **arreglárselas para** *to manage to* Reg.	hablar	41
arregostarse a *to take a liking to* Reg.	hablar	41
arrejuntarse *to live together, cohabit* Reg.	hablar	41
arrellanarse *to sprawl in one's seat* Reg.	hablar	41

arremangar *to turn up (sleeves); to tuck up* Reg.	pagar	52
arremangarse = **arremangar** Reg.	pagar	52
arremeter contra *to rush forth upon; to assault; to charge against* Reg.	comer	22
arremolinarse *to whirl; to mill about in a crowd* Reg.	hablar	41
arrendar *to rent; to lease*	cerrar	18
arrepentirse de *to repent of; to back down from*	sentir	78
arrestar *to arrest* Reg.	hablar	41
arrestarse a *to rush ahead boldly with; to charge headlong into* Reg.	hablar	41
arrezagar *to tuck up* Reg.	pagar	52
arriar *to lower (flag)*	liar	45
arriarse *to become flooded*	liar	45
arribar *to arrive; to make port* Reg.	hablar	41
arriesgar *to risk something* Reg.	pagar	52
arriesgarse *to take a risk* Reg.	pagar	52
arrimar a *to bring close to; to draw (something) close to* Reg.	hablar	41
arrimarse a *to come close to; to snuggle up to* Reg.	hablar	41
arrinconar *to corner; to abandon; to push away; to throw out* Reg.	hablar	41
arrizar *to reef; to lash down* Reg.	realizar	65
arrobar *to enchant; to fill with rapture* Reg.	hablar	41
arrobarse *to be enraptured* Reg.	hablar	41
arrodillarse *to kneel* Reg.	hablar	41
arrogarse *to arrogate* Reg.	pagar	52
arrojar *to throw; to fling* Reg.	hablar	41
arrojarse *to throw oneself; to leap* Reg.	hablar	41
arrollar *to trample upon; to flatten (opponents); to run down; to roll up* Reg.	hablar	41
arropar *to wrap up (with clothing)* Reg.	hablar	41

arroparse *to wrap up warm (with clothing)* Reg.	hablar	41
arrostrar *to face up to; to brave* Reg.	hablar	41
arrostrarse *to pitch into (a fight, the fray)* Reg.	hablar	41
arrugar *to wrinkle* (transitive) Reg.	pagar	52
arrugarse *to wrinkle* (intransitive) Reg.	hablar	41
arruinar *to ruin* Reg.	hablar	41
arruinarse *to go to ruin* Reg.	hablar	41
arrullar *to coo; to lull (to sleep)* Reg.	hablar	41
arrumbar *to take bearings (i.e. a ship)* Reg.	hablar	41
arrumbarse *to be seasick* (= **marearse**) Reg.	hablar	41
arrutinarse *to get into a rut/routine* Reg.	hablar	41
artesonar *to stucco; to put decorative panels on* Reg.	hablar	41
articular *to articulate; to join together; to draw up (rules)* Reg.	hablar	41
artificializar *to make artificial* Reg.	realizar	65
asalariar *to fix a salary; to put on the payroll* Reg.	hablar	41
asaltar *to assault* Reg.	hablar	41
asar *to roast; to broil; to grill* Reg.	hablar	41
asarse *to feel extremely hot* Reg.	hablar	41
ascender *to promote (= to raise someone's rank); to ascend*	perder	55
asear *to clean up; to adorn, embellish* Reg.	hablar	41
asearse *to get cleaned up; to smarten oneself up* Reg.	hablar	41
asediar *to besiege; to lay siege to* Reg.	hablar	41
asegurar *to make secure; to assure; to assert; to insure* Reg.	hablar	41
asegurarse *to get insured;* **a. de** *to make certain about* Reg.	hablar	41
asemejar *to make like* Reg.	hablar	41

asemejarse a *to be similar* (= **parecerse a**) Reg.	hablar	41
asenderear *to hound, harry* Reg.	hablar	41
asentar *to seat; to settle (someone, something); to lay down (rules, etc.)*	cerrar	18
asentarse *to settle; to settle down*	cerrar	18
asentir *to assent;* **a. a** *to assent to*	sentir	78
aserrar = **serrar**	cerrar	18
asertar *to assert* Reg.	hablar	41
asesinar *to murder* Reg.	hablar	41
asesorar *to advise* (= **aconsejar**) Reg.	hablar	41
asesorarse de *to seek advice from* Reg.	hablar	41
asestar *to aim (a blow);* **a. a** *to aim at* Reg.	hablar	41
aseverar *to assert* Reg.	hablar	41
asfaltar *to asphalt* Reg.	hablar	41
asfixiar *to asphyxiate* (= **ahogar**) Reg.	hablar	41
asfixiarse *to be asphyxiated* (= **ahogarse**) Reg.	hablar	41
asignar *to assign; to allocate* Reg.	hablar	41
asilar *to give refuge to; to give asylum to* Reg.	hablar	41
asilarse en *to take refuge in* Reg.	hablar	41
asimilar *to assimilate* (transitive) Reg.	hablar	41
asimilarse *to become assimilated;* **a. a** *to resemble* (= **parecerse a**) Reg.	hablar	41
asir *to grasp*	asir	10
asirse a *to grasp hold of*	asir	10
asistir *to assist* (= **ayudar**)*;* **a. a** *to attend (classes, etc.)* Reg.	vivir	89
asociar con *to associate with; to relate to* Reg.	hablar	41
asociarse *to associate* (intransitive)*; to act jointly* Reg.	hablar	41
asolanar *to parch* Reg.	hablar	41
asolar *to parch, dry up* (transitive) Reg.	hablar	41

asolar (formerly conjugated like **contar**)
   to raze, destroy Reg.   hablar   41
asolear *to sun* Reg.   hablar   41
asolearse *to get sun-tanned; to sun*
   oneself Reg.   hablar   41
asomar *to show something through an*
   opening; to stick out (head, etc.)
   Reg.   hablar   41
asomarse a/por *to lean out of* Reg.   hablar   41
asombrar *to astonish; to amaze* Reg.   hablar   41
asombrarse de *to be astonished at* Reg.   hablar   41
asordar = **ensordecer** Reg.   hablar   41
asosegar = **sosegar**   negar   49
aspirar *to inhale; to aspire;* **a. a** *to*
   aspire to Reg.   hablar   41
asquear *to disgust; to nauseate* Reg.   hablar   41
asquearse *to feel nauseated* Reg.   hablar   41
astillar *to splinter* Reg.   hablar   41
astringir *to constrict*   rugir   72
asumir *to assume (responsibility, task);*
   to suppose Reg.   vivir   89
asurar *to burn (food)* (= **quemar**)*; to*
   parch (land) Reg.   hablar   41
asustar *to scare* Reg.   hablar   41
asustarse de/por *to be scared about/by*
   Reg.   hablar   41
atacar *to attack; to assault* Reg.   sacar   74
atajar *to intercept; to take a shortcut*
   Reg.   hablar   41
atajarse *to feel ashamed*
   (= **avergonzarse**) Reg.   hablar   41
atañer *to concern* (= **concernir**. Third
   person only)   tañer   81
atar *to tie up* Reg.   hablar   41
atarse en *to get bogged down in* Reg.   hablar   41
atarantar *to stun* Reg.   hablar   41
atarantarse *to be stunned* Reg.   hablar   41

atardecer *to draw towards evening; to grow dark (day)*	parecer	53
atarear *to assign a task to* Reg.	hablar	41
atarearse *to work very hard* Reg.	hablar	41
atarugar *to make someone be quiet; to peg down* Reg.	pagar	52
atarugarse *to get confused; to choke* Reg.	pagar	52
atascar *to clog up* (transitive) Reg.	sacar	74
atascarse *to get stuck; to get clogged up* Reg.	sacar	74
ataviar *to attire; to adorn*	liar	45
ataviarse con *to dress oneself up in*	liar	45
atediar *to bore* (= **aburrir**) Reg.	hablar	41
atediarse *to get bored* (= **aburrirse**) Reg.	hablar	41
atemorizar *to frighten* Reg.	realizar	65
atemorizarse *to get frightened* Reg.	realizar	65
atemperar *to temper* Reg.	hablar	41
atender a *to attend to; to pay attention; to take care; to take into account; to wait on*	perder	55
atenerse a *to abide by*	tener	82
atentar contra *to make an attempt/ assault on* Reg.	hablar	41
atenuar *to lessen; to tone down*	continuar	25
aterirse *to become stiff with cold*	abolir	1
aterrar *to terrify* Reg.	hablar	41
aterrarse *to become frightened* Reg.	hablar	41
aterrar *to cover with earth; to demolish*	cerrar	18
aterrizar *to land* Reg.	realizar	65
aterrorizar *to terrify* Reg.	realizar	65
atesorar *to treasure; to hoard up; to amass* Reg.	hablar	41
atestar *to attest;* **a. de** *to cram, stuff with* (in latter meaning sometimes conj. like **cerrar**) Reg.	hablar	41
atestiguar *to testify; to attest*	averiguar	13

atezarse *to become tanned* Reg.	realizar	65
atiborrar *to stuff, cram full* Reg.	hablar	41
atiborrarse de *to gorge oneself on* Reg.	hablar	41
atiesar *to stiffen* Reg.	hablar	41
atildar *to spruce up* Reg.	hablar	41
atinar a *to guess right;* + infinitive *to manage to* Reg.	hablar	41
atisbar *to catch a glimpse of* Reg.	hablar	41
atizar *to stir up; to poke (a fire); to rouse* Reg.	realizar	65
atolondrar *to confuse, fluster* Reg.	hablar	41
atolondrarse *to get confused* Reg.	hablar	41
atollarse *to get stuck* Reg.	hablar	41
atomizar *to break into fragments; to spray with fine droplets* Reg.	realizar	65
atontar *to stupefy* Reg.	hablar	41
atontarse *to become stupefied* Reg.	hablar	41
atorar *to obstruct* Reg.	hablar	41
atorarse *to be choked* Reg.	hablar	41
atormentar *to torment* Reg.	hablar	41
atornillar *to screw in* Reg.	hablar	41
atosigar *to hassle* Reg.	pagar	52
atracar *to mug; to hold up (*i.e. rob*); to approach land* Reg.	sacar	74
atracarse de *to eat too much of* Reg.	sacar	74
atraer *to attract*	traer	83
atragantarse *to choke, get clogged up* Reg.	hablar	41
atramparse *to be trapped* Reg.	hablar	41
atrancar *to bar; to obstruct* Reg.	sacar	74
atrancarse *to get stuck, blocked* Reg.	sacar	74
atrapar *to trap* Reg.	hablar	41
atrasar *to slow down; to set back; to delay* Reg.	hablar	41
atrasarse *to go slow; to tail behind* Reg.	hablar	41
atravesar *to put or lay across; to cross; to pierce; to go through*	cerrar	18

atreverse a *to dare to* Reg.	comer	22
atribuir *to attribute*	construir	23
atribular *to afflict* Reg.	hablar	41
atrofiar *to atrophy* Reg.	hablar	41
atrofiarse = atrofiar Reg.	hablar	41
atronar *to deafen with noise*	contar	24
atropellar *to run over (*e.g. car*)* Reg.	hablar	41
atropellarse *to rush* Reg.	hablar	41
atufarse *to get angry* Reg.	hablar	41
aturdir *to stun* Reg.	vivir	89
aturdirse *to be stunned, flustered* Reg.	vivir	89
aturrullarse *to get flustered* Reg.	hablar	41
atusar *to smooth hair, clothes* Reg.	hablar	41
augurar *to augur; to foretell* Reg.	hablar	41
aullar *to howl*	aullar	11
aumentar *to increase* (transitive and intransitive) Reg.	hablar	41
aunar *to unite, combine*	aullar	11
auscultar *to examine with a stethoscope* Reg.	hablar	41
ausentarse *to absent oneself; to leave* Reg.	hablar	41
auspiciar *to sponsor* Reg.	hablar	41
autenticar *to authenticate* Reg.	sacar	74
For the conjugation of unlisted verbs beginning with **auto-**, see the root verb		
autoabastecerse *to be self-sufficient*	parecer	53
autofinanciarse *to be self-financing* Reg.	hablar	41
autografiar *to autograph*	liar	45
automatizar *to automate* Reg.	realizar	65
automedicarse con *to self-prescribe (medicine)* Reg.	sacar	74
autorizar *to authorize* Reg.	realizar	65
autorregularse *to be self-regulating* Reg.	hablar	41
auxiliar *to help* (= **ayudar**) Reg.	hablar	41
avalar *to guarantee; to underwrite* Reg.	hablar	41

avalorar *to estimate* Reg.	hablar	41
avanzar *to advance* (transitive and intransitive) Reg.	realizar	65
avasallar *to dominate; to subjugate* Reg.	hablar	41
avecindarse *to take up residence (in a city or town)* Reg.	hablar	41
avenir *to reconcile*	venir	87
avenirse en *to agree on*	venir	87
aventajar *to excel* Reg.	hablar	41
aventajarse *to get ahead of* Reg.	hablar	41
aventar *to fan (fire, flames)*	cerrar	18
aventurar *to venture (an opinion)* Reg.	hablar	41
aventurarse a *to venture to* Reg.	hablar	41
avergonzar *to shame* (transitive)	avergonzar	12
avergonzarse de *to be ashamed at*	avergonzar	12
averiar *to damage*	liar	45
averiarse *to break down (motors, etc.)*	liar	45
averiguar *to find out*	averiguar	13
avezar *to accustom* Reg.	realizar	65
avezarse *to become accustomed* Reg.	realizar	65
aviar *to prepare something; to ready*	liar	45
aviarse para *to get ready to*	liar	45
avinagrar *to sour* Reg.	hablar	41
avinagrarse *to turn sour* Reg.	hablar	41
avisar *to notify; to warn* Reg.	hablar	41
avispar *to put someone in the picture* Reg.	hablar	41
avisparse *to 'wise up', get smart* Reg.	hablar	41
avistar *to glimpse* Reg.	hablar	41
avivar *to enliven, arouse; to stir up (fire)* Reg.	hablar	41
avivarse *to become livelier* Reg.	hablar	41
ayudar *to help* Reg.	hablar	41
ayunar *to fast* Reg.	hablar	41
azorar *to embarrass* Reg.	hablar	41

azorarse *to be abashed, embarrassed*
Reg.   hablar   41
azotar *to whip* Reg.   hablar   41
azucarar *to sugar* Reg.   hablar   41
azular *to color/(Brit.) colour blue* Reg. hablar   41
azularse *to turn blue* Reg.   hablar   41
azulejar *to tile* Reg.   hablar   41
azuzar *to goad (animals); to incite* Reg. realizar 65

babear *to dribble, slobber* Reg.   hablar   41
babearse *to dribble, slobber over oneself*
Reg.   hablar   41
babosear = **babear** Reg.   hablar   41
bailar *to dance* Reg.   hablar   41
bajar *to lower; to take down; to come/go*
down; to get off Reg.   hablar   41
bajarse de *to get out of (vehicle); to get*
down from Reg.   hablar   41
balancear *to rock; to swing* Reg.   hablar   41
balancearse *to sway* Reg.   hablar   41
balar *to bleat* Reg.   hablar   41
balbucear *to stammer; to stutter; to*
babble Reg.   hablar   41
balbucir (= **balbucear**)   balbucir 14
baldar *to cripple* Reg.   hablar   41
baldear *to wash down, sluice* Reg.   hablar   41
balear *(Lat. Am.) to shoot* Reg.   hablar   41
balizar *to mark with buoys or flares*
Reg.   realizar 65
balsear *to cross by raft* Reg.   hablar   41
bambolear *to swing* Reg.   hablar   41
bambolearse *to sway* Reg.   hablar   41
banderillear *to stick banderillas into a*
bull's neck (in a bullfight) Reg.   hablar   41
bañar *to bathe* Reg.   hablar   41
bañarse *to take a bath; to go for a swim*
Reg.   hablar   41

barajar *to shuffle (cards, etc.)* Reg.	hablar	41
baratear *to sell at a bargain* Reg.	hablar	41
barnizar *to varnish* Reg.	realizar	65
barrenar *to drill* Reg.	hablar	41
barrer *to sweep* Reg.	comer	22
barruntar *to guess* Reg.	hablar	41
basar en *to base on* Reg.	hablar	41
basarse en *to base one's judgement on* Reg.	hablar	41
bascular *to swing* Reg.	hablar	41
bastar *to be enough* Reg.	hablar	41
bastarse *to be self-sufficient* Reg.	hablar	41
bastonear *to beat with a stick* Reg.	hablar	41
batallar *to battle* Reg.	hablar	41
batear *to bat* Reg.	hablar	41
batir *to beat (eggs, wings)* Reg.	vivir	89
bautizar *to baptize* Reg.	realizar	65
beatificar *to beatify* Reg.	sacar	74
beber *to drink* Reg.	comer	22
beberse *to drink up; to drink all of* Reg.	comer	22
becar *to grant a scholarship or fellowship* Reg.	sacar	74
befar *to scoff* Reg.	hablar	41
bendecir *to bless*	maldecir	47
beneficiar *to benefit (someone)* Reg.	hablar	41
beneficiarse de *to profit from* Reg.	hablar	41
besar *to kiss* Reg.	hablar	41
besuquear *to cover/smother with kisses* Reg.	hablar	41
bienquerer *to like*	querer	64
bienquistar *to reconcile* Reg.	hablar	41
bienquistarse *to become reconciled* Reg.	hablar	41
bifurcarse *to fork (= to divide into two branches)* Reg.	sacar	74
biografiar *to write the biography of*	liar	45
birlar *to filch* Reg.	hablar	41
bisecar *to bisect* Reg.	sacar	74

biselar *to bevel* Reg.	hablar	41
blandear *to soften* Reg.	hablar	41
blandir *to brandish*	abolir	1
blanquear *to whiten, bleach* Reg.	hablar	41
blanquecer *to whiten*	parecer	53
blasfemar *to blaspheme* Reg.	hablar	41
blasonar *to boast* Reg.	hablar	41
blindar *to armor/(Brit.) armour-plate* Reg.	hablar	41
bloquear *to block* Reg.	hablar	41
bobear *to talk nonsense* Reg.	hablar	41
bogar *to row* Reg.	pagar	52
boicotear *to boycott* Reg.	hablar	41
bombardear *to bomb; to bombard* Reg.	hablar	41
bombear *to pump* Reg.	hablar	41
bonificar *to subsidize; to give a discount* Reg.	sacar	74
bordear *to border; to go round the edge* Reg.	hablar	41
borrar *to erase* Reg.	hablar	41
borrarse *to fade* Reg.	hablar	41
borronear *to smudge* Reg.	hablar	41
bosquejar *to sketch* Reg.	hablar	41
botar *to throw away* (usu. Lat. Am.)*; to bounce; to launch* Reg.	hablar	41
boxear *to box (sport)* Reg.	hablar	41
bracear *to swing one's arms* Reg.	hablar	41
bramar *to bellow* Reg.	hablar	41
bravear *to boast* Reg.	hablar	41
bregar *to struggle* Reg.	pagar	52
brillar *to shine* Reg.	hablar	41
brincar *to hop; to jump* Reg.	sacar	74
brindar *to toast; to offer (as a favour)* Reg.	hablar	41
brindarse a *to volunteer to* Reg.	hablar	41
bromear *to joke* Reg.	hablar	41
broncear *to tan (someone)* Reg.	hablar	41

broncearse *to get a suntan* Reg.	hablar	41
brotar *to sprout* Reg.	hablar	41
bruñir *to polish*	gruñir	39
brutalizar *to brutalize, ill-treat* Reg.	realizar	65
bucear *to dive (= to swim or work under water)* Reg.	hablar	41
bufar *to snort; to blow* Reg.	hablar	41
bufonear *to clown* Reg.	hablar	41
bullir *to seethe*	bullir	15
burbujear *to bubble* Reg.	hablar	41
burilar *to engrave* Reg.	hablar	41
burlar *to mock; to deceive* Reg.	hablar	41
burlarse de *to make fun* Reg.	hablar	41
buscar *to look for* Reg.	sacar	74
cabalgar *to ride horseback; to gallop* Reg.	pagar	52
cabecear *to nod (in sleep); to nod off* Reg.	hablar	41
cabellar *to grow hair; to put on false hair* Reg.	hablar	41
caber *to fit in; to have enough room:* **¿quepo yo?** *is there room for me?*	caber	16
cablear *to wire; to cable* Reg.	hablar	41
cabrear (familiar) *to make annoyed* Reg.	hablar	41
cabrearse (familiar) *to get annoyed* Reg.	hablar	41
cacarear *to cackle; to crow* Reg.	hablar	41
cachear *to frisk* Reg.	hablar	41
cachondearse de (familiar) *to make fun of* Reg.	hablar	41
caducar *to expire (documents, etc.)* Reg.	sacar	74
caer *to fall; to be located*	caer	17
caerse *to fall over; to fall down*	caer	17
cagar (vulgar) *to shit* Reg.	pagar	52

calafatear *to caulk* Reg.	hablar	41
calar *to soak through; to see through a person* Reg.	hablar	41
calarse *to become soaked* Reg.	hablar	41
calcar *to trace; to copy* Reg.	sacar	74
calcificar *to calcify* Reg.	sacar	74
calcificarse *to become calcified* Reg.	sacar	74
calcinar *to burn* (= *to burn to death*) Reg.	hablar	41
calcular *to calculate* Reg.	hablar	41
caldear *to heat up* Reg.	hablar	41
caldearse *to become heated* Reg.	hablar	41
calefaccionar *to heat* Reg.	hablar	41
calentar *to heat; to warm; to annoy*	cerrar	18
calentarse *to get hot*	cerrar	18
calibrar *to calibrate* Reg.	hablar	41
calificar *to grade/(Brit.) to mark (exam paper);* **c. de** *to describe as* Reg.	sacar	74
callar *to silence, not to mention; to be silent* Reg.	hablar	41
callarse *to become silent* Reg.	hablar	41
callejear *to loaf around the street* Reg.	hablar	41
calzar *to put shoes on; to wear (shoes)* Reg.	realizar	65
calzarse *to put one's shoes on* Reg.	realizar	65
cambalachear *to barter; to swap* Reg.	hablar	41
cambiar *to change; to exchange* Reg.	hablar	41
cambiarse *to change clothes; to swap places; to move house* Reg.	hablar	41
caminar *to walk* Reg.	hablar	41
campanear *to ring the bells* Reg.	hablar	41
campar *to camp; to stand out* Reg.	hablar	41
campear *to wander freely; to fly freely* Reg.	hablar	41
camuflar *to camouflage* Reg.	hablar	41
canalizar *to channel* Reg.	realizar	65

cancelar *to cancel* Reg.	hablar	41
canjear *to exchange; to cash (a cheque)* Reg.	hablar	41
canonizar *to canonize* Reg.	realizar	65
cansar *to tire* Reg.	hablar	41
cansarse *to get tired* Reg.	hablar	41
cantar *to sing* Reg.	hablar	41
canturrear *to hum* Reg.	hablar	41
canonear *to cannonade* Reg.	hablar	41
capacitar *to enable; to prepare (= to train)* Reg.	hablar	41
capacitarse *to become qualified* Reg.	hablar	41
capar *to castrate* Reg.	hablar	41
capear *to duck out of; to weather (crises); to flourish a cape (bullfighting)* Reg.	hablar	41
capitalizar *to capitalize; to compound (interest)* Reg.	realizar	65
capitanear *to lead; to command* Reg.	hablar	41
capitular *to capitulate* Reg.	hablar	41
capotar *to overturn (car)* Reg.	hablar	41
capotear = **capear** Reg.	hablar	41
captar *to grasp (meaning); to receive (radio, TV signals)* Reg.	hablar	41
capturar *to capture* Reg.	hablar	41
caracolear *to caper* Reg.	hablar	41
caracterizar *to characterize* Reg.	realizar	65
caramelizar *to caramelize* Reg.	realizar	65
carbonatar *to carbonate* Reg.	hablar	41
carbonear *to make charcoal* Reg.	hablar	41
carbonizar *to char; to carbonize* Reg.	realizar	65
carbonizarse *to be reduced to ashes* Reg.	realizar	65
carcajearse *to howl with laughter* Reg.	hablar	41
carcomer *to eat away (envy, disease)* Reg.	comer	22
cardar *to card* Reg.	hablar	41

carduzar *to card* Reg.	realizar	65
carear *to bring face to face* Reg.	hablar	41
carecer *to lack*	parecer	53
cargar *to load; to charge (gun, battery, price)* Reg.	pagar	52
cargarse *to become loaded; to ruin; to kill* Reg.	pagar	52
cariar *to cause decay (in teeth)*	liar	45
cariarse *to become decayed (teeth)*	liar	45
caricaturizar *to caricature* Reg.	realizar	65
carnear *to slaughter; to butcher* Reg.	hablar	41
casar a alguien con alguien *to marry someone off to someone* Reg.	hablar	41
casarse *to get married* Reg.	hablar	41
cascabelear *to jingle* Reg.	hablar	41
cascar *to crack* Reg.	sacar	74
castañetear *to chatter (teeth)* Reg.	hablar	41
castigar *to punish* Reg.	pagar	52
castrar *to castrate* Reg.	hablar	41
catar *to taste (wine, etc.)* Reg.	hablar	41
catear *to flunk, to fail (a student) (transitive)* Reg.	hablar	41
causar *to cause* Reg.	hablar	41
cauterizar *to cauterize* Reg.	realizar	65
cautivar *to captivate; to charm* Reg.	hablar	41
cavar *to dig* Reg.	hablar	41
cavilar *to cavil; to quibble* Reg.	hablar	41
cazar *to hunt* Reg.	realizar	65
cebar *to fatten; to bait (a fishhook)* Reg.	hablar	41
cebarse en/con *to vent one's anger on* Reg.	hablar	41
cecear *to pronounce c before e or i, and also the letter z, as th (as in Spain); to lisp* Reg.	hablar	41
ceder *to yield; to give up* Reg.	comer	22
cegar *to blind*	negar	49

cegarse *to go blind*	negar	49
cejar *to back off; to back down* Reg.	hablar	41
celar *to keep an eye or check on; to conceal* Reg.	hablar	41
celarse de *to be jealous of* Reg.	hablar	41
celebrar *to celebrate; to hold (a meeting, etc.)* Reg.	hablar	41
cellisquear *to sleet* Reg.	hablar	41
cementar *to cement* Reg.	hablar	41
cenar *to have supper/dinner* Reg.	hablar	41
cencerrear *to jingle; to rattle* Reg.	hablar	41
centellear *to sparkle* Reg.	hablar	41
centralizar *to centralize* Reg.	realizar	65
centrar en *to center/(Brit.) centre on (e.g. gaze, attention)* Reg.	hablar	41
centrifugar *to centrifuge* Reg.	pagar	52
centuplicar *to increase a hundredfold* Reg.	sacar	74
ceñir *to gird; to encircle*	reñir	69
ceñirse a *to stick to (a text, a subject)*	reñir	69
cepillar *to brush; to plane* Reg.	hablar	41
cercar *to encircle; to fence in; to surround* Reg.	sacar	74
cercenar *to trim; to clip* Reg.	hablar	41
cerciorar *to assure* Reg.	hablar	41
cerciorarse de *to ascertain* Reg.	hablar	41
cerner *to sift*	perder	55
cernerse sobre *to hover over; to loom over*	perder	55
cernir = **cerner**	discernir	32
cernirse = **cernerse**	discernir	32
cerrar *to close* (transitive); *to lock*	cerrar	18
cerrarse *to close* (intransitive)	cerrar	18
certificar *to certify; to register (a letter)* Reg.	sacar	74
cesar de *to cease from; to quit* Reg.	hablar	41
chacharear *to chatter* Reg.	hablar	41

chacotearse de *to make fun* Reg.	hablar	41
chafar *to flatten* Reg.	hablar	41
chaflanar *to chamfer* Reg.	hablar	41
chalar *to make someone lose his head* Reg.	hablar	41
chalarse *to go crazy* Reg.	hablar	41
chamuscar *to singe* Reg.	sacar	74
chancar *to crush (stones)* Reg.	sacar	74
chancletear *to go around in slippers* Reg.	hablar	41
chapalear = **chapotear** Reg.	hablar	41
chapar *to plate (with metal sheets)* Reg.	hablar	41
chaparrear *to rain hard; to pour at intervals* Reg.	hablar	41
chapotear *to splash* Reg.	hablar	41
chapucear *to bodge; to do odd jobs* Reg.	hablar	41
chapurrear *to speak a language brokenly* Reg.	hablar	41
charlar *to chat* Reg.	hablar	41
charlatanear *to chatter* Reg.	hablar	41
charlotear *to chatter* Reg.	hablar	41
charolar *to varnish* Reg.	hablar	41
chascar = **chasquear** Reg.	sacar	74
chasquear *to click the tongue* Reg.	hablar	41
chequear *to check* Reg.	hablar	41
chichear *to hiss* Reg.	hablar	41
chicotear *to lash; to whip* Reg.	hablar	41
chiflar *to whistle at (in disapproval)* Reg.	hablar	41
chiflarse por *to go mad over* Reg.	hablar	41
chillar *to scream* Reg.	hablar	41
chinchar *to bother* Reg.	hablar	41
chiripear *to win by a fluke* Reg.	hablar	41
chirlar *to talk fast and loud* Reg.	hablar	41
chirriar *to squeak (e.g. door)*	liar	45
chismear *to gossip* Reg.	hablar	41

chismorrear = **chismear** Reg.	hablar	41
chispear *to spark; to sparkle; to spit with rain* Reg.	hablar	41
chisporrotear *to throw off sparks* Reg.	hablar	41
chistar *to mutter, grumble* Reg.	hablar	41
chitar *to mumble* Reg.	hablar	41
chivarse *to 'grass', 'squeal' (to the police)* Reg.	hablar	41
chocar *to collide; to shock; to knock together* Reg.	sacar	74
chocarrear *to tell coarse jokes* Reg.	hablar	41
chochear *to become doddery (with age)* Reg.	hablar	41
chorrear *to drip* Reg.	hablar	41
chotear *to make fun of; to jeer at* Reg.	hablar	41
chufletear *to jest* Reg.	hablar	41
chulear *to act as a pimp* Reg.	hablar	41
chulearse *to boast* Reg.	hablar	41
chupar *to suck* Reg.	hablar	41
chuparse *to get drunk* Reg.	hablar	41
churruscarse *to become crisp (food)* Reg.	sacar	74
chutar *to shoot (soccer)* Reg.	hablar	41
ciar *to back water (nautical)*	liar	45
cicatear *to be stingy* Reg.	hablar	41
cicatrizar *to heal* Reg.	realizar	65
cicatrizarse *to form a scar* Reg.	realizar	65
cifrar *to encipher; to abridge* Reg.	hablar	41
cimbrar *to shake around, swish (transitive)* Reg.	hablar	41
cimbrarse *to shake around, sway about (intransitive)* Reg.	hablar	41
cimbrearse = **cimbrarse** Reg.	hablar	41
cimentar *to found; to lay the foundation*	cerrar	18
or Reg. like	hablar	41
cincelar *to carve; to chisel* Reg.	hablar	41
cinchar *to cinch, girth* Reg.	hablar	41

circular *to circulate* Reg.	hablar	41
circuncidar *to circumcise* Reg.	hablar	41
circundar *to surround* Reg.	hablar	41
circunnavegar *to circumnavigate* Reg.	pagar	52
circunscribir *to circumscribe*	escribir	37
circunvalar *to surround* Reg.	hablar	41
circunvolar *to fly around*	contar	24
citar *to make an appointment with; to cite* Reg.	hablar	41
citarse con *to have an appointment with* Reg.	hablar	41
civilizar *to civilize* Reg.	realizar	65
cizañar *to sow discord* Reg.	hablar	41
clamar *to cry out for* Reg.	hablar	41
clarear *to grow clearer; to clear up* Reg.	hablar	41
clarearse *to show through; to be transparent (said of fabric)* Reg.	hablar	41
clarecer *to dawn*	parecer	53
clarificar *to clarify* Reg.	sacar	74
clasificar *to classify* Reg.	sacar	74
claudicar *to give in* Reg.	sacar	74
clausurar *to close (meeting, session)* Reg.	hablar	41
clavar *to nail* Reg.	hablar	41
clavetear *to stud* Reg.	hablar	41
claxonar *to sound one's horn (car)* Reg.	hablar	41
climatizar *to air-condition* Reg.	realizar	65
clocar = **cloquear**	trocar	84
cloquear *to cluck* Reg.	hablar	41
cloroformar = **cloroformizar** Reg.	hablar	41
cloroformizar *to chloroform* Reg.	realizar	65
coaccionar *to compel; to pressure* Reg.	hablar	41
coacervar *to heap up; to pile* Reg.	hablar	41
coactar *to coerce* Reg.	hablar	41
coadyuvar *to help* Reg.	hablar	41
coagular *to coagulate* Reg.	hablar	41
coartar *to limit* Reg.	hablar	41

cobardear *to be or act cowardly* Reg.	hablar	41
cobijar *to cover, protect* Reg.	hablar	41
cobrar *to be paid (wages, etc.); to take (money)* Reg.	hablar	41
cocear *to kick (horses)* Reg.	hablar	41
cocer *to cook; to boil; to bake*	cocer	19
cocinar *to do the cooking* Reg.	hablar	41
codear *to elbow* Reg.	hablar	41
codearse con *to hobnob with, mix with (socially)* Reg.	hablar	41
codiciar *to covet* Reg.	hablar	41
codificar *to codify* Reg.	sacar	74
coeditar *to publish jointly* Reg.	hablar	41
coercer *to coerce* Reg.	vencer	86
coexistir con *to coexist with* Reg.	vivir	89
coger *to seize; to pick; to catch; to get* Reg.	proteger	62
cohabitar *to live together* Reg.	hablar	41
cohechar *to bribe* Reg.	hablar	41
cohibir *to restrain; to repress*	prohibir	61
coincidir *to coincide* Reg.	vivir	89
cojear *to limp* Reg.	hablar	41
colaborar *to collaborate* Reg.	hablar	41
colar *to strain (liquids)*	contar	24
colarse en *to slip or sneak in*	contar	24
colchar *to quilt* Reg.	hablar	41
colear *to wag the tail* Reg.	hablar	41
coleccionar *to collect* Reg.	hablar	41
colectar *to collect* Reg.	hablar	41
colegir *to infer, deduce*	regir	66
colgar *to hang; to dangle*	colgar	20
coligarse *to join forces* Reg.	pagar	52
colindar con *to border on* Reg.	hablar	41
colmar *to fill to the brim; c. de to shower with (e.g. blessings)* Reg.	hablar	41
colocar *to place; to lay out* Reg.	sacar	74

colocarse *to get placed; to find a job* Reg.	sacar	74
colonizar *to settle; to colonize* Reg.	realizar	65
colorar *to color/(Brit.) to colour* Reg.	hablar	41
colorear = **colorar***; to blush, grow red* Reg.	hablar	41
colorir = **colorar, colorear**	abolir	1
coludir *to be in collusion* Reg.	vivir	89
columbrar *to glimpse* Reg.	hablar	41
columpiar *to swing* (transitive) Reg.	hablar	41
columpiarse *to swing (*i.e. *on a swing)* Reg.	hablar	41
comadrear *to go around gossiping* Reg.	hablar	41
comandar *to command* Reg.	hablar	41
comanditar *to invest in an undertaking as a silent partner* Reg.	hablar	41
comarcar con *to border on* Reg.	sacar	74
combar *to bend* (transitive) Reg.	hablar	41
combarse *to warp, bend* (intransitive) Reg.	hablar	41
combatir *to combat* Reg.	vivir	89
combatirse con *to struggle against* Reg.	vivir	89
combinar *to combine* Reg.	hablar	41
combinarse para *to get together in order to* Reg.	hablar	41
comedirse *to behave politely/civilly*	pedir	54
comentar *to comment on* Reg.	hablar	41
comenzar a *to begin to; to start to*	comenzar	21
comer *to eat* Reg.	comer	22
comerse *to eat up; to eat the whole of* Reg.	comer	22
comercializar *to market; to commercialize* Reg.	realizar	65
comerciar en *to trade in* Reg.	hablar	41
cometer *to commit* Reg.	comer	22
comisionar *to commission* Reg.	hablar	41
compactar *to compact* Reg.	hablar	41

compadecer *to pity; to feel sorry for*	parecer	53
compaginar *to put in order;* **compaginar con** *to bring in to line with* Reg.	hablar	41
compaginarse con *to tally with* Reg.	hablar	41
comparar *to compare* Reg.	hablar	41
comparecer *to appear (in court)*	parecer	53
compartir *to divide; to share out* Reg.	vivir	89
compartimentar *to compartmentalize* Reg.	hablar	41
compasar *to measure with a compass* Reg.	hablar	41
compeler *to compel* Reg.	comer	22
compendiar *to summarize* Reg.	hablar	41
compenetrarse con *to share feelings and outlook with* Reg.	hablar	41
compensar *to compensate;* **no me compensa** *it isn't worth it for me* Reg.	hablar	41
competer a *to be the responsibility of* Reg.	comer	22
competir con *to compete with*	pedir	54
compilar *to compile (dictionaries, programs)* Reg.	hablar	41
complacer *to please*	parecer	53
complacerse en *to be pleased to*	parecer	53
complementar *to complement* Reg.	hablar	41
completar *to complete* Reg.	hablar	41
complicar *to complicate; to involve* Reg.	sacar	74
complicarse *to get complicated, entangled* Reg.	sacar	74
complotar *to plot* Reg.	hablar	41
componer *to fix; to compose*	poner	58
componerse de *to be composed of; to consist of*	poner	58
comportar *to tolerate; to bear* Reg.	hablar	41
comportarse *to behave* Reg.	hablar	41
comprar *to buy* Reg.	hablar	41

comprender *to include; to understand*
  (= **entender**) Reg.   comer   22
comprimir *to compress; to hold back*
  (tears) Reg.   vivir   89
comprimirse *to control oneself, hold*
  oneself back Reg.   vivir   89
comprobar *to verify; to check*   contar   24
comprometer *to compromise; to commit*
  (someone) Reg.   comer   22
comprometerse a *to undertake, be*
  committed to Reg.   comer   22
compulsar = **comparar** *(legal language)*
  Reg.   hablar   41
compungir *to make remorseful*   rugir   72
compungirse *to feel remorse*   rugir   72
computar *to compute* Reg.   hablar   41
computarizar = **computerizar** Reg.   realizar   65
computerizar *to computerize* Reg.   realizar   65
comulgar *to take communion;* **c. con** *to*
  sympathize with Reg.   pagar   52
comunicar *to inform* Reg.   sacar   74
comunicarse con *to get in touch,*
  communicate with Reg.   sacar   74
concadenar = **concatenar** Reg.   hablar   41
concatenar *to link together* Reg.   hablar   41
concebir *to conceive*   pedir   54
conceder *to concede; to grant* Reg.   comer   22
concentrar *to concentrate (in one place)*
  Reg.   hablar   41
concentrarse en *to concentrate on* Reg.   hablar   41
conceptuar *to judge; to deem*   continuar 25
concernir *to concern* (third person only)   discernir 32
concertar *to arrange (e.g.*
  appointment); to harmonize   cerrar   18
concertarse con *to come to terms with*   cerrar   18
conchabar *to join, mix* Reg.   hablar   41

conchabarse para *to gang together in order to* Reg.	hablar	41
concienciar = **concientizar** Reg.	hablar	41
concientizar *to make aware, raise consciousness in* Reg.	realizar	65
conciliar *to conciliate, reconcile* Reg.	hablar	41
concitar *to incite, stir up* Reg.	hablar	41
concluir *to conclude*	construir	23
concluirse *to come to an end*	construir	23
concordar *to agree*	contar	24
concretar *to make specific* Reg.	hablar	41
concretarse *to become definite, specific, tangible;* **c. a** *to confine oneself to* Reg.	hablar	41
conculcar *to violate, infringe* Reg.	sacar	74
concurrir en *to concur in; to come together in* Reg.	vivir	89
concursar *to declare bankrupt* Reg.	hablar	41
condecorar *to decorate (with medals, etc.)* Reg.	hablar	41
condenar *to condemn* Reg.	hablar	41
condenarse *to acknowledge one's guilt* Reg.	hablar	41
condensar *to condense* (transitive) Reg.	hablar	41
condensarse *to condense* (intransitive) Reg.	hablar	41
condescender *to condescend*	perder	55
condicionar *to condition* Reg.	hablar	41
condimentar *to season (with spices, etc.)* Reg.	hablar	41
condolerse de *to sympathize over*	mover	48
condonar *to cancel (a debt)* Reg.	hablar	41
conducir *to conduct; to drive*	producir	60
conducirse *to behave*	producir	60
conectar *to connect;* **c. con** *to communicate well with* Reg.	hablar	41

conexionarse con *to get in touch with*
   Reg.   hablar   41
confabularse con *to connive; to scheme*
   with Reg.   hablar   41
confederarse *to confederate* Reg.   hablar   41
conferenciar con *to confer with* Reg.   hablar   41
conferir a *to bestow on (an award)*   sentir   78
confesar *to confess*   cerrar   18
confesarse = **confesar** Reg.   cerrar   18
confiar *to entrust; to confide*   liar   45
confiarse *to trust; to become confident*   liar   45
configurar *to shape; to form; to*
   configure Reg.   hablar   41
configurarse *to take shape; to take form*
   Reg.   hablar   41
confinar *to confine; to lock up;* **c. con** *to*
   border on Reg.   hablar   41
confinarse *to keep oneself locked away*
   Reg.   hablar   41
confirmar *to confirm* Reg.   hablar   41
confiscar *to confiscate* Reg.   sacar   74
confitar *to preserve in sugar; to candy*
   Reg.   hablar   41
confluir *to come together; to flow*
   together   construir   23
conformar *to shape, fashion* Reg.   hablar   41
conformarse con *to conform to; to*
   reconcile oneself to Reg.   hablar   41
confortar *to comfort* Reg.   hablar   41
confraternizar *to fraternize* Reg.   realizar   65
confrontar *to confront* Reg.   hablar   41
confrontarse con *to confront* Reg.   hablar   41
confundir *to confuse* Reg.   vivir   89
confundirse *to become confused; to*
   make an error Reg.   vivir   89
congelar *to freeze (food, funds)* Reg.   hablar   41

congeniar con *to get along well with*
Reg.   hablar   41
congestionar *to make congested* Reg.   hablar   41
congestionarse *to become congested*
Reg.   hablar   41
conglomerar *to conglomerate*
(transitive) Reg.   hablar   41
conglomerarse *to become*
conglomerated Reg.   hablar   41
congraciar *to win over* Reg.   hablar   41
congraciarse con *to get into the good*
books of Reg.   hablar   41
congratular *to congratulate* Reg.   hablar   41
congregar *to congregate* Reg.   pagar   52
conjeturar *to guess* Reg.   hablar   41
conjugar *to conjugate; to bring together*
(qualities) Reg.   pagar   52
conjugarse *to fit together; to be*
conjugated Reg.   pagar   52
conjurar *to conspire; to conjure* Reg.   hablar   41
conllevar *to imply; to entail; to tolerate;*
to put up with Reg.   hablar   41
conmemorar *to commemorate* Reg.   hablar   41
conmensurar *to make commensurate*
Reg.   hablar   41
conminar con *to threaten with* Reg.   hablar   41
conmover *to move (emotionally)*   mover   48
conmoverse *to be moved, touched*
(emotionally)   mover   48
conmutar *to exchange* Reg.   hablar   41
connaturalizarse con *to become*
accustomed to Reg.   realizar   65
connotar *to connote* Reg.   hablar   41
connumerar *to enumerate* Reg.   hablar   41
conocer *to know; to meet*   parecer   53
conocerse a *to know someone only too*
well   parecer   53

conquistar *to conquer; to win over* Reg.	hablar	41
consagrar *to consecrate; to devote* Reg.	hablar	41
consagrarse a *to devote oneself to* Reg.	hablar	41
conseguir *to obtain; to get*	seguir	77
consensuar *to reach a consensus on*	continuar	25
consentir *to allow; to consent*	sentir	78
consentirse *to give way (in an argument)*	sentir	78
conservar *to preserve* Reg.	hablar	41
considerar *to consider* Reg.	hablar	41
consignar *to consign; to dispatch* Reg.	hablar	41
consistir en *to consist in/of* Reg.	vivir	89
consolar *to console*	contar	24
consolarse con *to take consolation in*	contar	24
consolidar *to consolidate* Reg.	hablar	41
consonar *to be in harmony*	contar	24
conspirar contra *to conspire against* Reg.	hablar	41
constar *to be on the record; to be a fact that; c. de = consistir en* Reg.	hablar	41
constatar *to verify* Reg.	hablar	41
consternar *to dismay, fill with consternation* Reg.	hablar	41
consternarse por *to be dismayed that* Reg.	hablar	41
constiparse *to catch a cold* Reg.	hablar	41
constituir *to constitute; to set up*	construir	23
constreñir *to constrain*	reñir	69
construir *to construct; to build*	construir	23
consultar *to consult* Reg.	hablar	41
consumar *to consummate, complete, carry through* Reg.	hablar	41
consumir *to consume, use up* Reg.	vivir	89
consumirse *to waste away; to be used up* Reg.	vivir	89
contactar *to contact* Reg.	hablar	41

contagiar *to infect (with an illness)*
  Reg.   hablar   41
contagiarse *to become infected* Reg.   hablar   41
contaminar *to contaminate; to pollute*
  Reg.   hablar   41
contaminarse *to become contaminated,*
  polluted Reg.   hablar   41
contar *to count; to tell (story);* **c. con** *to*
  count on   contar   24
contemplar *to contemplate* Reg.   hablar   41
contemporizar *to comply; to be flexible,*
  compliant Reg.   realizar   65
contender *to contend*   perder   55
contener *to contain*   tener   82
contenerse *to control oneself*   tener   82
contenerizar *to containerize* Reg.   realizar   65
contentar *to content* Reg.   hablar   41
contentarse con *to be content with* Reg. hablar   41
contestar *to answer* Reg.   hablar   41
contextualizar *to back with quotations;*
  to provide a context for Reg.   realizar   65
continuar *to continue;* + gerund *to*
  continue to   continuar   25
contonearse *to swagger, strut* Reg.   hablar   41
contorcerse *to writhe*   cocer   19
contornear *to trace the contour of; to go*
  around Reg.   hablar   41
contornearse *to strut* Reg.   hablar   41
For the conjugation of unlisted verbs beginning with
  contra-, see the root verb (e.g. **contramarchar** will be
  conjugated like **marchar**)
contratacar = contraatacar
contraatacar *to counterattack* Reg.   sacar   74
contrabalancear *to counterbalance* Reg.   hablar   41
contrabandear *to smuggle* Reg.   hablar   41
contradecir *to contradict*   decir   28

contraer *to contract (*e.g. *debt, marriage); to make tighter*	traer	83
contraerse *to contract (= to become smaller)*	traer	83
contrahacer *to copy; to counterfeit*	hacer	42
contramarcar *to countermark* Reg.	sacar	74
contrapesar *to counterbalance, counterweigh* Reg.	hablar	41
contraponer *to oppose; to compare*	poner	58
contrariar *to oppose; to vex*	liar	45
contrarrestar *to counteract* Reg.	hablar	41
contrastar *to contrast; to resist* Reg.	hablar	41
contratar *to contract, sign up (a person)* Reg.	hablar	41
contravenir *to transgress*	venir	87
contribuir *to contribute*	construir	23
contristar *to sadden* Reg.	hablar	41
controlar *to check (passports, tickets, etc.); to control* Reg.	hablar	41
controvertir *to dispute*	sentir	78
contundir *to contuse, bruise* Reg.	vivir	89
conturbar *to perturb* Reg.	hablar	41
conturbarse *to be perturbed* Reg.	hablar	41
contusionar *to bruise, damage* Reg.	hablar	41
convalecer *to recover from an illness*	parecer	53
convalidar *to confirm; to validate* Reg.	hablar	41
convencer *to convince*	vencer	86
convenir en *to agree on; to be suitable, appropriate*	venir	87
converger *to converge* Reg.	proteger	62
convergir = **converger**	rugir	72
conversar *to converse* Reg.	hablar	41
convertir *to convert*	sentir	78
convertirse en *to change into, turn into*	sentir	78
convidar *to invite* Reg.	hablar	41
convivir con *to live amicably with* Reg.	vivir	89

convocar *to summon; to call (elections, meeting)* Reg.   sacar   74
convoyar *to escort, convoy* Reg.   hablar   41
convulsionar *to convulse* Reg.   hablar   41
cooperar *to co-operate* Reg.   hablar   41
coordinar *to co-ordinate* Reg.   hablar   41
copar *to surround, corner (an enemy)* Reg.   hablar   41
copear *to have a drink* Reg.   hablar   41
copiar *to copy; to copy down* Reg.   hablar   41
copular *to join one thing with another* Reg.   hablar   41
copularse con *to copulate with* Reg.   hablar   41
coquetear con *to flirt with* Reg.   hablar   41
corcovar *to bend over* Reg.   hablar   41
corcovear *to buck (horse); to prance about* Reg.   hablar   41
corear *to chorus* Reg.   hablar   41
coreografiar *to choreograph*   liar   45
cornear *to butt; to gore* Reg.   hablar   41
coronar *to crown; to cap* Reg.   hablar   41
corregir *to correct*   regir   66
corregirse *to mend one's ways*   regir   66
correlacionar *to correlate* Reg.   hablar   41
correr *to run; to flow; to rush* Reg.   comer   22
corresponder a/con *to correspond to/ with;* **me corresponde a mí** *it's my affair/turn* Reg.   comer   22
corresponderse *to correspond (= to harmonize)* Reg.   comer   22
corroborar *to corroborate* Reg.   hablar   41
corroer *to corrode*   roer   71
corromper *to corrupt* Reg.   comer   22
corromperse *to become corrupt, rotten* Reg.   comer   22
corrugar *to corrugate* Reg.   pagar   52
cortar *to cut; to cut off; to omit* Reg.   hablar   41

cortarse *to cut oneself; to be
  embarrassed* Reg.   hablar   41
cortejar *to court* Reg.   hablar   41
cosechar *to harvest* Reg.   hablar   41
coser *to sew* Reg.   comer   22
cosquillear *to tickle* Reg.   hablar   41
costar *to cost*   contar   24
costear *to defray or pay the cost of; to
  sail along the coast of* Reg.   hablar   41
cotejar *to collate; to compare* Reg.   hablar   41
cotillear *to gossip* Reg.   hablar   41
cotizar *to quote (price); to contribute
  one's share* Reg.   realizar   65
cotizarse a *to be priced/quoted at* Reg.   realizar   65
cotorrear *to chatter; to gossip* Reg.   hablar   41
crear *to create* Reg.   hablar   41
crecer *to grow (in size)*   parecer   53
crecerse *to grow (morally, emotionally,
  in status); to get haughty*   parecer   53
creer *to believe; to think*   poseer   59
creerse *to believe mistakenly*   poseer   59
crepitar *to crackle* Reg.   hablar   41
criar *to rear, breed, bring up*   liar   45
criarse *to be brought up*   liar   45
cribar *to sieve* Reg.   hablar   41
criminalizar *to criminalize* Reg.   realizar   65
crispar *to make tense; to contract
  (muscles)* Reg.   hablar   41
cristalizar *to crystallize* Reg.   realizar   65
cristianizar *to Christianize* Reg.   realizar   65
criticar *to criticize* Reg.   sacar   74
croar *to croak* Reg.   hablar   41
cronometrar *to clock; to time* Reg.   hablar   41
crucificar *to crucify* Reg.   sacar   74
crujir *to creak; to gnash (one's teeth)*
  Reg.   vivir   89

cruzar *to cross over (= to go to the other side)* Reg.	realizar	65
cruzarse *to cross (= one over another)* Reg.	realizar	65
cuadrar *to square; to balance (books)* Reg.	hablar	41
cuadrarse *to stand to attention; to square up* Reg.	hablar	41
cuadricular *to divide into squares* Reg.	hablar	41
cuadruplicar *to quadruple* Reg.	sacar	74
cuajar *to coagulate, clot* Reg.	hablar	41
cuajarse *to curdle* Reg.	hablar	41
cualificar *to qualify* Reg.	sacar	74
cuantificar *to quantify* Reg.	sacar	74
cuartear *to cut up (carcass)* Reg.	hablar	41
cubicar *to cube (math)* Reg.	sacar	74
cubrir *to cover*	cubrir	26
cubrirse *to put one's hat on*	cubrir	26
cucharear *to spoon* Reg.	hablar	41
cuchichear *to whisper* Reg.	hablar	41
cuchufletear *to make fun; to joke* Reg.	hablar	41
cuestionar *to question (a statement, assertion)* Reg.	hablar	41
cuidar *to take care of; to watch over; to take good care of* Reg.	hablar	41
cuidarse *to take care of oneself; c. de to refrain from* Reg.	hablar	41
culebrear *to wiggle* Reg.	hablar	41
culminar *to culminate* Reg.	hablar	41
culpar *to blame* Reg.	hablar	41
cultivar *to cultivate* Reg.	hablar	41
cumplimentar *to carry out (a duty)* Reg.	hablar	41
cumplir *to fulfill/(Brit.) fulfil; to keep a promise* Reg.	vivir	89
cumplirse *to come to pass; to come true* Reg.	vivir	89

cundir *to spread; to yield abundantly; to propagate* Reg.   vivir   89

curar *to cure; to treat (a sick person)* Reg.   hablar   41

curarse *to get well* Reg.   hablar   41

curiosear *to browse around* Reg.   hablar   41

cursar *to take a course in* Reg.   hablar   41

curtir *to tan; to harden, toughen a person* Reg.   vivir   89

curtirse *to become tanned; to become hardened to difficulties* Reg.   vivir   89

custodiar *to watch over; to guard* Reg.   hablar   41

danzar = **bailar** Reg.   realizar   65

dañar *to hurt, damage* (transitive) Reg.   hablar   41

dañarse *to spoil; to get damaged* (intransitive) Reg.   hablar   41

dar *to give; to hit*   dar   27

darse a *to devote oneself to*   dar   27

datar *to date (a document, etc.)* Reg.   hablar   41

deambular *to wander about* Reg.   hablar   41

debatir *to debate, discuss* Reg.   vivir   89

debatirse entre *to struggle between (e.g. two opposing ideas)* Reg.   vivir   89

deber *to owe; + infinitive must* Reg.   comer   22

debilitar *to make weak* Reg.   hablar   41

debilitarse *to grow weak* Reg.   hablar   41

debutar *to make one's debut* Reg.   hablar   41

decaer *to decay (= to lessen, decline)*   caer   17

decantar *to decant* Reg.   hablar   41

decantarse por *to opt for* Reg.   hablar   41

decapar *to remove, strip (paint)* Reg.   hablar   41

decapitar *to behead* Reg.   hablar   41

decepcionar *to disappoint* Reg.   hablar   41

decidir *to decide* Reg.   vivir   89

decidirse a *to make up one's mind to* Reg.   vivir   89

decir *to say*	decir	28
declamar *to declaim* Reg.	hablar	41
declarar *to declare* Reg.	hablar	41
declinar *to decline (= reject)* Reg.	hablar	41
decolorar = **descolorar** Reg.	hablar	41
decomisar *to confiscate* Reg.	hablar	41
decorar *to decorate* Reg.	hablar	41
decrecer *to decrease*	parecer	53
decrepitar *to crackle* Reg.	hablar	41
decretar *to decree* Reg.	hablar	41
decuplar *to multiply by ten* Reg.	hablar	41
dedicar *to dedicate* Reg.	sacar	74
dedicarse a *to dedicate oneself to* Reg.	sacar	74
deducir *to deduce; to deduct*	producir	60
defecar *to defecate* Reg.	sacar	74
defeccionar *to defect* Reg.	hablar	41
defender *to defend*	perder	55
defenderse *to manage;* **me defiendo en español** *I can get by in Spanish*	perder	55
deferir a *to defer to*	sentir	78
definir *to define* Reg.	vivir	89
definirse *to make one's position clear* Reg.	vivir	89
defoliar *to defoliate* Reg.	hablar	41
deforestar *to deforest* Reg.	hablar	41
deformar *to deform* Reg.	hablar	41
deformarse *to become deformed* Reg.	hablar	41
defraudar *to defraud; to disappoint* Reg.	hablar	41
degenerar *to degenerate* Reg.	hablar	41
degenerarse *to go to seed; to become degenerate* Reg.	hablar	41
deglutir *to swallow* Reg.	vivir	89
degollar *to behead; to slit someone's throat*	agorar	4
degradar *to degrade; to demote* Reg.	hablar	41
degradarse *to become degraded* Reg.	hablar	41
degustar *to taste (*e.g. *wines)* Reg.	hablar	41

deificar *to deify* Reg.	sacar	74
dejar *to leave; to abandon; to lend; to allow* Reg.	hablar	41
dejarse *to let oneself go (to seed)* Reg.	hablar	41
delatar *to denounce (= to inform on someone)* Reg.	hablar	41
delegar *to delegate* Reg.	pagar	52
deleitar *to delight* Reg.	hablar	41
deletrear *to spell (a word)* Reg.	hablar	41
deliberar *to deliberate* Reg.	hablar	41
delimitar *to delimit* Reg.	hablar	41
delinear *to delineate; to draw* Reg.	hablar	41
delinquir *to transgress; to offend (* i.e. *act criminally)* Reg.	delinquir	29
delirar *to be delirious* Reg.	hablar	41
deludir *to delude* Reg.	vivir	89
demandar *to sue; to demand* Reg.	hablar	41
demarcar *to demarcate* Reg.	sacar	74
demeritar *to discredit (a person)* Reg.	hablar	41
democratizar *to democratize* Reg.	realizar	65
demoler *to demolish*	mover	48
demorar en *to delay in* Reg.	hablar	41
demorarse en *to be late, slow in* Reg.	hablar	41
demostrar *to demonstrate (the truth of)*	contar	24
demudar *to change, alter (*e.g. *facial expression)* Reg.	hablar	41
denegar *to refuse, reject (a request)*	negar	49
denegrir *to blacken*	abolir	1
denigrar *to denigrate* Reg.	hablar	41
denominar *to name (things, not people)* Reg.	hablar	41
denostar *to insult*	contar	24
denotar *to denote* Reg.	hablar	41
dentar *to tooth*	cerrar	18
denudar *to denude* Reg.	hablar	41
denunciar *to denounce; to report (a crime to the police)* Reg.	hablar	41

deparar *to hold in store (*i.e. *fate, the future)* Reg.	hablar	41
departir *to converse* Reg.	vivir	89
depauperarse *to become poor* Reg.	hablar	41
depender de *to depend on* Reg.	comer	22
depilar *to depilate, remove hair* Reg.	hablar	41
deplorar *to deplore* Reg.	hablar	41
deponer *to depose; to lay down (arms)*	poner	58
deportar *to deport* Reg.	hablar	41
depositar *to deposit, place, pay in* Reg.	hablar	41
depositarse *to be deposited (sediment)* Reg.	hablar	41
depravar *to deprave* Reg.	hablar	41
deprecar *to implore* Reg.	sacar	74
depreciar *to depreciate* Reg.	hablar	41
deprimir *to depress* Reg.	vivir	89
deprimirse *to become depressed* Reg.	vivir	89
depurar *to purify (water)* Reg.	hablar	41
derivar de *to derive from* Reg.	hablar	41
derogar *to revoke* Reg.	pagar	52
derramar *to spill (tears)* Reg.	hablar	41
derramarse *to flow, overflow* Reg.	hablar	41
derrengarse *to be exhausted*	negar	49
derretir *to melt (something)*	pedir	54
derretirse *to melt (snow, ice)*	pedir	54
derribar *to tear down, demolish* Reg.	hablar	41
derrocar *to overthrow; to fling down* Reg.	sacar	74
derrochar *to squander* Reg.	hablar	41
derrotar *to defeat* Reg.	hablar	41
derruir = **derribar**	construir	23
derrumbar *to overthrow, demolish* Reg.	hablar	41

For the conjugation of unlisted verbs beginning with **des-** see the root verb.

desabollar *to knock the dents out* Reg.	hablar	41
desabotonar *to undo (buttons)* Reg.	hablar	41
desabotonarse *to unbutton oneself* Reg.	hablar	41

desabrigar *to deprive of shelter; to take off (someone's coat, sweater, etc.)* Reg. — pagar — 52

desabrigarse *to take off one's coat, sweater* Reg. — pagar — 52

desabrirse *to become embittered* Reg. — vivir — 89

desabrochar *to unfasten* Reg. — hablar — 41

desacatar *to fail to obey (law)* Reg. — hablar — 41

desacelerar *to decelerate* Reg. — hablar — 41

desacertar *to make a mistake* — cerrar — 18

desacostumbrarse a *to lose the habit of* Reg. — hablar — 41

desacreditar *to discredit* Reg. — hablar — 41

desactivar *to defuse (bomb)* Reg. — hablar — 41

desadaptar *to unsettle* Reg. — hablar — 41

desadaptarse *to become unsettled* Reg. — hablar — 41

desafiar *to defy* — liar — 45

desafilar *to make blunt* Reg. — hablar — 41

desafinar *to be out of tune* Reg. — hablar — 41

desafinarse *to get out of tune* Reg. — hablar — 41

desagradar *to displease* Reg. — hablar — 41

desagradecer *to be ungrateful* — parecer — 53

desagraviar *to make amends for* Reg. — hablar — 41

desaguar *to drain* — averiguar — 13

desahogar *to relieve from pain or trouble; to give vent to (passions, desires)* Reg. — pagar — 52

desahogarse *to let off steam* Reg. — pagar — 52

desahuciar *declare a patient past recovery; to evict* — aullar — 11

desajustar *to loosen* Reg. — hablar — 41

desajustarse *to get loose (bolt, etc.)* Reg. — hablar — 41

desalentar *to discourage* — cerrar — 18

desalentarse por *to get discouraged* — cerrar — 18

desalinizar *desalinate* Reg. — realizar — 65

desaliñar *to make shabby, unkempt* — hablar — 41

desamarrar *to unhitch* Reg.	hablar	41
desamortizar = **confiscar** Reg.	realizar	65
desamparar *to abandon* Reg.	hablar	41
desatentarse *to become discouraged*	cerrar	18
desalojar *to evict; to oust* Reg.	hablar	41
desamoblar = **desamueblar**	contar	24
desamueblar *to remove the furniture* Reg.	hablar	41
desandar *to retrace (steps)*	andar	7
desangrar *to bleed* Reg.	hablar	41
desanimar *to discourage* Reg.	hablar	41
desanimarse *to grow discouraged* Reg.	hablar	41
desanudar *to unknot, untie* Reg.	hablar	41
desaparecer *to disappear*	parecer	53
desaparejar *to unharness* Reg.	hablar	41
desapoderar *to remove someone's powers, withdraw authority* Reg.	hablar	41
desaprender *to unlearn* Reg.	comer	22
desapretar *to loosen, slacken* (transitive)	cerrar	18
desapretarse *to become loose*	cerrar	18
desaprobar *to disapprove of*	contar	24
desaprovechar *to use to no advantage* Reg.	hablar	41
desarmar *to disarm; to dismantle* Reg.	hablar	41
desarraigar *to root out* Reg.	pagar	52
desarraigarse *to become uprooted* Reg.	pagar	52
desarreglar *to mess up* Reg.	hablar	41
desarrollar *to develop* (transitive) Reg.	hablar	41
desarrollarse *to evolve, develop* (intransitive) Reg.	hablar	41
desarropar *to pull off bedclothes* Reg.	hablar	41
desarroparse *to throw off one's bedclothes* Reg.	hablar	41
desarrugar *to unwrinkle* Reg.	pagar	52
desarticular *to smash up (e.g. a criminal organization); to dislocate* Reg.	hablar	41

desarticularse *to become dislocated*
Reg. .... hablar   41
desasirse de *to get free from (clutches, etc.)* .... asir   10
desasistir *to abandon* Reg. .... vivir   89
desasnar (familiar) *to educate* Reg. .. hablar   41
desasnarse (familiar) *to get educated*
Reg. .... hablar   41
desasociar *to disassociate* Reg. .... hablar   41
desasosegar *to disquiet* .... negar   49
desasosegarse *to become disquieted* .. negar   49
desatar *to untie; to unknot; to unleash*
Reg. .... hablar   41
desatarse *to come untied; to break loose*
Reg. .... hablar   41
desatascar *to unclog* Reg. .... sacar   74
desatinar *to talk or act foolishly* Reg. .. hablar   41
desatornillar *to unscrew* Reg. .... hablar   41
desatrancar *to break down (door)* Reg. .. sacar   74
desautorizar *to deprive of authority; to
discredit* Reg. .... realizar   65
desavenirse *to fall out (friends, etc.)* .. venir   87
desaviar *to mislead; to lead astray; to
deprive someone of something
necessary* .... liar   45
desayunar *to breakfast; to eat breakfast*
Reg. .... hablar   41
desayunarse = **desayunar** (esp. Lat.
Am.) Reg. .... hablar   41
desazonar *to upset, make anxious* .... hablar   41
desazonarse *to get upset, worried* .... hablar   41
desbancar *to relegate, push to one side*
Reg. .... sacar   74
desbandarse *to stampede, scatter in all
directions* Reg. .... hablar   41
desbarajustar *to disorder* Reg. .... hablar   41
desbaratar *to spoil* Reg. .... hablar   41

desbaratarse *to fall into pieces* Reg.	hablar	41
desbarrancarse *to go off the road (vehicle)* Reg.	sacar	74
desbarrar *to talk nonsense* Reg.	hablar	41
desbastar *to rough out; to plane down* Reg.	hablar	41
desbastarse *to become polished* Reg.	hablar	41
desbocarse *to bolt (horse)* Reg.	sacar	74
desbordar *to overflow (limits, channel)* Reg.	hablar	41
desbordarse *to overflow* (intransitive) Reg.	hablar	41
desbravar *to tame; to break in* Reg.	hablar	41
descabalgar *to dismount* Reg.	pagar	52
descabezar *to chop off the head of (an organization)* Reg.	realizar	65
descaecer *to decrease*	parecer	53
descafeinar *to decaffeinate* Reg.	hablar	41
descalabrar *to hit on the head* Reg.	hablar	41
descalabrarse *to fracture one's skull; to hurt one's head* Reg.	hablar	41
descalcificar *to soften (water)* Reg.	sacar	74
descalzarse *to take one's shoes off* Reg.	realizar	65
descansar *to rest* Reg.	hablar	41
descararse *to be insolent* Reg.	hablar	41
descargar *to unload; to discharge* Reg.	pagar	52
descargarse *to go flat (battery); to break (storm)* Reg.	pagar	52
descarriarse *to go wild, off the rails*	liar	45
descarrilar *to derail (a train)* Reg.	hablar	41
descarrilarse *to become derailed* Reg.	hablar	41
descartar *to rule out (an option)* Reg.	hablar	41
descender *to drop (temperature); to descend*	perder	55
descentralizar *decentralize* Reg.	realizar	65
descentrar *to put off center/(Brit.) centre* Reg.	hablar	41

descentrarse *to get off center/(Brit.)* *centre* Reg.	hablar	41
descerrajar *to break the lock off* Reg.	hablar	41
descifrar *to decipher* Reg.	hablar	41
desclavar *to unnail* Reg.	hablar	41
descolgar *to take down (from a peg, wall, etc.); to pick up (a phone)*	colgar	20
descolgarse *to climb down (a rope)*	colgar	20
descollar *to excel*	contar	24
descolonizar *to decolonize* Reg.	realizar	65
descolorar *to discolor/(Brit.) discolour* Reg.	hablar	41
descolorir = **descolorar**	abolir	1
descompaginar *to disorder, turn upside down (plans)* Reg.	hablar	41
descompaginarse *to go to pieces* Reg.	hablar	41
descomponer *to decompose; to break down into arts*	poner	58
descomponerse *to decay, break up into parts; to feel upset*	poner	58
desconcertar *to disconcert*	cerrar	18
desconcertarse *to get out of order*	cerrar	18
desconchar *to chip* Reg.	hablar	41
desconectar *to disconnect* (transitive and intransitive); *to switch off* Reg.	hablar	41
desconfiar de *to distrust; to have no confidence in*	liar	45
descongelar *to defrost (something)* Reg.	hablar	41
descongelarse *to defrost (i.e. to thaw itself out)* Reg.	hablar	41
descongestionar *to decongest* Reg.	hablar	41
desconocer *to fail to recognize, not to know*	parecer	53
desconsolar *to grieve*	contar	24
desconsolarse *to become grieved*	contar	24
descontaminar *to decontaminate* Reg.	hablar	41

descontar *to discount*	contar	24
descontentar *to displease; to dissatisfy* Reg.	hablar	41
descontinuar *to discontinue*	continuar	25
descontrolarse *to go out of control* Reg.	hablar	41
descorazonar *to dishearten* Reg.	hablar	41
descorazonarse *to become disheartened* Reg.	hablar	41
descorchar *to uncork* Reg.	hablar	41
descornar *to dehorn (cattle)*	contar	24
descorrer *to draw (a curtain)* Reg.	comer	22
descortezar *to remove bark, crust* Reg.	realizar	65
descoser *to unstitch* Reg.	comer	22
descoserse *to become unstitched* Reg.	comer	22
descoyuntar *to dislocate* Reg.	hablar	41
descoyuntarse *to become dislocated* Reg.	hablar	41
descremar *to skim (cream)* Reg.	hablar	41
describir *to describe*	escribir	37
descuartizar *to chop into pieces (a carcass)* Reg.	realizar	65
descubrir *to discover; to uncover*	cubrir	26
descubrirse *to take off one's hat*	cubrir	26
descuerar *to flay* Reg.	hablar	41
descuidar *to neglect* Reg.	hablar	41
desdecir *to fail to confirm (qualities)*	decir	28
desdecirse de *to go back on (a promise)*	decir	28
desdentar *to pull or break the teeth of*	cerrar	18
desdeñar *to disdain* Reg.	hablar	41
desdibujar *to blur* Reg.	hablar	41
desdoblar *to unfold (a sheet of paper, etc.)* Reg.	hablar	41
desdoblarse *to split into two* Reg.	hablar	41
desear *to desire* Reg.	hablar	41
desecar *to dry something out* Reg.	sacar	74
desechar *to discard; to reject* Reg.	hablar	41

desedificar *to give a bad example to*
  Reg.   sacar   74
desembalar *to unpack* Reg.   hablar   41
desembarazar *to disembarrass, remove*
  hindrances Reg.   realizar   65
desembarazarse de *to get rid of* Reg.   realizar   65
desembarcar *to disembark* Reg.   sacar   74
desembargar *to lift an embargo; to*
  remove impediments from Reg.   pagar   52
desembocar en *to flow into (rivers); to*
  lead to Reg.   sacar   74
desembolsar *to pay out (a sum of*
  money) Reg.   hablar   41
desembozar *to unmask* Reg.   realizar   65
desembragar *to declutch (car)* Reg.   pagar   52
desembuchar *to tell the truth; to come*
  clean (about something) Reg.   hablar   41
desempacar *to unpack* Reg.   sacar   74
desempañar *to demist* Reg.   hablar   41
desempatar *to break the tie between*
  Reg.   hablar   41
desempeñar *to carry out (a role); to*
  play (a part) Reg.   hablar   41
desempolvar *to blow the dust off* Reg.   hablar   41
desencadenar *to unchain, unleash* Reg.   hablar   41
desencadenarse *to break out (storms,*
  etc.) Reg.   hablar   41
desencajar *to put out of joint* Reg.   hablar   41
desencajarse *to be thrown out of joint*
  Reg.   hablar   41
desencantar *to disillusion; to disenchant*
  Reg.   hablar   41
desenchufar *to unplug* Reg.   hablar   41
desenfadarse *to calm down* Reg.   hablar   41
desenfocar *to go out of focus, become*
  unfocussed Reg.   sacar   74

desenfrenarse *to lose all one's inhibitions* Reg.	hablar	41
desenganchar *to unhitch* Reg.	hablar	41
desengañar *to disillusion* Reg.	hablar	41
desengañarse *to become disillusioned; to become disappointed* Reg.	hablar	41
desenhebrar *to unthread* Reg.	hablar	41
desenlazar *to untie* Reg.	realizar	65
desenlazarse *to turn out (* i.e. *a story, in the end)* Reg.	realizar	65
desenmarañar *to disentangle* Reg.	hablar	41
desenmascarar *to unmask* Reg.	hablar	41
desenredar *to disentangle* Reg.	hablar	41
desenrollar *to unroll something* Reg.	hablar	41
desenrollarse *to become unrolled* Reg.	hablar	41
desenroscar *to unbolt* Reg.	sacar	74
desentenderse *to ignore; to pretend not to know*	perder	55
desenterrar *to unearth*	cerrar	18
desentonar *to be out of tune; to clash (hue, etc.)* Reg.	hablar	41
desentumecer *to relieve of stiffness*	parecer	53
desentumecerse *to become less stiff*	parecer	53
desenvainar *to unsheath* Reg.	hablar	41
desenvolver *to unwrap*	volver	90
desenvolverse *to do well in (a situation)*	volver	90
desequilibrar *to unbalance* Reg.	hablar	41
desequilibrarse *to become unbalanced* Reg.	hablar	41
desertar *to desert* Reg.	hablar	41
desescombrar *to clear away rubble*	hablar	41
desesperar *to drive to despair* Reg.	hablar	41
desesperarse de *to despair of* Reg.	hablar	41
desestimar *to hold in low esteem* Reg.	hablar	41
desfalcar *to embezzle* Reg.	sacar	74
desfallecer *to grow weak*	parecer	53

desfavorecer *to cease to support (cause,*
person)   parecer   53
desfigurar *to disfigure* Reg.   hablar   41
desfilar *to parade; to march past* Reg.   hablar   41
desflorar *to deflower* Reg.   hablar   41
desfogarse *to vent one's anger* Reg.   pagar   52
desfondar *to knock the bottom out of*
Reg.   hablar   41
desfondarse *to be utterly distraught; to*
go to pieces Reg.   hablar   41
desgajar *to break off (a branch)* Reg.   hablar   41
desgajarse *to split off* (intransitive) Reg.   hablar   41
desganarse *to lose one's appetite; to*
become indifferent Reg.   hablar   41
desgarrar *to rip* Reg.   hablar   41
desgastar *to wear away* Reg.   hablar   41
desgastarse *to become worn down* Reg.   hablar   41
desglosar *to break down (figures)* Reg.   hablar   41
desgobernar *to misrule; to govern badly*   cerrar   18
desgoznar *to take (a door) off its hinges*
Reg.   hablar   41
desgoznarse *to become unhinged* Reg.   hablar   41
desgraciar *to make ugly, unattractive*
Reg.   hablar   41
desgraciarse *to come to a bad end; to*
fail Reg.   hablar   41
desgranar *to remove the grain from*
Reg.   hablar   41
desgranarse : **esta planta se está**
desgranando *this plant is dropping its*
seeds Reg.   hablar   41
desguarnecer *to dismantle, strip down*
(mechanism)   parecer   53
desguazar *to break up (for scrap,* e.g.
cars, planes) Reg.   realizar   65
deshabituar *to disaccustom; to make*
someone break a habit   continuar   25

deshabituarse de *to lose the habit of*	continuar	25
deshacer *to undo; to take apart; to untie*	hacer	42
deshacerse *to dissolve; to break up into pieces*	hacer	42
deshebrar *to unpick* Reg.	hablar	41
deshechizar *to remove a spell or incantation from* Reg.	realizar	65
deshelar *to thaw something*	cerrar	18
deshelarse *to melt* (intransitive)	cerrar	18
desherbar *to weed*	cerrar	18
desheredar *to disinherit* Reg.	hablar	41
deshidratar *to dehydrate* Reg.	hablar	41
deshilachar *to fray (material)* Reg.	hablar	41
deshilar *to unravel* Reg.	hablar	41
deshilvanar *to unbaste (sewing)* Reg.	hablar	41
deshinchar *to deflate* Reg.	hablar	41
deshincharse *to go flat (tires, etc.)* Reg.	hablar	41
deshojar *to defoliate, strip leaves off* Reg.	hablar	41
deshojarse *to lose leaves* Reg.	hablar	41
deshonorar *to dishonor/(Brit.) dishonour* Reg.	hablar	41
deshonrar *to affront; to insult; to seduce (a woman)* Reg.	hablar	41
deshuesar *to bone* Reg.	hablar	41
deshumanizar *to dehumanize* Reg.	realizar	65
deshumedecer *to dehumidify*	parecer	53
designar *to designate* Reg.	hablar	41
desilusionar *to disappoint* Reg.	hablar	41
desilusionarse *to be disappointed* Reg.	hablar	41
desincrustar *to descale* Reg.	hablar	41
desinfectar *to disinfect* Reg.	hablar	41
desinfestar *to rid of vermin, disease* Reg.	hablar	41
desinflar *to deflate something* Reg.	hablar	41
desinflarse *to go flat (tires, etc.)* Reg.	hablar	41
desinformar *to disinform* Reg.	hablar	41

desinhibir *to remove inhibitions from*
Reg.   vivir   89

desinhibirse *to lose one's inhibitions*
Reg.   vivir   89

desintegrar *to disintegrate something*
Reg.   hablar   41

desintegrarse *to become disintegrated*
Reg.   hablar   41

desinteresarse *to lose interest* Reg.   hablar   41

desintoxicar *to detoxify; to cure of*
alcoholism Reg.   sacar   74

desistir de *to desist from* Reg.   vivir   89

deslavar *to wash partially, incompletely*
Reg.   hablar   41

deslegitimar *to discredit* Reg.   hablar   41

desleír *to dilute; to dissolve* (transitive)   reír   68

desleírse *to become diluted; to dissolve*
(intransitive)   reír   68

deslenguarse *to talk too much*   averiguar   13

desliar *to undo*   liar   45

desligar *to untie* Reg.   pagar   52

desligarse *to become undone* Reg.   pagar   52

deslindar *to mark out boundaries* Reg.   hablar   41

deslizar *to slide* Reg.   realizar   65

deslizarse *to skid; slip; to slide into bad*
ways Reg.   realizar   65

deslucir *to tarnish*   lucir   46

deslucirse *to do poorly*   lucir   46

deslumbrar *to dazzle* Reg.   hablar   41

deslustrar *to tarnish, remove the shine*
from Reg.   hablar   41

desmanchar *to remove stains* Reg.   hablar   41

desmandarse *to get out of control*
(person) Reg.   hablar   41

desmantelar *to dismantle* Reg.   hablar   41

desmaquillarse *to take off one's make-*
up Reg.   hablar   41

desmarcarse de *to step out of line from*
    Reg.   sacar   74
desmayar *to lose heart* Reg.   hablar   41
desmayarse *to faint* Reg.   hablar   41
desmedirse *to be impudent*   pedir   54
desmedrar *to damage, impair* Reg.   hablar   41
desmedrarse *to become impaired; to*
    decline (from a previous standard)
    Reg.   hablar   41
desmejorar *to impair; to make worse*
    Reg.   hablar   41
desmejorarse *to deteriorate* Reg.   hablar   41
desmelenar *to tousle (hair)* Reg.   hablar   41
desmembrar *to dismember*   cerrar   18
desmentir *to contradict; to deny*   sentir   78
desmenuzar *to crumble something* Reg.   realizar   65
desmenuzarse *to crumble* (intransitive)
    Reg.   realizar   65
desmerecer *to be unworthy of*   parecer   53
desmesurarse *to become impudent,*
    insolent Reg.   hablar   41
desmilitarizar *to demilitarize* Reg.   realizar   65
desmitificar *to demythify* Reg.   sacar   74
desmochar *to chop off (the top or tip)*
    Reg.   hablar   41
desmontar *to take apart (mechanism);*
    dismantle Reg.   hablar   41
desmontarse de *to alight from* Reg.   hablar   41
desmoralizar *to demoralize* Reg.   realizar   65
desmoronar *to wear something down*
    Reg.   hablar   41
desmoronarse *to crumble away* Reg.   hablar   41
desmotivar *to discourage, demotivate*
    Reg.   hablar   41
desmovilizar *to demobilize* Reg.   realizar   65
desnatar *to skim (milk)* Reg.   hablar   41
desnaturalizar *to denaturalize* Reg.   realizar   65

desnaturalizarse *to give up one's*
nationality Reg.   realizar   65
desnivelar *to make uneven* Reg.   hablar   41
desnivelarse *to become uneven* Reg.   hablar   41
desnucar *to poleaxe; to break the neck*
of Reg.   sacar   74
desnudar *to undress someone* Reg.   hablar   41
desnudarse *to undress oneself* Reg.   hablar   41
desnutrirse *to become undernourished*
Reg.   vivir   89
desobedecer *to disobey*   parecer   53
desocupar *to vacate* Reg.   hablar   41
desodorizar *to deodorize* Reg.   realizar   65
desoír *to turn a deaf ear to*   oír   50
desolar *to make desolate*   contar   24
desollar *to skin; to flay*   contar   24
desordenar *to throw into disorder* Reg.   hablar   41
desorbitar *to exaggerate wildly* Reg.   hablar   41
desorbitarse *to go to wild extremes* Reg. hablar   41
desordenar *to disorder, disarray* Reg.   hablar   41
desorganizar *to disorganize* Reg.   realizar   65
desorientar *to misdirect; to confuse*
Reg.   hablar   41
desorientarse *to lose one's way; to*
become confused Reg.   hablar   41
desosar = **deshuesar**   desosar   30
desovar *to spawn*   hablar   41
desovillar *to unwind (a ball of string,*
etc.) Reg.   hablar   41
desovillarse *to become unwound* Reg.   hablar   41
desoxidar *to de-rust* Reg.   hablar   41
despachar *to complete, carry out; to*
finish a task; to dispatch Reg.   hablar   41
despacharse *to finish work; to get on*
with something Reg.   hablar   41
despachurrar *to squash* Reg.   hablar   41
despampanar *to trim, prune* Reg.   hablar   41

desparpajar = **desmontar** Reg.	hablar	41
desparramar *to scatter; to spread all over the place* Reg.	hablar	41
desparramarse *to be scattered, spread* Reg.	hablar	41
despatarrar *to dumbfound* Reg.	hablar	41
despatarrarse *to do the splits, open one's legs wide* Reg.	comer	22
despechar *to enrage* Reg.	hablar	41
despedazar *to break to pieces* Reg.	realizar	65
despedir *to fire (dismiss); to give off; to see off*	pedir	54
despedirse de *to say good-bye to*	pedir	54
despegar *to take off (aircraft)* Reg.	pagar	52
despegarse *to come off; to come unstuck* Reg.	pagar	52
despeinar *to mess up the hair* Reg.	hablar	41
despejar *to remove obstacles; also =* **despejarse** Reg.	hablar	41
despejarse *to clear (weather)* Reg.	hablar	41
despellejar *to skin* Reg.	hablar	41
despenalizar *to decriminalize* Reg.	realizar	65
despeñar *to fling down a precipice* Reg.	hablar	41
despeñarse *to fall down a precipice; to plummet* Reg.	hablar	41
despepitar *to remove the seeds, pips* Reg.	hablar	41
despepitarse *to holler* Reg.	hablar	41
desperdiciar *to waste, squander* Reg.	hablar	41
desperdigar *to scatter* Reg.	pagar	52
desperezarse *to stretch oneself* Reg.	realizar	65
despertar *to wake someone up*	cerrar	18
despertarse *to awake* (intransitive)	cerrar	18
despilfarrar *to squander* Reg.	hablar	41
despintar *to strip the paint off* Reg.	hablar	41
despistar *to throw off the trail or course; to confuse* Reg.	hablar	41

despistarse *to get confused* Reg.	hablar	41
desplacer = **disgustar**	parecer	53
desplazar *to shift something* Reg.	realizar	65
desplazarse *to shift* (intransitive)*; to move; to commute* Reg.	realizar	65
desplegar *to unfold something; to display*	negar	49
desplegarse *to unfold* (intransitive)	negar	49
desplomarse *to tilt over; to collapse* Reg.	hablar	41
desplumar *to pluck* Reg.	hablar	41
despoblar *to depopulate*	contar	24
despojar *to despoil; to deprive of* Reg.	hablar	41
despojarse de *to divest oneself of* Reg.	hablar	41
desportillar *to chip the edge of* Reg.	hablar	41
desposar = **casar** Reg.	hablar	41
desposarse = **casarse** Reg.	hablar	41
desposeer de *to deprive, dispossess of* Reg.	poseer	59
despotricar contra *to rave about/against* Reg.	sacar	74
despreciar *to despise; to scorn* Reg.	hablar	41
desprender *to loosen; to unfasten; to emit* Reg.	comer	22
desprenderse de *to work loose from; to fall off* Reg.	comer	22
despreocuparse de *not to worry about* Reg.	hablar	41
desprestigiar *to discredit; to disparage* Reg.	hablar	41
desprivatizar *to nationalize, de-privatize* Reg.	realizar	65
desproveer de *to deprive of*	proveer	63
despuntar *to blunt; to show (dawn, day)* Reg.	hablar	41
desquiciar *to unhinge* Reg.	hablar	41

desquiciarse *to become unhinged, mad* Reg.	hablar	41
desquitar *to make good (a loss)* Reg.	hablar	41
desquitarse con *to get even with* Reg.	hablar	41
destacar *to make something stand out; to emphasize* Reg.	sacar	74
destacarse *to stand out* Reg.	sacar	74
destapar *to uncover; to open* Reg.	hablar	41
destaparse *to become uncovered; to strip oneself naked* Reg.	hablar	41
destejar *to remove roofing tiles* Reg.	hablar	41
destellar *to twinkle; to flash (lights)* (intransitive) Reg.	hablar	41
destemplar *to put out of tune* Reg.	hablar	41
destemplarse *to get out of tune* Reg.	hablar	41
desteñir *to take the color/(Brit.)colour out of*	reñir	69
desteñirse *to lose color/(Brit.) colour*	reñir	69
desterrar *to exile*	cerrar	18
destetar *to wean* Reg.	hablar	41
destilar *to distill/(Brit.) distil; to drip* Reg.	hablar	41
destinar *to destine; to post (i.e. soldiers, officials to a posting)* Reg.	hablar	41
destituir *to dismiss from office*	construir	23
destorcer *to untwist*	cocer	19
destornillar *to unscrew* Reg.	hablar	41
destranquilizar *to make someone worried* Reg.	realizar	65
destranquilizarse *to get worried, upset* Reg.	realizar	65
destripar *to gut; to rip out intestines* Reg.	hablar	41
destroncar *to lop off* Reg.	sacar	74
destronar *to dethrone* Reg.	hablar	41
destrozar *to shatter* Reg.	realizar	65
destruir *to destroy*	construir	23

desvainar *to shell (peas)* Reg.   hablar   41
desvaír *to empty; to vacate*   desvaír   31
desvalijar *to rob; to ransack* Reg.   hablar   41
desvalorar *to devalue* Reg.   hablar   41
desvalorizar = **desvalorar** Reg.   realizar   65
desvanecerse *to vanish*   parecer   53
desvariar *to rave; to talk nonsense*   liar   45
desvelar *to keep someone awake* Reg.   hablar   41
desvelarse *to stay awake; to be sleepless*
  Reg.   hablar   41
desvencijar *to weaken, wear down* Reg.   hablar   41
desvergonzarse *to speak or act in a*
  shameless manner   avergonzar   12
desvestir *to undress someone*   pedir   54
desvestirse *to undress oneself*   pedir   54
desviar *to deflect*   liar   45
desviarse *to go awry, off course*   liar   45
desvincular de *to disconnect from* Reg.   hablar   41
desvincularse de *to break off one's*
  connections with Reg.   hablar   41
desvirtuar *to spoil (quality)*   continuar   25
desvivirse por *to be crazy about; to do*
  one's best for Reg.   vivir   89
detallar *to detail* Reg.   hablar   41
detectar *to detect* Reg.   hablar   41
detener *to stop (someone); to arrest*   tener   82
detenerse *to stop (= to come to a halt);*
  to pause   tener   82
detentar *to hold (records, titles)* Reg.   hablar   41
deteriorar *to damage* Reg.   hablar   41
deteriorarse *to deteriorate* Reg.   hablar   41
determinar *to determine; to fix (price,*
  etc.) Reg.   hablar   41
determinarse a *to make up one's mind to*
  Reg.   hablar   41
detestar *to detest* Reg.   hablar   41
detonar *to detonate* Reg.   hablar   41

detractar *to detract; to defame* Reg.	hablar	41
detraer *to separate; to defame*	traer	83
devaluar *to devalue*	continuar	25
devanarse (los sesos) *to rack one's brains* Reg.	hablar	41
devanear *to rave* Reg.	hablar	41
devastar *to devastate* Reg.	hablar	41
devengar *to accrue (interest)* Reg.	pagar	52
devenir *to become*	venir	87
devolver *to give back; to vomit*	volver	90
devorar *to devour* Reg.	hablar	41
diagnosticar *to diagnose* Reg.	sacar	74
dialogar *to dialogue* Reg.	pagar	52
dibujar *to draw* Reg.	hablar	41
dibujarse *to be outlined* Reg.	hablar	41
dictaminar en *to pass judgement on* Reg.	hablar	41
dictar *to dictate* Reg.	hablar	41
diezmar *to decimate* Reg.	hablar	41
difamar *to slander, libel* Reg.	hablar	41
diferenciar *to differentiate* Reg.	hablar	41
diferenciarse de *to differ from* Reg.	hablar	41
diferir *to defer;* **d. de** *to differ from*	sentir	78
dificultar *to make difficult; to hinder* Reg.	hablar	41
difuminar *to blur* Reg.	hablar	41
difundir *to diffuse; to broadcast* Reg.	vivir	89
difundirse *to spread (news, etc.)* Reg.	vivir	89
digerir *to digest*	sentir	78
digitalizar *to digitalize* Reg.	realizar	65
dignarse a *to condescend to* Reg.	hablar	41
dignificar *to dignify* Reg.	sacar	74
dignificarse *to become dignified* Reg.	sacar	74
dilapidar *to squander* Reg.	hablar	41
dilatar *to expand (metal); to dilate, enlarge (orifice); to defer (plan, etc.)* (transitive) Reg.	hablar	41

dilatarse *to stretch (space, time); to*
   expand (intransitive) Reg.   hablar   41
diligenciar *to get busy with; to get*
   something moving Reg.   hablar   41
dilucidar *to elucidate* Reg.   hablar   41
diluir *to dilute*   construir   23
diluviar *to rain hard; to pour* Reg.   hablar   41
dimanar de *to emanate, flow from* Reg.   hablar   41
dimitir *to resign* Reg.   vivir   89
dinamitar *to dynamite* Reg.   hablar   41
diputar *to delegate* Reg.   hablar   41
dirigir *to steer, direct; to address*   rugir   72
dirigirse a *to proceed towards*   rugir   72
dirimir *to settle (a dispute); to dissolve,*
   annul (a contract) Reg.   vivir   89
discapacitar *to disable (a person); to*
   handicap Reg.   hablar   41
discernir *to distinguish; to discern*   discernir   32
disciplinar *to discipline* Reg.   hablar   41
discontinuar *to discontinue*   continuar   25
disconvenir *to disagree*   venir   87
discordar *to disagree; to be out of tune*   contar   24
discrepar de *to dissent from* Reg.   hablar   41
discriminar *to discriminate against* Reg.   hablar   41
disculpar *to excuse, pardon* Reg.   hablar   41
disculparse de *to say sorry for* Reg.   hablar   41
discurrir *to think up, invent (some*
   prank, etc.); to flow (rivers, time)
   Reg.   vivir   89
discursear *to make speeches* Reg.   hablar   41
discutir *to have an argument; to discuss*
   Reg.   vivir   89
disecar *to stuff and mount (a dead*
   animal) Reg.   sacar   74
diseccionar *to dissect* Reg.   hablar   41
diseminar *to disseminate* Reg.   hablar   41
disentir de *to dissent from*   sentir   78

diseñar *to sketch* Reg.	hablar	41
disertar acerca de *to hold forth about* Reg.	hablar	41
disfrazar *to disguise* (transitive) Reg.	realizar	65
disfrazarse *to disguise oneself* Reg.	realizar	65
disfrutar *to enjoy* Reg.	hablar	41
disgregar *to disintegrate, break up* (transitive) Reg.	pagar	52
disgregarse *to become disintegrated, broken up* Reg.	pagar	52
disgustar *to displease* Reg.	hablar	41
disgustarse *to be displeased* Reg.	hablar	41
disimular *to hide one's feelings; to dissimulate* Reg.	hablar	41
disipar *to dissipate; to disperse something* Reg.	hablar	41
disiparse *to vanish away* Reg.	hablar	41
dislocar *to dislocate* Reg.	sacar	74
disminuir *to diminish* (transitive and intransitive)	construir	23
disonar *to be discordant; to sound unfamiliar*	contar	24
disociar *to disassociate* Reg.	hablar	41
disolver *to dissolve*	volver	90
disonar *to be discordant*	contar	24
disparar *to shoot (a gun)* Reg.	hablar	41
dispararse *to go off (guns, bombs)* Reg.	hablar	41
disparatar *to talk nonsense* Reg.	hablar	41
dispensar *to excuse; to grant (honours, titles)* Reg.	hablar	41
dispersar *to disperse (a group)* Reg.	hablar	41
dispersarse *to scatter* (intransitive) Reg.	hablar	41
displacer = **desplacer**	parecer	53
disponer *to dispose; to order;* **d. de** *to dispose of (= to possess)*	poner	58
disponerse a *to get ready to*	poner	58
disputar *to dispute* Reg.	hablar	41

distanciar *to place at a distance* Reg.	hablar	41
distanciarse de *to distance oneself from* Reg.	hablar	41
distar de *to be far from; to be different from* Reg.	hablar	41
distender *to distend*	perder	55
distinguir *to distinguish* Reg.	distinguir	33
distinguirse por *to distinguish oneself by* Reg.	distinguir	33
distraer *to distract*	traer	83
distraerse *to be distracted*	traer	83
distribuir *to distribute*	construir	23
disturbar *to disturb* Reg.	hablar	41
disuadir de *to dissuade from* Reg.	vivir	89
divagar *to digress, go off the point* Reg.	pagar	52
divergir *to diverge*	rugir	72
diversificar *to diversify* Reg.	sacar	74
divertir *to amuse*	sentir	78
divertirse *to have a good time; to amuse oneself*	sentir	78
dividir *to divide* Reg.	vivir	89
divinizar *to deify* Reg.	realizar	65
divisar *to sight; to make out (in the distance)* Reg.	hablar	41
divorciarse *to get divorced* Reg.	hablar	41
divulgar *to make public* Reg.	pagar	52
divulgarse *to become widespread* Reg.	pagar	52
doblar *to bend something; to fold; to turn (a corner)* Reg.	hablar	41
doblegar *to break (resistance)* Reg.	pagar	52
doblegarse *to submit, knuckle under* Reg.	pagar	52
documentar *to document* Reg.	hablar	41
dogmatizar *to dogmatize* Reg.	realizar	65
doler *to hurt, ache*	mover	48
dolerse de *to suffer because of; to regret*	mover	48
domar *to tame* Reg.	hablar	41

domeñar *to tame; to restrain* Reg.	hablar	41
domesticar *to domesticate* Reg.	sacar	74
domiciliar *to pay by direct billing/ (Brit.) by direct debit* Reg.	hablar	41
domiciliarse *to reside* Reg.	hablar	41
dominar *to dominate; to master* Reg.	hablar	41
dominarse *to control oneself* Reg.	hablar	41
donar *to donate* Reg.	hablar	41
dorar *to gild* Reg.	hablar	41
dormir *to sleep*	dormir	34
dormirse *to fall asleep*	dormir	34
dormitar *to doze* Reg.	hablar	41
dosificar *to measure out (doses)* Reg.	sacar	74
dotar de *to endow with; to equip with* Reg.	hablar	41
dramatizar *to dramatize* Reg.	realizar	65
drenar *to drain* Reg.	hablar	41
driblar *to dribble (soccer)* Reg.	hablar	41
drogar *to drug* Reg.	pagar	52
duchar *to give a shower* Reg.	hablar	41
ducharse *to take a shower* Reg.	hablar	41
dudar *to doubt* Reg.	hablar	41
duplicar *to duplicate* Reg.	sacar	74
durar *to last* Reg.	hablar	41
echar *to throw out; to pour out* (consult dictionary for idiomatic meanings) Reg.	hablar	41
echarse *to throw, move oneself* Reg.	hablar	41
eclipsar *to eclipse something* Reg.	hablar	41
eclipsar *to be eclipsed* Reg.	hablar	41
economizar *to economize on, save (money, fuel, etc.)* Reg.	realizar	65
edificar *to build* Reg.	sacar	74
editar *to publish; to edit* Reg.	hablar	41
educar *to educate; to bring up (children)* Reg.	sacar	74

efectuar *to effect; to carry out*	continuar	25
ejecutar *to execute (plan or criminal);*		
to perform (task) Reg.	hablar	41
ejemplificar *to exemplify* Reg.	sacar	74
ejercer *to practice/(Brit.) practise (a*		
profession) Reg.	vencer	86
ejercitar *to exercise* Reg.	hablar	41
elaborar *to manufacture; to work out (a*		
plan) Reg.	hablar	41
electrificar *to electrify* Reg.	sacar	74
electrizar = **electrificar** Reg.	realizar	65
electrocutar *to electrocute* Reg.	hablar	41
elegir *to elect; to choose*	regir	66
elevar *to elevate* Reg.	hablar	41
elevarse *to rise* Reg.	hablar	41
eliminar *to eliminate* Reg.	hablar	41
elogiar *to praise* Reg.	hablar	41
eludir *to elude* Reg.	vivir	89
emanar *to emanate* Reg.	hablar	41
emancipar *to emancipate* Reg.	hablar	41
emanciparse *to become emancipated*		
Reg.	hablar	41
embadurnar de *to daub with* Reg.	hablar	41
embaír *to deceive* (archaic = **engañar**)	desvaír	31
embalar *to pack (e.g. an article in a*		
crate)	hablar	41
embalarse *to rush, hurry* Reg.	hablar	41
embalsamar *to embalm* Reg.	hablar	41
embalsar *to dam* Reg.	hablar	41
embarazar *to make pregnant; to get in*		
the way of, hamper Reg.	realizar	65
embarcar *to embark, go on board* Reg.	sacar	74
embarcarse en *to go on board* Reg.	sacar	74
embargar *to embargo; to distrain* Reg.	pagar	52
embarrancar *to run aground* Reg.	sacar	74
embarrancarse = **embarrancar** Reg.	sacar	74
embarrar *to stain with mud* Reg.	hablar	41

embarullar *to make a mess of; to confuse* Reg.	hablar	41
embarullarse *to get confused* Reg.	hablar	41
embaucar *to bamboozle* Reg.	sacar	74
embeberse en *to get absorbed (in a task)* Reg.	comer	22
embelesar *to charm, captivate* Reg.	hablar	41
embelesarse *to be charmed, captivated* Reg.	hablar	41
embestir *to charge (like a bull)*	pedir	54
emblandecer *to soften*	parecer	53
embobar *to enchant; to fascinate* Reg.	hablar	41
embobarse *to be captivated, spellbound* Reg.	hablar	41
embolsarse *to pocket (money, etc.)* Reg.	hablar	41
emborrachar *to intoxicate* Reg.	hablar	41
emborracharse *to get drunk* Reg.	hablar	41
emborronar *to blot* Reg.	hablar	41
emboscar *to ambush* Reg.	sacar	74
embotar *to dull* Reg.	hablar	41
embotarse *to get sluggish, dull* Reg.	hablar	41
embotellar *to bottle* Reg.	hablar	41
embozarse *to cover one's face with a cloak or muffler* Reg.	realizar	65
embragar *to engage the clutch* Reg.	pagar	52
embravecer *to infuriate*	parecer	53
embravecerse *to get stormy (weather)*	parecer	53
embrear *to cover or soak with tar* Reg.	hablar	41
embriagar *to enrapture* = **emborrachar** Reg.	pagar	52
embriagarse = **emborracharse** Reg.	pagar	52
embrollar *to embroil, entangle* Reg.	hablar	41
embrollarse *to become entangled, embroiled* Reg.	hablar	41
embromar *to tease; to trick* Reg.	hablar	41
embrujar *to bewitch* Reg.	hablar	41

embrutecer *to brutalize*	parecer	53
embutir de *to stuff with* Reg.	vivir	89
emerger *to surface; to come to light* Reg.	proteger	62
emigrar *to emigrate; to migrate* Reg.	hablar	41
emitir *to emit* Reg.	vivir	89
emocionar *to cause emotion; to excite (emotionally)* Reg.	hablar	41
emocionarse *to be excited (emotionally)* Reg.	hablar	41
empacar *to pack* Reg.	sacar	74
empacarse *to become obstinate, dig in one's heels* Reg.	sacar	74
empachar *to cause indigestion* Reg.	hablar	41
empacharse *to have indigestion* Reg.	hablar	41
empadronar *to register (in a census)* Reg.	hablar	41
empalagar: esto me empalaga *I find this sickly* Reg.	pagar	52
empalagarse de *to stuff oneself with* Reg.	pagar	52
empalar *to impale* Reg.	hablar	41
empalizar *to stockade* Reg.	realizar	65
empalmar *to splice together; to connect* Reg.	hablar	41
empanar *to bread* Reg.	hablar	41
empantanar *to swamp* Reg.	hablar	41
empantanarse *to get bogged down* Reg.	hablar	41
empañar *to fog; to tarnish* Reg.	hablar	41
empapar *to soak* Reg.	hablar	41
empaparse *to get soaked* Reg.	hablar	41
empapelar *to wallpaper* Reg.	hablar	41
empaquetar *to pack* Reg.	hablar	41
emparejar *to pair someone off* Reg.	hablar	41
emparentar con *to become related to by marriage* Reg.	hablar	41
empastar *to fill (a tooth)* Reg.	hablar	41

empatar *to tie (in games, etc.)* Reg.	hablar	41
empatarse con *to be dead level with, neck and neck with* Reg.	hablar	41
empecinarse en *to get it into one's head that* Reg.	hablar	41
empedernir *to harden*	abolir	1
empedrar *to pave with stones*	cerrar	18
empeñar *to pawn* Reg.	hablar	41
empeñarse en *to insist on* Reg.	hablar	41
empeorar *to make worse; to get worse* Reg.	hablar	41
empequeñecer *to get smaller*	parecer	53
emperejilarse *to dress up smart* Reg.	hablar	41
emperrarse en *to get stubborn about* Reg.	hablar	41
empezar a *to begin to*	comenzar	21
empinar *to raise (cup, elbow)* Reg.	hablar	41
empinarse *to rise high* Reg.	hablar	41
emplazar *to locate, site (a building)* Reg.	realizar	65
emplear *to employ; to use* Reg.	hablar	41
emplumar *to feather, adorn with feathers* Reg.	hablar	41
empobrecer *to impoverish*	parecer	53
empobrecerse *to become impoverished*	parecer	53
empollar *to hatch (eggs)* Reg.	hablar	41
empolvarse *to get dusty* Reg.	hablar	41
empotrar *to embed, build in (*e.g. **armario empotrado** *built-in cupboard)* Reg.	hablar	41
emprender *to undertake* Reg.	comer	22
empujar *to push* Reg.	hablar	41
empuñar *to brandish (a stick)* Reg.	hablar	41
emular *to emulate* Reg.	hablar	41
enajenar *to alienate; to drive out of one's mind* Reg.	hablar	41

enajenarse *to go mad; to become alienated* Reg.	hablar	41
enaltecer *to exalt*	parecer	53
enaltecerse *to be exalted*	parecer	53
enamorar *to make someone fall in love* Reg.	hablar	41
enamorarse de *to fall in love with* Reg.	hablar	41
enarbolar *to raise, hoist (a banner)* Reg.	hablar	41
enardecerse *to get excited (passions)*	parecer	53
encabezar *to head; to put a heading to* Reg.	realizar	65
encabritarse *to rear (horse)* Reg.	hablar	41
encadenar *to chain* Reg.	hablar	41
encajar en *to fit something to* Reg.	hablar	41
encajarse con *to fit (i.e. match)* Reg.	hablar	41
encajonar *to box, crate* Reg.	hablar	41
encalar *to whitewash* Reg.	hablar	41
encallar *to run aground; to get entangled* Reg.	hablar	41
encallecerse *to get callused/(Brit.) calloused, rough (skin)*	parecer	53
encalvecer *to become bald*	parecer	53
encaminar *to channel; to direct* Reg.	hablar	41
encaminarse a *to be on the way to* Reg.	hablar	41
encanecerse *to become gray/(Brit.)grey haired*	parecer	53
encantar *to charm* Reg.	hablar	41
encañonar *to point a gun at* Reg.	hablar	41
encapotarse *to get cloudy* Reg.	hablar	41
encapricharse con *to get a thing about; to get crazy about* Reg.	hablar	41
encaramarse a *to climb up (trees, ladders)* Reg.	hablar	41
encarar *to face up to* Reg.	hablar	41
encararse con *to come face to face with* Reg.	hablar	41

encarcelar *to incarcerate* Reg.	hablar	41
encarecer *to extol; to raise the price of*	parecer	53
encarecerse *to get dearer*	parecer	53
encargar *to order (goods, etc.); to entrust* Reg.	pagar	52
encargarse de *to undertake to* Reg.	pagar	52
encariñarse con *to get fond of* Reg.	hablar	41
encarnar *to embody (qualities); to play (a theatrical role)* Reg.	hablar	41
encarnizarse *to get furious, vicious* Reg.	realizar	65
encarrilar *to put on the right track* Reg.	hablar	41
encarrilarse *to get back on the right track* Reg.	hablar	41
encasillar *to pigeonhole* Reg.	hablar	41
encauzar *to direct; to channel (stream)* Reg.	realizar	65
encauzarse hacia *to be channeled/ (Brit.) channelled towards; to tend to* Reg.	realizar	65
encenagar *to smear with mud* Reg.	pagar	52
encender *to light; to set on fire; to turn on (TV, etc.)*	perder	55
encenderse *to catch fire; to light (intransitive)*	perder	55
encerar *to wax* Reg.	hablar	41
encerrar *to lock up; to contain*	cerrar	18
encharcar *to turn into a puddle; to flood* Reg.	sacar	74
enchufar *to plug in; to switch on* Reg.	hablar	41
encizañar *to sow discord* Reg.	hablar	41
enclaustrarse *to shut oneself away* Reg.	hablar	41
encoger *to shrink* (transitive)*; to shrug* Reg.	proteger	62
encogerse *to shrink* (intransitive) Reg.	proteger	62
encolar *to glue* Reg.	hablar	41
encolerizar *to anger* Reg.	realizar	65
encolerizarse *to become angry* Reg.	realizar	65

encomendar a *to recommend to; to
  entrust to*   cerrar   18
encomiar *to praise* Reg.   hablar   41
enconar *to inflame (resentment, hatred)*
  Reg.   hablar   41
enconarse *to become aggravated; to
  fester* Reg.   hablar   41
encontrar *to find; to meet*   contar   24
encontrarse *to be located; to find by
  chance;* **e. con** *to come across, meet* contar   24
encorvarse *to bend over, hunch up* Reg. hablar   41
encrespar *to ruffle, make curly* Reg.   hablar   41
encresparse *to become choppy; to rise
  (bad temper)* Reg.   hablar   41
encuadernar *to bind (a book)* Reg.   hablar   41
encuadrar *to frame; to fit; to classify*
  Reg.   hablar   41
encubrir *to hide; to conceal*   cubrir   26
enderezar *to straighten; to put on the
  right path* Reg.   realizar   65
enderezarse *to sort oneself out* Reg. realizar   65
endeudarse *to get into debt* Reg.   hablar   41
endiosar *to deify* Reg.   hablar   41
endiosarse *to be stuck-up* Reg.   hablar   41
endomingarse *to dress up in one's
  Sunday clothes* Reg.   pagar   52
endosar *to endorse (a cheque)* Reg.   hablar   41
endulzar *to sweeten* Reg.   realizar   65
endurecer *to harden, toughen*   parecer   53
endurecerse *to become hard*   parecer   53
enemistar *to cause enmity between* Reg. hablar   41
enemistarse con *to fall out with* Reg. hablar   41
enervar *to get on one's nerves* Reg. hablar   41
enfadar *to anger* Reg.   hablar   41
enfadarse *to get angry* Reg.   hablar   41
enfatizar *to emphasize* Reg.   realizar   65
enfermar *to become ill* Reg.   hablar   41

enfermarse (Lat. Am.) = **enfermar** Reg.	hablar	41
enfervorizar *to arouse* Reg.	realizar	65
enfervorizarse *to become heated, aroused* Reg.	realizar	65
enfilar *to take (a road, turning)* Reg.	hablar	41
enfocar *to focus* Reg.	sacar	74
enfrascarse en *to become engrossed in* Reg.	sacar	74
enfrentar *to confront* Reg.	hablar	41
enfrentarse con *to meet face to face* Reg.	hablar	41
enfriar *to cool, chill*	liar	45
enfriarse *to grow cool*	liar	45
enfundar *to put in a case* Reg.	hablar	41
enfurecer *to infuriate*	parecer	53
enfurecerse *to become infuriated*	parecer	53
enfurruñarse *to sulk*	hablar	41
enganchar *to hook* Reg.	hablar	41
engancharse *to get hooked (drugs, passions)* Reg.	hablar	41
engañar *to deceive* Reg.	hablar	41
engañarse *to be mistaken* Reg.	hablar	41
engarzar *to set (precious stones)* Reg.	realizar	65
engatusar *to take in (someone gullible)* Reg.	hablar	41
engendrar *to engender* Reg.	hablar	41
englobar *to include; to lump together* Reg.	hablar	41
engolfarse *to become deeply absorbed* Reg.	hablar	41
engomar *to gum* Reg.	hablar	41
engordar *to fatten; to grow fatter* Reg.	hablar	41
engranar *to mesh; to engage (gears)* Reg.	hablar	41
engrandecer *to enlarge; to enhance; to extol*	parecer	53
engrapar *to staple* Reg.	hablar	41

engrasar *to lubricate; to grease* Reg.	hablar	41
engreír *to make vain*	reír	68
engreírse *to become vain*	reír	68
engrosar *to enlarge; to swell (numbers)*	contar	24
engullir *to gulp down*	bullir	15
enhebrar *to thread* Reg.	hablar	41
enjabonar *to soap* Reg.	hablar	41
enjalbegar = **encalar** Reg.	pagar	52
enjambrar *to swarm* Reg.	hablar	41
enjaular *to cage* Reg.	hablar	41
enjuagar *to rinse off* Reg.	pagar	52
enjugar *to dry off, wipe away* Reg.	pagar	52
enjuiciar *to pass judgement on; to indict* Reg.	hablar	41
enlazar *to link* Reg.	realizar	65
enlodar *to muddy* Reg.	hablar	41
enlodarse *to get muddied* Reg.	hablar	41
enloquecer *to madden; to craze*	parecer	53
enloquecerse *to become crazy*	parecer	53
enlosar *to pave with slabs* Reg.	hablar	41
enlutar *to plunge into mourning* Reg.	hablar	41
enmarañar *to entangle; to tangle* Reg.	hablar	41
enmarañarse *to become entangled* Reg.	hablar	41
enmarcar *to frame* Reg.	sacar	74
enmascarar *to mask* Reg.	hablar	41
enmascararse *to put on a mask; to masquerade* Reg.	hablar	41
enmendar *to amend; to emend*	cerrar	18
enmohecerse *to get moldy/(Brit.) mouldy*	parecer	53
enmudecer *to silence*	parecer	53
ennegrecer *to make black*	parecer	53
ennegrecerse *to grow black*	parecer	53
enojar *to anger* Reg.	hablar	41
enojarse *to get angry* Reg.	hablar	41
enorgullecer *to make proud*	parecer	53
enorgullecerse *to be proud*	parecer	53

enraizar *to take root*	arcaizar	8
enredar *to tangle up; to complicate* Reg.	hablar	41
enriquecer *to enrich*	parecer	53
enristrar *to string (onions, etc.)* Reg.	hablar	41
enrojecer *to make red; to turn red*	parecer	53
enrojecerse *to go red*	parecer	53
enrolar *to recruit* Reg.	hablar	41
enrolarse en *to sign up for; to enlist* Reg.	hablar	41
enrollar *to roll up; to coil up* Reg.	hablar	41
enrollarse *to roll up, coil up* (intransitive) Reg.	hablar	41
enronquecer *to make hoarse*	parecer	53
enroscar *to screw in/on (nut, bottle-cap, etc.)* Reg.	sacar	74
enroscarse *to curl up in a ball* Reg.	sacar	74
ensalzar *to extol* Reg.	realizar	65
ensamblar *to assemble (mechanisms, computer programs); to joint* Reg.	hablar	41
ensanchar *to widen* (transitive) Reg.	hablar	41
ensancharse *to get wider* Reg.	hablar	41
ensangrentar *to stain with blood*	cerrar	18
ensangrentarse *to get bloody (wars, etc.)*	cerrar	18
ensañar *to enrage* Reg.	hablar	41
ensañarse con *to act cruelly towards* Reg.	hablar	41
ensartar *to string (beads, etc.); to string together (words)* Reg.	hablar	41
ensayar *to rehearse; to try out* Reg.	hablar	41
enseñar *to teach; to show* Reg.	hablar	41
enseñorearse de *to take possession of* Reg.	hablar	41
ensillar *to saddle* Reg.	hablar	41
ensimismarse *to become absorbed in thought* Reg.	hablar	41
ensombrecer *to make something dark*	parecer	53

ensombrecerse *to become gloomy*	parecer	53
ensordecer *to deafen*	parecer	53
ensuciar *to dirty; to soil* Reg.	hablar	41
ensuciarse *to get dirty* Reg.	hablar	41
entablar *to start (conversation, friendship)* Reg.	hablar	41
entallar *to carve; to engrave* Reg.	hablar	41
entarimar *to floor with boards* Reg.	hablar	41
entender *to understand*	perder	55
entenderse con *to reach an understanding with*	perder	55
entenebrecer *to make dark*	parecer	53
enterar *to inform* Reg.	hablar	41
enterarse de *to find out about* Reg.	hablar	41
enternecer *to move to pity*	parecer	53
enternecerse *to be moved to pity*	parecer	53
enterrar *to bury*	cerrar	18
entibiar *to make lukewarm* Reg.	hablar	41
entibiarse *to cool down; to become lukewarm* Reg.	hablar	41
entoldar *to cover with an awning* Reg.	hablar	41
entonar *to intone; to sing in tune* Reg.	hablar	41
entontecer *to make foolish*	parecer	53
entornar *to half-close (door, eyes)* Reg.	hablar	41
entorpecer *to stupefy; to obstruct (traffic)*	parecer	53
entrampar *to trap; to trick* Reg.	hablar	41
entrañar *to entail* Reg.	hablar	41
entrar en/a *to enter* Reg.	hablar	41
entreabrir *to half-open (door, eyes)*	abrir	2
entregar *to deliver (goods to home, etc.); to hand over* Reg.	pagar	52
entregarse *to surrender* Reg.	pagar	52
entrelazar *to entwine; to interweave* Reg.	realizar	65
entrenar *to train* (transitive and intransitive) Reg.	hablar	41

entrenarse *to train* (intransitive)	hablar	41
entretejer *to weave together* Reg.	comer	22
entretener *to entertain; to delay someone*	tener	82
entrever *to see vaguely; to glimpse*	ver	88
entrevistar *to interview* Reg.	hablar	41
entrevistarse con *to have an interview with* Reg.	hablar	41
entristecer *to sadden*	parecer	53
entristecerse *to grow sad*	parecer	53
entrometerse *to butt in; to intrude* Reg.	comer	22
entroncar con *to be related to; to be connected to* Reg.	sacar	74
entronizar *to enthrone* Reg.	realizar	65
entumecerse *to become numb*	parecer	53
enturbiar *to make cloudy* Reg.	hablar	41
enturbiarse *to become cloudy* Reg.	hablar	41
entusiasmar *to excite; to make enthusiastic* Reg.	hablar	41
entusiasmarse *to get enthusiastic* Reg.	hablar	41
enunciar *to enunciate* Reg.	hablar	41
envainar *to sheathe* Reg.	hablar	41
envalentonar *to make courageous* Reg.	hablar	41
envalentonarse *to get bolder* Reg.	hablar	41
envanecer *to make vain*	parecer	53
envanecerse *to become vain*	parecer	53
envasar *to bottle; to package* Reg.	hablar	41
envejecer *to make old; to make look old; to grow old*	parecer	53
envenenar *to poison* Reg.	hablar	41
enviar *to send*	liar	45
envidiar *to envy* Reg.	hablar	41
envilecer *to vilify*	parecer	53
envilecerse *to debase oneself; to become degraded*	parecer	53
enviudar *to be widowed* Reg.	hablar	41
envolver *to wrap; to imply; to involve*	volver	90

enyesar *to plaster (e.g. broken leg)* Reg.	hablar	41
enzarzarse en *to be entangled in difficulties* Reg.	realizar	65
epitomar *to epitomize* Reg.	hablar	41
equilibrar *to balance something* Reg.	hablar	41
equilibrarse *to be balanced* Reg.	hablar	41
equidistar de *to be equidistant from* Reg.	hablar	41
equipar con *to equip with* Reg.	hablar	41
equiparar con *to equate with; to put on the same level as* Reg.	hablar	41
equivaler a *to be equivalent to*	valer	85
equivocar *to make someone make a mistake* Reg.	sacar	74
equivocarse *to make a mistake* Reg.	sacar	74
erguir *to erect; to set up straight; to prick up (ears)*	erguir	35
erguirse *to sit upright; to sit up straight; to rear up (snakes, etc.)*	erguir	35
erigir *to erect*	rugir	72
erigirse en *to set out to be; to set oneself up as*	rugir	72
erizar *to make hair/fur bristle* Reg.	realizar	65
erizarse *to bristle* Reg.	realizar	65
erosionar *to erode* Reg.	hablar	41
erradicar *to eradicate* Reg.	sacar	74
errar *to err; to wander*	errar	36
eructar *to belch* Reg.	hablar	41
esbozar *to sketch* Reg.	realizar	65
escabechar *to pickle* Reg.	hablar	41
escabullirse *to slip away; to skive off*	bullir	15
escalar *to scale (a ladder)* Reg.	hablar	41
escaldar *to scald* Reg.	hablar	41
escalfar *to poach (eggs)* Reg.	hablar	41
escalonar *to stagger (timetable); to scale (wages, figures)* Reg.	hablar	41

escamar *to scale (a fish); to cause suspicion* Reg.	hablar	41
escamotear *to make something disappear by sleight of hand or cunning* Reg.	hablar	41
escampar *to clear up (weather); to stop raining* Reg.	hablar	41
escanciar *to pour wine* Reg.	hablar	41
escandalizar *to scandalize* Reg.	realizar	65
escandalizarse *to be scandalized* Reg.	realizar	65
escapar a *to escape (justice)* Reg.	hablar	41
escaparse de *to escape from (prisoners)* Reg.	hablar	41
escaramuzar *to skirmish* Reg.	realizar	65
escarbar *to scratch about; to pry into* Reg.	hablar	41
escarchar *to frost, crystallize* Reg.	hablar	41
escardar *to weed; to hoe* Reg.	hablar	41
escarmentar *to learn a lesson (through experience)*	cerrar	18
escarnecer *to ridicule*	parecer	53
escasear *to be scarce* Reg.	hablar	41
escatimar *to skimp* Reg.	hablar	41
escayolar *to put in plaster* Reg.	hablar	41
escenificar *to stage (play, etc.)* Reg.	sacar	74
escindirse *to split (into factions, e.g. political party)* Reg.	vivir	89
esclarecer *to make clear*	parecer	53
esclavizar *to enslave* Reg.	realizar	65
escocer *to smart, sting*	cocer	19
escoger *to choose, select* Reg.	proteger	62
escolarizar *to educate; to provide schooling for* Reg.	realizar	65
escoltar *to escort* Reg.	hablar	41
esconder *to hide (something)* Reg.	comer	22
esconderse *to hide oneself* Reg.	comer	22

escorar *to heel over; to list (boat)* (intransitive); *to prop up* (transitive)	hablar	41
escribir *to write*	escribir	37
escrutar *to scrutinize* Reg.	hablar	41
escuchar *to listen to; to heed* Reg.	hablar	41
escudar *to shield* Reg.	hablar	41
escudriñar *to pry into* Reg.	hablar	41
esculpir *to sculpture* Reg.	vivir	89
escupir *to spit* Reg.	vivir	89
escurrir *to drain* (transitive); *to wring out* Reg.	vivir	89
escurrirse *to drain, drip (dry)* (intransitive); *to slip away; to skive off* Reg.	vivir	89
esforzar *to encourage; to push (a person into trying harder)*	almorzar	6
esforzarse por *to try hard to*	almorzar	6
esfumar *to tone down* Reg.	hablar	41
esfumarse *to melt away, disappear* Reg.	hablar	41
esgrimir *to brandish; to fence* Reg.	vivir	89
eslabonar *to link together* Reg.	hablar	41
esmaltar *to enamel* Reg.	hablar	41
esmerarse por *to do one's best to; to take pains to* Reg.	hablar	41
espabilar *to wake someone up (figuratively)* Reg.	hablar	41
espabilarse *to wake up (= to get 'clued up')* Reg.	hablar	41
espaciar *to space out* Reg.	hablar	41
espantar *to scare; to frighten away* Reg.	hablar	41
espantarse *to be scared, startled* Reg.	hablar	41
españolizar *to Hispanify, make Spanish* Reg.	realizar	65
esparcir *to scatter* Reg.	zurcir	92
esparcirse por *to be scattered over* Reg.	zurcir	92
especificar *to specify* Reg.	sacar	74
especular *to speculate* Reg.	hablar	41

esperar *to hope; to expect; to wait* Reg.	hablar	41
espesar *to thicken* (transitive and intransitive) Reg.	hablar	41
espetar: espetar una pregunta *to fire/rap out a question*	hablar	41
espiar *to spy*	liar	45
espigar *to form ears (wheat, barley, etc.); to glean* Reg.	pagar	52
espigarse *to grow tall* Reg.	pagar	52
espirar *to exhale* Reg.	hablar	41
espolear *to spur* Reg.	hablar	41
espolvorear *to sprinkle* Reg.	hablar	41
esponjar *to make fluffy* Reg.	hablar	41
esponjarse *to become fluffy* Reg.	hablar	41
esposar *to handcuff* Reg.	hablar	41
espumar *to skim (the foam off)* Reg.	hablar	41
esquematizar *to sketch; to outline* Reg.	realizar	65
esquiar *to ski*	liar	45
esquilar *to shear* Reg.	hablar	41
esquilmar *to exhaust (reserves); to harvest* Reg.	hablar	41
esquivar *to dodge, avoid* Reg.	hablar	41
estabilizar *to stabilize something* Reg.	realizar	65
estabilizarse *to become stable* Reg.	realizar	65
establecer *to establish*	parecer	53
establecerse *to settle in*	parecer	53
estacionar *to park* (transitive) Reg.	hablar	41
estacionarse *to park* (intransitive) Reg.	hablar	41
estafar *to swindle* Reg.	hablar	41
estallar *to explode* Reg.	hablar	41
estampar *to stamp (a sign, seal)* Reg.	hablar	41
estancar *to staunch, dam up* Reg.	sacar	74
estancarse *to stagnate* Reg.	sacar	74
estandarizar *to standardize* Reg.	realizar	65
estañar *to solder* Reg.	hablar	41
estar *to be* (consult a dictionary for idiomatic uses)	estar	38

estarse *to stay*	estar	38
estatuir *to establish, lay down (a law, statute)*	construir	23
estereotipar *to stereotype* Reg.	hablar	41
esterilizar *to sterilize* Reg.	realizar	65
estigmatizar *to stigmatize* Reg.	realizar	65
estilarse *to be in style* Reg.	hablar	41
estilizar *to stylize* Reg.	realizar	65
estimar *to esteem; to estimate* Reg.	hablar	41
estimular *to stimulate* Reg.	hablar	41
estipular *to stipulate* Reg.	hablar	41
estirar *to stretch; to tense* Reg.	hablar	41
estofar *to stew* Reg.	hablar	41
estorbar *to be in the way; to obstruct; to annoy* Reg.	hablar	41
estornudar *to sneeze* Reg.	hablar	41
estrangular *to strangle* Reg.	hablar	41
estratificar *to stratify* Reg.	sacar	74
estrechar *to make narrow, tighter* Reg.	hablar	41
estrecharse *to get narrower, tighter* Reg.	hablar	41
estrellar *to shatter* Reg.	hablar	41
estrellarse *to crash (vehicles)* Reg.	hablar	41
estremecer *to shake something; to shudder*	parecer	53
estremecerse *to tremble*	parecer	53
estrenar *to use, display or wear for the first time* Reg.	hablar	41
estrenarse *to make one's debut* Reg.	hablar	41
estreñir *to constipate*	reñir	69
estreñirse *to become constipated*	reñir	69
estresar *to stress (psychologically)* Reg.	hablar	41
estribar *to be based on (argument, belief)* Reg.	hablar	41
estropear *to spoil* Reg.	hablar	41
estropearse *to break down* Reg.	hablar	41
estructurar *to organize, structure* Reg.	hablar	41
estrujar *to squeeze; to crumple* Reg.	hablar	41

estudiar *to study* Reg.	hablar	41
eternizar *to make endless* Reg.	realizar	65
eternizarse *never to finish; to go on for ever* Reg.	realizar	65
etiquetar *to label* Reg.	hablar	41
europeizar *to Europeanize*	arcaizar	8
evacuar (formerly conjugated like **continuar**) *to evacuate* Reg.	hablar	41
evadir *to evade* Reg.	vivir	89
evadirse *to escape* Reg.	vivir	89
evaluar *to evaluate*	continuar	25
evangelizar *to evangelize* Reg.	realizar	65
evaporar *to evaporate* Reg.	hablar	41
evaporizar *to vaporize* Reg.	realizar	65
evidenciar *to make evident* Reg.	hablar	41
evitar *to avoid* Reg.	hablar	41
evocar *to evoke* Reg.	sacar	74
evolucionar *to evolve* Reg.	hablar	41
exacerbar *to exacerbate* Reg.	hablar	41
exagerar *to exaggerate* Reg.	hablar	41
exaltar *to exalt* Reg.	hablar	41
exaltarse *to become excited* Reg.	hablar	41
examinar *to examine; to inspect* Reg.	hablar	41
examinarse *to take an examination* Reg.	hablar	41
excavar *to excavate* Reg.	hablar	41
exceder *to exceed* Reg.	comer	22
exceptuar *to except*	continuar	25
excitar *to excite* Reg.	hablar	41
excitarse *to become excited* Reg.	hablar	41
exclamar *to exclaim* Reg.	hablar	41
excluir *to exclude*	construir	23
excogitar *to think out; to devise* Reg.	hablar	41
excomulgar *to excommunicate* Reg.	pagar	52
excusar *to excuse; to avoid; to exempt* Reg.	hablar	41
excusarse *to apologize* Reg.	hablar	41

exhalar *to emit; to exhale* Reg.	hablar	41
exhibir *to exhibit* Reg.	vivir	89
exhibirse *to show off* (intransitive) Reg.	vivir	89
exhortar *to exhort* Reg.	hablar	41
exhumar *to exhume* Reg.	hablar	41
exigir *to require; to demand*	rugir	72
eximir *to exempt* Reg.	vivir	89
exonerar *to exonerate* Reg.	hablar	41
exorcizar *to exorcise* Reg.	realizar	65
expansionar *to expand* (transitive) Reg.	hablar	41
expansionarse *to open one's heart* Reg.	hablar	41
expatriar *to expatriate*	liar	45
expedir *to issue*	pedir	54
expeditar *to expedite* Reg.	hablar	41
experimentar *to experience; to experiment* Reg.	hablar	41
expiar *to atone for*	liar	45
expirar *to expire* Reg.	hablar	41
explanar *to level; to explain* Reg.	hablar	41
explayar *to extend* Reg.	hablar	41
explayarse *to discourse at large* Reg.	hablar	41
explicar *to explain* Reg.	sacar	74
explicarse *to make sense of* Reg.	sacar	74
explorar *to explore* Reg.	hablar	41
explosionar *to detonate, fire (explosives); to explode* (transitive and intransitive)	hablar	41
explotar *to exploit; to explode* Reg.	hablar	41
expoliar *to plunder* Reg.	hablar	41
exponer *to expose; to show*	poner	58
exportar *to export* Reg.	hablar	41
expresar *to express* Reg.	hablar	41
exprimir *to squeeze out* Reg.	vivir	89
expropiar *to expropriate* Reg.	hablar	41
expugnar *to take by storm* Reg.	hablar	41
expulsar *to expel* Reg.	hablar	41
expurgar *to expurgate* Reg.	pagar	52

extasiar *to delight*	liar	45
extasiarse *to be in ecstasy*	liar	45
extender *to extend; to draw up (a document)*	perder	55
extenuar *to make exhausted*	continuar	25
exteriorizar *to make manifest* Reg.	realizar	65
exterminar *to exterminate* Reg.	hablar	41
extinguir *to extinguish* Reg.	distinguir	33
extinguirse *to be extinguished* Reg.	distinguir	33
extirpar *to extirpate; to root out* Reg.	hablar	41
extorsionar *to extort* Reg.	hablar	41
extractar *to make a summary of (a text)* Reg.	hablar	41
extradir *to extradite* Reg.	vivir	89
extraditar *to extradite* Reg.	hablar	41
extraer *to extract*	traer	83
extralimitarse *to overstep* Reg.	hablar	41
extranjerizarse *to adopt foreign ways* Reg.	realizar	65
extrañar *to miss (i.e. feel longing for)* Reg.	hablar	41
extrañarse de *to be surprised at* Reg.	hablar	41
extrapolar *to extrapolate* Reg.	hablar	41
extraviar *to mislead; to misplace*	liar	45
extraviarse *to get lost*	liar	45
extremar *to carry to an extreme* Reg.	hablar	41
extremarse *to exert oneself to the utmost* Reg.	hablar	41
extrudir *to extrude* Reg.	vivir	89
exultar *to exult* Reg.	hablar	41
eyacular *to ejaculate* Reg.	hablar	41
fabricar *to manufacture* Reg.	sacar	74
facilitar *to make easier* Reg.	hablar	41
facturar *to check baggage (at airport); to invoice* Reg.	hablar	41

facultar para *to authorize someone to*
   Reg.   hablar   41

facultar para *to authorize someone to* Reg.	hablar	41
faenar *to fish (trawlers)* Reg.	hablar	41
fajar *to girdle; to bind with a bandage or sash* Reg.	hablar	41
fallar *to fail; to make a ruling* Reg.	hablar	41
fallecer *to die*	parecer	53
falsear *to misrepresent* Reg.	hablar	41
falsificar *to falsify; to counterfeit* Reg.	sacar	74
faltar *to be lacking; to be absent* Reg.	hablar	41
familiarizar *to familiarize* Reg.	realizar	65
fanatizar *to make fanatical* Reg.	realizar	65
fanfarronear *to brag* Reg.	hablar	41
fantasear *to daydream; to fantasize* Reg.	hablar	41
farfullar *to jabber; to gabble* Reg.	hablar	41
farolear *to show off* Reg.	hablar	41
fascinar *to fascinate* Reg.	hablar	41
fastidiar *to annoy* Reg.	hablar	41
fatigar *to make tired* Reg.	pagar	52
fatigarse *to get tired* Reg.	pagar	52
favorecer *to favor/(Brit.) favour*	parecer	53
fechar *to date (a document, etc.)* Reg.	hablar	41
fecundar *to inseminate* Reg.	hablar	41
fecundizar *to make fertile* Reg.	realizar	65
felicitar *to congratulate* Reg.	hablar	41
fermentar *to ferment* Reg.	hablar	41
fertilizar *to fertilize* Reg.	realizar	65
festejar *to laugh at (a joke); to celebrate (an occasion)* Reg.	hablar	41
fiar *to sell on credit*	liar	45
fiarse de *to trust*	liar	45
fichar *to put on file* Reg.	hablar	41
figurar *to figure (e.g. on a list)* Reg.	hablar	41
figurarse *to imagine* Reg.	hablar	41
fijar *to fix* Reg.	hablar	41
fijarse en *to pay attention to* Reg.	hablar	41

filmar *to film* Reg.	hablar	41
filosofar *to philosophize* Reg.	hablar	41
filtrar *to filter* Reg.	hablar	41
filtrarse *to leak out (information)* Reg.	hablar	41
finalizar *to finalize, finish* (transitive) Reg.	realizar	65
finalizarse *to come to an end* Reg.	realizar	65
financiar *to finance* Reg.	hablar	41
fingir *to pretend*	rugir	72
firmar *to sign* Reg.	hablar	41
fiscalizar *to oversee (e.g. expenditure)* Reg.	realizar	65
fisgar *to pry* Reg.	pagar	52
fisgonear *to pry constantly* Reg.	hablar	41
flagelar *to whip* Reg.	hablar	41
flamear *to flame* Reg.	hablar	41
flanquear *to flank* Reg.	hablar	41
flaquear *to grow weak; to falter* Reg.	hablar	41
fletar *to charter (plane, etc.)* Reg.	hablar	41
flexibilizar *to make more flexible* Reg.	realizar	65
flirtear *to flirt* Reg.	hablar	41
flojear *to slacken; to weaken; to go off an idea; to laze around* Reg.	hablar	41
florear *to decorate with flowers* Reg.	hablar	41
florecer *to blossom, flourish*	parecer	53
flotar *to float* Reg.	hablar	41
fluctuar *to fluctuate*	continuar	25
fluir *to flow*	construir	23
fluorizar *to fluoridize* Reg.	realizar	65
fomentar *to promote (idea, campaign, etc.)* Reg.	hablar	41
fondear *to sound (i.e. measure the depth of water)* Reg.	hablar	41
forjar *to forge* Reg.	hablar	41
formalizar *to formalize; to formulate,* Reg.	realizar	65
formar *to form, shape* Reg.	hablar	41

formatear *to format (disk, etc.)* Reg.	hablar	41
formular *to formulate* Reg.	hablar	41
fornicar *to fornicate* Reg.	sacar	74
forrar *to line; to cover* Reg.	hablar	41
forrarse *to rake it in (money)* Reg.	hablar	41
fortalecer *to strengthen*	parecer	53
fortificar *to fortify* Reg.	sacar	74
forzar *to force*	almorzar	6
fosilizarse *to fossilize* Reg.	realizar	65
fotograbar *to photoengrave* Reg.	hablar	41
fotografiar *to photograph*	liar	45
fracasar *to fail* (intransitive) Reg.	hablar	41
fraccionar *to divide into fractions, small portions* Reg.	hablar	41
fracturar *to fracture* Reg.	hablar	41
fragmentar *to break something into fragments* Reg.	hablar	41
fragmentarse *to fragment* (intransitive) Reg.	hablar	41
fraguar *to forge; to concoct (a scheme, plot)*	averiguar	13
franquear *to frank (a letter); to exempt* Reg.	hablar	41
fraternizar *to fraternize* Reg.	realizar	65
frecuentar *to frequent* Reg.	hablar	41
fregar *to rub; to scrub; to do the washing up*	negar	49
freír (past participle **frito**) *to fry*	reír	68
frenar *to brake* Reg.	hablar	41
fresar *to mill (engineering)* Reg.	hablar	41
friccionar *to rub; to massage* Reg.	hablar	41
frisar en : **frisaba en los sesenta años** *he wasn't far off sixty years old* Reg.	hablar	41
frotar *to rub* Reg.	hablar	41
fruncir *to wrinkle (brows)* Reg.	zurcir	92
frustrar *to frustrate* Reg.	hablar	41
fugarse *to run away* Reg.	pagar	52

fulgurar *to flash* Reg.	hablar	41
fulminar *to fulminate* Reg.	hablar	41
fumar *to smoke* Reg.	hablar	41
fumarse (familiar) *to skip (class, seminar)* Reg.	hablar	41
fumigar *to fumigate* Reg.	pagar	52
funcionar *to function; to work (machines)* Reg.	hablar	41
fundamentar *to lay the bases of* Reg.	hablar	41
fundar *to found; to base* Reg.	hablar	41
fundarse en *to be based on* Reg.	hablar	41
fundir *to smelt; to fuse* (transitive) Reg.	vivir	89
fundirse *to melt; to blow (fuse)* (intransitive) Reg.	vivir	89
fusilar *to execute by firing squad* Reg.	hablar	41
fusionar *to merge* Reg.	hablar	41
fustigar *to lash; to censure severely* Reg.	pagar	52
galantear *to flirt with (a woman)* Reg.	hablar	41
galardonar *to reward; to award a prize to (novel, etc.)* Reg.	hablar	41
galopar *to gallop* Reg.	hablar	41
galvanizar *to galvanize, electroplate* Reg.	realizar	65
gallardear *to act dashingly, elegantly* Reg.	hablar	41
ganar *to earn; to gain; to win* Reg.	hablar	41
gandulear *to loaf; to idle* Reg.	hablar	41
gangrenarse *to grow gangrenous* Reg.	hablar	41
garabatear *to scribble* Reg.	hablar	41
garantir = **garantizar**	abolir	1
garantizar *to guarantee* Reg.	realizar	65
gargajear *to spit phlegm* Reg.	hablar	41
gargarear = **gargarizar** Reg.	hablar	41
gargarizar *to gargle* Reg.	realizar	65
garrapatear *to scribble, scrawl* Reg.	hablar	41
garuar = **lloviznar**	continuar	25

gasear *to gas* Reg.	hablar	41
gastar *to spend; to waste; to wear out;* *to use up* Reg.	hablar	41
gatear *to crawl* Reg.	hablar	41
gemir *to moan; to whine*	pedir	54
generalizar *to generalize* Reg.	realizar	65
generalizarse *to become generalized,* *widely known* Reg.	realizar	65
generar *to generate* Reg.	hablar	41
germinar *to germinate* Reg.	hablar	41
gestar *to gestate* Reg.	hablar	41
gesticular *to gesture* Reg.	hablar	41
gestionar *to manage* Reg.	hablar	41
gimotear *to whimper* Reg.	hablar	41
girar *to revolve; to spin* Reg.	hablar	41
gloriarse *to boast; to be proud*	liar	45
glorificar *to glorify* Reg.	sacar	74
gobernar *to govern; to steer (boat)*	cerrar	18
golear *to score a goal* (usually **marcar**)	hablar	41
golpear *to beat* Reg.	hablar	41
golpetear *to beat repeatedly; to tap* Reg.	hablar	41
gorjear *to warble* Reg.	hablar	41
gotear *to drip; to sprinkle* Reg.	hablar	41
gozar *to enjoy* Reg.	realizar	65
grabar *to engrave; to record (on tape)* Reg.	hablar	41
graduar *to adjust*	continuar	25
graduarse *to graduate, get a degree*	continuar	25
granar *to seed (plants)* Reg.	hablar	41
granear = **granar** Reg.	hablar	41
granizar *to hail* Reg.	realizar	65
granjear *to win (by one's efforts)* Reg.	hablar	41
granular *to granulate* Reg.	hablar	41
grapar *to staple* Reg.	hablar	41
gratificar *to reward (* i.e. *to give a* *reward)* Reg.	sacar	74

gratinar *to brown (food, under the grill)*
    Reg.   hablar   41
gravar *to levy (a tax)* Reg.   hablar   41
gravitar *to gravitate;* **g. sobre** *to weight*
    *upon (*e.g. *a burden, responsibility)*
    Reg.   hablar   41
graznar *to croak; to caw; to quack*
    (ducks) Reg.   hablar   41
gritar *to shout* Reg.   hablar   41
gruñir *to grunt; to growl; to grumble*   gruñir   39
guadañar *to scythe* Reg.   hablar   41
guardar *to guard; to keep;* Reg.   hablar   41
guardarse *to keep for/to oneself* Reg.   hablar   41
guarecer *to shelter*   parecer   53
guarecerse *to take shelter*   parecer   53
guarnecer de *to garnish with*   parecer   53
guatear *to pad, wad* Reg.   hablar   41
guerrear *to war* Reg.   hablar   41
guerrillear *to wage guerrilla warfare*
    Reg.   hablar   41
guiar *to guide; to steer*   liar   45
guiarse por *to be guided by*   liar   45
guillotinar *to guillotine* Reg.   hablar   41
guiñar *to wink* (transitive and
    intransitive) Reg.   hablar   41
guisar *to cook; to stew* Reg.   hablar   41
gustar *to please;* **me gusta** *I like it* Reg.   hablar   41

haber auxiliary verb or *there is/are*   haber   40
habilitar *to equip; to authorize* Reg.   hablar   41
habitar *to inhabit; to live in* Reg.   hablar   41
habituar *to habituate*   continuar   25
habituarse a *to get into the habit of*   continuar   25
hablar *to speak; to talk* Reg.   hablar   41
hacendar *to confer land upon (a knight,*
    etc.) Reg.   hablar   41
                              or   perder   55

hacer *to do; to make* (consult a
   dictionary for idiomatic uses)   hacer   42
hacerse *to become*   hacer   42
hacinar *to jam together; to heap up*
   (transitive)   hablar   41
hacinarse *to be crowded together*   hablar   41
halagar *to flatter* Reg.   pagar   52
hallar *to find* (**encontrar** is more
   common) Reg.   hablar   41
hallarse *to find oneself; to be located*
   Reg.   hablar   41
haraganear *to loaf; to lounge* Reg.   hablar   41
hartar *to satiate; to make fed up* Reg.   hablar   41
hartarse de *to get sick of* Reg.   hablar   41
hastiar *to annoy*   liar   45
hastiarse de *to get sick/tired of*   liar   45
hechizar *to bewitch; to charm* Reg.   realizar   65
heder *to stink*   perder   55
helar *to freeze* (transitive); *to astonish*   cerrar   18
helarse *to freeze* (intransitive)   cerrar   18
henchir *to fill, swell (e.g. a river)*   pedir   54
hender *to cleave*   perder   55
heredar *to inherit* Reg.   hablar   41
herir *to wound; to hurt*   sentir   78
hermanar *to unite (people in a feeling,*
   ideal); to twin (cities) Reg.   hablar   41
hermosear *to beautify* Reg.   hablar   41
herrar *to shoe (a horse)*   cerrar   18
hervir *to boil*   sentir   78
hibernar *to hibernate* Reg.   hablar   41
hidratar *to moisturize* Reg.   hablar   41
hidrolizar *to hydrolize* Reg.   realizar   65
higienizar *to sanitize* Reg.   realizar   65
hilar *to spin (thread)* Reg.   hablar   41
hilvanar *to baste, tack (sewing); to*
   connect (ideas, phrases) Reg.   hablar   41

hincar en *to drive, sink into (teeth, stakes)* Reg.	sacar	74
hincarse *to kneel down* Reg.	sacar	74
hinchar *to inflate* Reg.	hablar	41
hincharse *to swell up* Reg.	hablar	41
hipar *to hiccup* Reg.	hablar	41
hipnotizar *to hypnotize* Reg.	realizar	65
hispanizar *to Hispanize* Reg.	realizar	65
historiar *to write the history of* Reg.	hablar	41
hocicar *to nuzzle; to root around* Reg.	sacar	74
hojear *to leaf through (a book, etc.)* Reg.	hablar	41
holgar *to be useless, pointless;* **huelga decir que** *there is no need to say that*	colgar	20
hollar *to tread upon; to trample*	contar	24
homenajear *to pay tribute to (= to praise)* Reg.	hablar	41
homogeneizar *to homogenize*	arcaizar	8
homologar *to make equal; to endorse* Reg.	pagar	52
honrar *to honor/(Brit.) honour* Reg.	hablar	41
horadar *to perforate; to bore/drill through* Reg.	hablar	41
hormiguear *to swarm* Reg.	hablar	41
hornear *to bake* Reg.	hablar	41
horrorizar *to horrify* Reg.	realizar	65
horrorizarse de *to be horrified at* Reg.	realizar	65
hospedar *to lodge, accommodate (people)* Reg.	hablar	41
hospedarse *to stay (in a hotel, etc.)* Reg.	hablar	41
hospitalizar *to hospitalize* Reg.	realizar	65
hostigar *to harass* Reg.	pagar	52
huir *to flee, run away*	construir	23
humanizar *to humanize* Reg.	realizar	65
humedecer *to moisten, wet*	parecer	53
humedecerse *to become moist, damp*	parecer	53

humillar *to humiliate* Reg.	hablar	41
hundir *to sink* (transitive) Reg.	vivir	89
hundirse *to sink* (intransitive) Reg.	vivir	89
hurgar *to poke, rummage* Reg.	pagar	52
hurtar *to steal* (= **robar**) Reg.	hablar	41
husmear *to sniff around* Reg.	hablar	41
idealizar *to idealize* Reg.	realizar	65
idear *to devise (a scheme, plan)* Reg.	hablar	41
identificar *to identify* Reg.	sacar	74
idiotizarse *to become completely stupid* Reg.	realizar	65
idolatrar *to idolize* Reg.	hablar	41
ignorar *not to know; to ignore* Reg.	hablar	41
igualar *to make equal, even, level* Reg.	hablar	41
igualarse con *to be equal to; to match* Reg.	hablar	41
ilegalizar *to make illegal* Reg.	realizar	65
iluminar *to illuminate* Reg.	hablar	41
ilusionar *to fill with excitement (*e.g. *plans, dreams)* Reg.	hablar	41
ilusionarse por *to look forward to; to get excited about* Reg.	hablar	41
ilustrar *to illustrate; to enlighten* Reg.	hablar	41
imaginar *to imagine; to invent* Reg.	hablar	41
imaginarse *to imagine* Reg.	hablar	41
imanar *to magnetize* Reg.	hablar	41
imantar = **imanar** Reg.	hablar	41
imbuir *to imbue*	construir	23
imbuirse de *to become imbued with*	construir	23
imitar *to imitate* Reg.	hablar	41
impacientar *to make impatient* Reg.	hablar	41
impacientarse *to get impatient* Reg.	hablar	41
impactar *to make an impression; to shock* Reg.	hablar	41
impartir *to impart* Reg.	vivir	89
impedir *to prevent*	pedir	54

impeler *to impel* Reg.	comer	22
imperar *to prevail* Reg.	hablar	41
impermeabilizar *to make waterproof* Reg.	realizar	65
implementar *to implement* Reg.	hablar	41
implicar *to imply* Reg.	sacar	74
implicarse *to become implicated* Reg.	sacar	74
implorar *to implore* Reg.	hablar	41
imponer *to impose*	poner	58
imponerse *to prevail; to become established (idea, etc.)*	poner	58
importar *to import; to be worth; to matter* Reg.	hablar	41
importunar *to importune* Reg.	hablar	41
imposibilitar *to make impossible; to prevent* Reg.	hablar	41
imposibilitarse *to become disabled* Reg.	hablar	41
imprecar *to imprecate, curse* Reg.	sacar	74
impregnar *to impregnate, soak* Reg.	hablar	41
impresionar *to impress* Reg.	hablar	41
imprimir *to print* Reg.	vivir	89
improvisar *to improvise* Reg.	hablar	41
impugnar *to impugn; to challenge (an idea, etc.)* Reg.	hablar	41
impulsar *to propel* Reg.	hablar	41
imputar a *to attribute to* Reg.	hablar	41
inactivar *to deactivate* Reg.	hablar	41
inaugurar *to inaugurate* Reg.	hablar	41
incapacitar *to incapacitate; to disqualify* Reg.	hablar	41
incautar *to seize, confiscate* Reg.	hablar	41
incendiar *to set fire to* Reg.	hablar	41
incendiarse *to catch fire* Reg.	hablar	41
incensar *to incense*	cerrar	18
incidir en *to affect, influence; to impinge on* Reg.	vivir	89
incinerar *to incinerate* Reg.	hablar	41

incitar *to incite* Reg.	hablar	41
inclinar *to incline; to tilt* (transitive) Reg.	hablar	41
inclinarse *to lean over; to bow* Reg.	hablar	41
incluir *to include*	construir	23
incoar *to initiate* Reg.	hablar	41
incomodar *to make someone feel awkward* Reg.	hablar	41
incomodarse *to feel embarrassed, awkward* Reg.	hablar	41
incomunicar *to isolate, cut off* Reg.	sacar	74
incordiar (familiar) *to annoy* Reg.	hablar	41
incorporar *to incorporate; to stir in* Reg.	hablar	41
incorporarse a *to sit up; to join (a club, etc.)* Reg.	hablar	41
incrementar *to increase* (transitive) Reg.	hablar	41
incrementarse *to increase* (intransitive) Reg.	hablar	41
increpar *to reprimand* Reg.	hablar	41
incriminar *to incriminate* Reg.	hablar	41
incrustar *to set (a precious stone); to embed* Reg.	hablar	41
incrustarse *to become embedded* Reg.	hablar	41
incubar *to incubate* Reg.	hablar	41
inculcar *to inculcate* Reg.	sacar	74
inculpar *to accuse; to charge (with a crime)* Reg.	hablar	41
incumbir *to concern* (third person only) Reg.	vivir	89
incumplir *to break (promises, laws); to fail to abide by* Reg.	vivir	89
incurrir en *to commit (an error); to incur (expenses)* Reg.	vivir	89
indagar *to investigate, enquire* Reg.	pagar	52
indemnizar *to indemnify* Reg.	realizar	65
independizar *to make independent* Reg.	realizar	65

independizarse *to become independent*
   Reg.   realizar   65
indexar *to index* Reg.   hablar   41
indicar *to point to; to indicate* Reg.   sacar   74
indiciar = **indexar** Reg.   hablar   41
indigestarse *to cause indigestion; se me*
   indigestó *I couldn't stomach it* Reg.   hablar   41
indignar *to anger, make indignant* Reg.   hablar   41
indignarse *to become angry* Reg.   hablar   41
indisponer *to upset; to indispose*   poner   58
indisponerse *to get upset; to become ill*   poner   58
individualizar *to individualize; to single*
   out by name Reg.   realizar   65
inducir a *to induce to; to persuade to*   producir   60
indultar *to pardon* Reg.   hablar   41
industrializar *to industrialize* Reg.   realizar   65
industrializarse *to become industrialized*
   Reg.   realizar   65
infamar *to defame* Reg.   hablar   41
infatuar *to make conceited*   continuar 25
infatuarse *to become conceited*   continuar 25
infectar *to infect* Reg.   hablar   41
infectarse *to become infected* Reg.   hablar   41
inferir de *to infer from*   sentir   78
infestar *to infest* Reg.   hablar   41
infiltrar *to infiltrate* (transitive) Reg.   hablar   41
infiltrarse *to infiltrate* (intransitive)*; to*
   sneak in Reg.   hablar   41
inflamar *to inflame* Reg.   hablar   41
inflar *to inflate; to exaggerate* Reg.   hablar   41
inflarse *to swell up* Reg.   hablar   41
infligir *to inflict*   rugir   72
influir *to influence*   construir 23
informar *to inform* Reg.   hablar   41
informarse sobre *to find out about* Reg.   hablar   41
infringir *to infringe*   rugir   72

infundir *to infuse; to instill/(Brit.) instil*
Reg. vivir 89
ingeniar *to think up (plan, idea)* Reg. hablar 41
ingeniarse *to manage* Reg. hablar 41
ingerir *to ingest* sentir 78
ingresar *to deposit (money);* **i. en** *to*
enter (an organization) Reg. hablar 41
inhabilitar *to disqualify* Reg. hablar 41
inhalar *to inhale* Reg. hablar 41
inhibir *to inhibit* Reg. vivir 89
inhumar *to inter* (= **enterrar**) Reg. hablar 41
iniciar *to initiate* Reg. hablar 41
iniciarse *to begin; to be initiated* Reg. hablar 41
injerirse en *to interfere* sentir 78
injertar *to graft (shoots on a plant, etc.)*
Reg. hablar 41
injuriar *to insult; to injure* Reg. hablar 41
inmergir *to immerse* rugir 72
inmigrar *to immigrate* Reg. hablar 41
inmiscuirse en *to interfere in* construir 23
inmolar *to immolate* (= **sacrificar**) Reg. hablar 41
inmortalizar *to immortalize* Reg. realizar 65
inmovilizar *to immobilize* Reg. realizar 65
inmunizar *to immunize* Reg. realizar 65
inmutar *to change, perturb* Reg. hablar 41
innovar *to innovate* Reg. hablar 41
inocular *to inoculate* Reg. hablar 41
inquietar *to worry, disturb* Reg. hablar 41
inquirir sobre *to inquire about* adquirir 3
inscribir *to enter something in a register* escribir 37
inscribirse *to enroll/(Brit.) enrol; to*
register escribir 37
inseminar *to inseminate* Reg. hablar 41
insensibilizar *to desensitize* Reg. realizar 65
insertar *to insert* Reg. hablar 41
insidiar *to plot against* Reg. hablar 41
insinuar *to insinuate, hint* continuar 25

insinuarse *to show through; to become just visible*	continuar	25
insistir en *to insist on* Reg.	vivir	89
insolentarse *to become insolent* Reg.	hablar	41
insonorizar *to soundproof* Reg.	realizar	65
inspeccionar *to inspect* Reg.	hablar	41
inspirar *to inspire* Reg.	hablar	41
instalar *to install* Reg.	hablar	41
instalarse *to settle in* Reg.	hablar	41
instar a *to urge to* Reg.	hablar	41
instaurar *to establish (regime, etc.)* Reg.	hablar	41
instigar a *to instigate; to incite to* Reg.	pagar	52
instilar *to instill/(Brit.) instil* Reg.	hablar	41
institucionalizar *to institutionalize* Reg.	realizar	65
instituir *to institute*	construir	23
instruir *to instruct*	construir	23
insubordinarse *to rebel* Reg.	hablar	41
insuflar *to breathe into, inspire with (e.g. spirit, enthusiasm)* Reg.	hablar	41
insultar *to insult* Reg.	hablar	41
insumir = **invertir** Reg.	vivir	89
integrar *to make up (numbers);* **i. en** *to incorporate into* Reg.	hablar	41
integrarse en *to become integrated in;* **i. a** *to join (organization)* Reg.	hablar	41
intensificar *to intensify* Reg.	sacar	74
intentar *to try* Reg.	hablar	41
interactuar *to interact*	continuar	25
intercalar en *to insert; to place between; to interpose* Reg.	hablar	41
intercambiar *to exchange* Reg.	hablar	41
interceder *to intercede* Reg.	comer	22
interceptar *to intercept* Reg.	hablar	41
interconectar *to interconnect (transitive)* Reg.	hablar	41
interdecir *to interdict*	decir	28

interesar *to interest* Reg.	hablar	41
interesarse por/en *to be interested in* Reg.	hablar	41
interferir *to interfere*	sentir	78
interiorizar *to internalize* Reg.	realizar	65
interiorizarse sobre *to make oneself familiar with* Reg.	realizar	65
intermediar *to intermediate* Reg.	hablar	41
internacionalizar *to internationalize* Reg.	realizar	65
internar *to intern, put away (e.g. in an asylum)* Reg.	hablar	41
internarse en *to penetrate into (territory, etc.)* Reg.	hablar	41
interpelar sobre *to demand explanations about* Reg.	hablar	41
interpolar *to interpolate* Reg.	hablar	41
interponer *to place between, interpose*	poner	58
interponerse *to intervene (e.g. between two enemies)*	poner	58
interpretar *to interpret; to play (a film or theatre role)* Reg.	hablar	41
interrogar *to interrogate* Reg.	pagar	52
interrumpir *to interrupt* Reg.	vivir	89
intervenir *to intervene; to take part in (performance, debate, etc.); to tap (phone calls)*	venir	87
intimar con *to be emotionally close to* Reg.	hablar	41
intimidar *to intimidate, threaten* Reg.	hablar	41
intoxicar *to intoxicate, poison* Reg.	sacar	74
intranquilizar *to disquiet; to worry* (transitive) Reg.	realizar	65
intranquilizarse *to be worried* Reg.	realizar	65
intrigar *to intrigue* Reg.	pagar	52
introducir *to introduce (e.g. legislation);* **i. en** *to insert in*	producir	60

introducirse *to get in; to gain access*	producir	60
intuir *to know or sense by intuition*	construir	23
inundar *to flood* Reg.	hablar	41
inundarse *to be flooded* Reg.	hablar	41
inutilizar *to make useless* Reg.	realizar	65
inutilizarse *to become useless* Reg.	realizar	65
invadir *to invade* Reg.	vivir	89
invalidar *to invalidate* Reg.	hablar	41
inventar *to invent* Reg.	hablar	41
inventariar *to make an inventory of*	liar	45
invernar *to winter; to hibernate*	cerrar	18
invertir *to invest; to reverse* (transitive)	sentir	78
investigar *to investigate* Reg.	pagar	52
investir *to invest (i.e. an official with a title or powers)*	pedir	54
invitar *to invite;* **invito yo** *it's on me/I'm paying* Reg.	hablar	41
invocar *to invoke* Reg.	sacar	74
involucrar *to involve* Reg.	hablar	41
involucrarse en *to be involved in* Reg.	hablar	41
inyectar *to inject* Reg.	hablar	41
ionizar *to ionize* Reg.	realizar	65
ir *to go* (consult a dictionary for idiomatic uses)	ir	43
irse *to go away*	ir	43
irisar *to iridesce; to give off the colors/ (Brit.) colours of the rainbow* Reg.	hablar	41
irradiar *to radiate; to irradiate* Reg.	hablar	41
irrigar *to irrigate* Reg.	pagar	52
irritar *to irritate* Reg.	hablar	41
irritarse *to get irritated* Reg.	hablar	41
irrumpir *to burst in* Reg.	vivir	89
iterar *to iterate, repeat* Reg.	hablar	41
izar *to hoist (flags)* Reg.	realizar	65
jabonar *to soap* Reg.	hablar	41
jactarse de *to boast about* Reg.	hablar	41

jadear *to pant* Reg.	hablar	41
jalar *to pull, haul* (Lat. Am.) Reg.	hablar	41
jalear *to cheer on (performers)* Reg.	hablar	41
jaquear *to put into check (chess)* Reg.	hablar	41
jorobar *to annoy; to bother* Reg.	hablar	41
jubilar *to pension off (an employee)* Reg.	hablar	41
jubilarse *to retire* Reg.	hablar	41
jugar *to play*	jugar	44
jugarse *to risk* (e.g. *one's life*)	jugar	44
juntar *to join together* (transitive) Reg.	hablar	41
juntarse *to join up, unite* (intransitive) Reg.	hablar	41
juramentar *to swear in (e.g. a jury)* Reg.	hablar	41
jurar *to swear* Reg.	hablar	41
justificar *to justify* Reg.	sacar	74
juzgar *to judge* Reg.	pagar	52
laborar *to labor/(Brit.) labour* Reg.	hablar	41
laborear *to work the land; also =* **laborar** Reg.	hablar	41
labrar *to carve; to work the land* Reg.	hablar	41
lacerar *to lacerate* Reg.	hablar	41
lactar *to nurse; to feed with milk* Reg.	hablar	41
ladear *to tilt* (transitive) Reg.	hablar	41
ladearse *to tilt over, become crooked* Reg.	hablar	41
ladrar *to bark* Reg.	hablar	41
ladrillar *to pave with bricks* Reg.	hablar	41
ladronear *to go around thieving* Reg.	hablar	41
lagrimar *to weep* Reg.	hablar	41
lagrimear *to water (eyes); to sob* Reg.	hablar	41
laicizar *to secularize* Reg.	realizar	65
lamentar *to regret, deplore* Reg.	hablar	41
lamentarse *to complain* Reg.	hablar	41
lamer *to lick* Reg.	comer	22

laminar *to laminate* Reg.	hablar	41
languidecer *to languish; to flag (= to grow feeble)*	parecer	53
lanzar *to throw; to launch* Reg.	realizar	65
lanzarse *to throw oneself; to leap; to pounce* Reg.	realizar	65
lapidar *to stone* Reg.	hablar	41
laquear *to lacquer* Reg.	hablar	41
largar *to let go; to let out (rope, etc.)* Reg.	pagar	52
largarse *to go away* (familiar) Reg.	pagar	52
lastimar *to hurt* (transitive) Reg.	hablar	41
lastimarse *to hurt oneself* Reg.	hablar	41
latir *to throb; to beat (heart)* Reg.	vivir	89
laurear *to honor/(Brit.) honour with a prize* Reg.	hablar	41
lavar *to wash* (transitive) Reg.	hablar	41
lavarse *to wash oneself* Reg.	hablar	41
lazar *to lasso* Reg.	realizar	65
leer *to read*	poseer	59
legalizar *to legalize* Reg.	realizar	65
legar *to bequeath* Reg.	pagar	52
legislar *to legislate* Reg.	hablar	41
legitimar *to legitimate, authenticate* Reg.	hablar	41
lesionar *to injure* Reg.	hablar	41
lesionarse *to be injured* Reg.	hablar	41
levantar *to raise; to lift* Reg.	hablar	41
levantarse *to stand up; to get up* Reg.	hablar	41
levar *to weigh (anchor)* Reg.	hablar	41
liar *to tie up in a bundle; to embroil*	liar	45
liarse *to get into a mess, jam; to get complicated*	liar	45
liberalizar *to liberalize* Reg.	realizar	65
liberar *to free* Reg.	hablar	41
liberarse de *to free oneself from* Reg.	hablar	41
libertar *to liberate* Reg.	hablar	41

librar de *to free, save from* Reg.	hablar	41
librarse de *to avoid (danger, inconvenience); to save oneself from* Reg.	hablar	41
licenciarse *to graduate (from university)* Reg.	hablar	41
licitar *to put out to tender* Reg.	hablar	41
licuar *to liquidize; to liquefy* (transitive) Reg.	continuar	25
licuarse *to liquefy* (intransitive)	continuar	25
licuefacer *to liquefy* (= **licuar**)	satisfacer	76
lidiar con *to fight, struggle with* Reg.	hablar	41
ligar *to bind, tie* Reg.	pagar	52
ligarse con *to 'pick up' (a person)* Reg.	pagar	52
lijar *to sandpaper* Reg.	hablar	41
limar *to file* (e.g. *nails, metal*) Reg.	hablar	41
limitar *to limit;* **l. con** *to border on* Reg.	hablar	41
limitarse a *to limit oneself to* Reg.	hablar	41
limpiar *to clean* Reg.	hablar	41
lindar con = **limitar con** Reg.	hablar	41
liquidar *to pay off (debt); to sell off (goods); to liquidate* Reg.	hablar	41
lisiar *to cripple* Reg.	hablar	41
lisonjear *to flatter* Reg.	hablar	41
listar *to list* Reg.	hablar	41
litigar *to litigate* Reg.	pagar	52
litografiar *to lithograph*	liar	45
llagar *to wound; to create a sore* Reg.	pagar	52
llamar *to call; to phone* Reg.	hablar	41
llamarse *to be called* Reg.	hablar	41
llamear *to flame* Reg.	hablar	41
llegar *to arrive;* **l. a** *to arrive at/in* Reg.	pagar	52
llenar *to fill* (transitive); *to fulfill/*(Brit.) *fulfil (* i.e. *emotionally, intellectually)* Reg.	hablar	41
llenarse *to fill* (intransitive) Reg.	hablar	41

llevar *to carry; to take* (consult a dictionary for idiomatic meanings) Reg.	hablar	41
llevarse *to take away* Reg.	hablar	41
llorar *to cry; to weep* Reg.	hablar	41
lloriquear *to whine* Reg.	hablar	41
llover *to rain* (usually third person only)	mover	48
lloviznar *to drizzle* (usually third person only) Reg.	hablar	41
loar *to praise* Reg.	hablar	41
lobreguecer *to make gloomy; to grow dark; to make dark*	parecer	53
localizar *to locate* Reg.	realizar	65
localizarse *to be localized* Reg.	realizar	65
lograr *to achieve; to manage to* Reg.	hablar	41
lotear *to divide into lots* Reg.	hablar	41
lozanear *to look fresh and luxuriant* Reg.	hablar	41
lubricar *to lubricate* Reg.	sacar	74
luchar *to fight; to struggle; to wrestle* Reg.	hablar	41
lucir *to shine; to show off* (transitive)	lucir	46
lucirse *to come off well; to excel*	lucir	46
lucrar *to profit* Reg.	hablar	41
lucrarse = **lucrar** Reg.	hablar	41
lustrar *to polish* Reg.	hablar	41
macanear *to joke; to tell lies* (R. Plate region) Reg.	hablar	41
macerar *to marinade, soak* Reg.	hablar	41
machacar *to crush; to nag* Reg.	sacar	74
madrugar *to get up early* Reg.	pagar	52
madurar *to ripen; to mature* Reg.	hablar	41
madurarse = **madurar** Reg.	hablar	41
magnetizar *to magnetize* Reg.	realizar	65
magnificar *to magnify* Reg.	sacar	74
magullar *to bruise* (transitive) Reg.	hablar	41

magullarse *to bruise* (intransitive) Reg.	hablar	41
malbaratar *to squander* Reg.	hablar	41
malcriar *to spoil (a child)*	liar	45
maldecir *to curse*	maldecir	47
malear *to corrupt, pervert* Reg.	hablar	41
malearse *to become corrupted* Reg.	hablar	41
malgastar *to waste, squander* Reg.	hablar	41
malherir *to wound seriously*	sentir	78
maliciar *to suspect* (esp. Lat. Am.) Reg.	hablar	41
maliciarse = **maliciar** Reg.	hablar	41
malograr *to wreck (plans)* Reg.	hablar	41
malograrse *to fail, come to nothing (plans)* Reg.	hablar	41
malquerer *to dislike*	querer	64
malquistarse con *to fall out with* Reg.	hablar	41
maltratar *to mistreat* Reg.	hablar	41
malvender *to sell off at a loss* Reg.	comer	22
malversar *to embezzle* Reg.	hablar	41
mamar *to suckle; to feed at the breast*	hablar	41
mamarse *to get drunk* Reg.	hablar	41
manar *to pour forth* (transitive and intransitive) Reg.	hablar	41
manchar *to stain* Reg.	hablar	41
mancillar *to besmirch* Reg.	hablar	41
mancomunar *to pool (resources)* Reg.	hablar	41
mandar *to command; to send* Reg.	hablar	41
manejar *to handle;* (Lat. Am.) *to drive (cars)* Reg.	hablar	41
manejarse *to cope, manage* (intransitive) Reg.	hablar	41
mangonear *to boss around* Reg.	hablar	41
maniatar *to tie the hands; to shackle* Reg.	hablar	41
manifestar *to declare, state*	cerrar	18
manifestarse *to demonstrate (* i.e. *protest); to become obvious*	cerrar	18

maniobrar *to maneuver/(Brit.)*		
manoeuvre Reg.	hablar	41
manipular *to manipulate; to handle*		
(goods, etc.) Reg.	hablar	41
manosear *to handle; to grope* Reg.	hablar	41
manotear *to gesture* Reg.	hablar	41
mantener *to maintain (machinery,*		
etc.); to support (e.g. *financially)*	tener	82
mantenerse de *to survive on*	tener	82
manufacturar *to manufacture* Reg.	hablar	41
mapear *to map* Reg.	hablar	41
maquinar *to plot; to scheme* Reg.	hablar	41
maravillar *to amaze* Reg.	hablar	41
maravillarse de *to be amazed at* Reg.	hablar	41
marcar *to mark (with a sign); to dial;*		
to score (sport) Reg.	sacar	74
marchar *to march; to walk; to run*		
(machinery) Reg.	hablar	41
marcharse *to go away; to leave* Reg.	hablar	41
marchitarse *to wilt; to wither* Reg.	hablar	41
marear *to make someone feel nauseated*		
Reg.	hablar	41
marearse *to feel nauseated* Reg.	hablar	41
marginar *to marginalize, push to one*		
side Reg.	hablar	41
marinar *to marinate* Reg.	hablar	41
mariposear *to flutter around* Reg.	hablar	41
martillar *to hammer* Reg.	hablar	41
martillear = **martillar** Reg.	hablar	41
martirizar *to martyrize; to torment* Reg.	realizar	65
mascar *to chew* Reg.	sacar	74
mascullar *to mumble (words)* Reg.	hablar	41
masificarse *to get overcrowded* Reg.	sacar	74
masticar *to chew* Reg.	sacar	74
masturbarse *to masturbate* (intransitive)		
Reg.	hablar	41
matar *to kill; to butcher* Reg.	hablar	41

materializar *to fulfill/(Brit.) fulfil (a plan, etc.)* Reg. — realizar — 65

materializarse *to be fulfilled (plans)* Reg. — realizar — 65

matizar *to modify, qualify (a statement)* Reg. — realizar — 65

matricular *to register, enroll/(Brit.) enrol* (transitive) Reg. — hablar — 41

matricularse *to register, enroll* (intransitive) Reg. — hablar — 41

maximizar *to maximize* Reg. — realizar — 65

maullar *to meow* — aullar — 11

mecanizar *to mechanize* Reg. — realizar — 65

mecanografiar *to type* — liar — 45

mecer *to rock* (transitive) Reg. — vencer — 86

mecerse *to sway* Reg. — vencer — 86

mediar *to mediate; to elapse (time); to lie between (space)* Reg. — hablar — 41

medir *to measure* — pedir — 54

meditar *to meditate* Reg. — hablar — 41

medrar *to thrive, prosper* Reg. — hablar — 41

mejorar *to improve* (transitive and intransitive) Reg. — hablar — 41

mejorarse *to recover (from an illness)* Reg. — hablar — 41

mellar *to notch; to nick* Reg. — hablar — 41

mencionar *to mention* Reg. — hablar — 41

mendigar *to beg (i.e. be a beggar)* Reg. — pagar — 52

menear *to wag* Reg. — hablar — 41

menguar *to diminish* (transitive and intransitive) — averiguar — 13

menoscabar *to impair* Reg. — hablar — 41

menospreciar *to despise* Reg. — hablar — 41

menstruar *to menstruate* — continuar — 25

mensurar *to measure* Reg. — hablar — 41

mentalizar *to make someone aware* Reg. — realizar — 65

mentalizarse *to become aware; to get a clear idea* Reg.	realizar	65
mentar *to mention*	cerrar	18
mentir *to lie*	sentir	78
menudear *to be frequent* Reg.	hablar	41
mercadear *to haggle* Reg.	hablar	41
merecer *to deserve*	parecer	53
merendar *to have an afternoon snack*	cerrar	18
mermar *to decrease* (transitive and intransitive) Reg.	hablar	41
merodear *to prowl* Reg.	hablar	41
metalizarse *to become mercenary* Reg.	realizar	65
meter *to insert* Reg.	comer	22
meterse en *to get involved in* Reg.	comer	22
mezclar *to mix, blend* (transitive) Reg.	hablar	41
mezclarse *to mix, mingle* (intransitive) Reg.	hablar	41
migar *to crumble* Reg.	pagar	52
militar *to be an active member* (e.g. *of a political party*) Reg.	hablar	41
militarizar *to militarize* Reg.	realizar	65
mimar *to pamper; to spoil* (*a child*) Reg.	hablar	41
minar *to mine; to undermine* Reg.	hablar	41
minimizar *to minimize* Reg.	realizar	65
modelar *to model* Reg.	hablar	41
moderar *to moderate* Reg.	hablar	41
moderarse *to control oneself* Reg.	hablar	41
modernizar *to modernize* Reg.	realizar	65
modificar *to modify* Reg.	sacar	74
modular *to modulate* Reg.	hablar	41
mofarse de *to scoff at* Reg.	hablar	41
mojar *to wet* Reg.	hablar	41
mojarse *to get wet* Reg.	hablar	41
moldear *to shape; to mold/(Brit.) mould* Reg.	hablar	41
moler *to grind*	mover	48

molestar *to disturb; to bother* Reg.	hablar	41
molestarse *to be annoyed; to be bothered* Reg.	hablar	41
momificar *to mummify* Reg.	sacar	74
mondar *to peel* Reg.	hablar	41
monologar *to talk without listening* Reg.	pagar	52
monopolizar *to monopolize* Reg.	realizar	65
montar *to mount* (transitive)*; to set up (organization, etc.)* Reg.	hablar	41
montarse en *to get into/onto (vehicle, horse, etc.)* Reg.	hablar	41
moralizar *to moralize* Reg.	realizar	65
morar *to dwell* (= **habitar**) Reg.	hablar	41
morder *to bite*	mover	48
mordisquear *to nibble* Reg.	hablar	41
morir *to die* (past participle **muerto**)	dormir	34
morirse (past participle **muerto**) = **morir** (familiar or figurative usage)	dormir	34
mortificar *to mortify* Reg.	sacar	74
mosquear *to annoy* (transitive) Reg.	hablar	41
mosquearse *to get annoyed* Reg.	hablar	41
mostrar *to show*	contar	24
motear *to speckle* Reg.	hablar	41
motejar *to call names* Reg.	hablar	41
motivar *to motivate* Reg.	hablar	41
mover *to move* (transitive)	mover	48
moverse *to move* (intransitive)	mover	48
movilizar *to mobilize* Reg.	realizar	65
mudar de *to change (e.g. opinion)* (transitive) Reg.	hablar	41
mudarse *to move house; to change clothes* Reg.	hablar	41
mugir *to moo* Reg.	rugir	72
mullir *to fluff up*	bullir	15
multiplicar *to multiply* Reg.	sacar	74
murmurar *to murmur, mutter* Reg.	hablar	41
mutilar *to mutilate* Reg.	hablar	41

mutarse *to mutate* Reg.   hablar   41

nacer *to be born*   parecer   53
nacionalizar *to nationalize; to*
naturalize Reg.   realizar   65
naturalizar *to naturalize* Reg.   realizar   65
naufragar *to be shipwrecked; to come to*
grief (plans) Reg.   pagar   52
navegar *to navigate* Reg.   pagar   52
necesitar *to need* Reg.   hablar   41
negar *to deny*   negar   49
negarse a *to refuse to*   negar   49
negociar *to negotiate* Reg.   hablar   41
neutralizar *to neutralize* Reg.   realizar   65
nevar *to snow* (usu. third person only)   cerrar   18
neviscar *to snow lightly; to sleet* (usu.
third person only) Reg.   sacar   74
nivelar *to level; to even* Reg.   hablar   41
nombrar *to name; to appoint* Reg.   hablar   41
nominar *to nominate* Reg.   hablar   41
normalizar *to normalize* Reg.   realizar   65
notar *to note, notice* Reg.   hablar   41
novelar *to write up in the form of a novel*
Reg.   hablar   41
nublar *to cloud, obscure* (transitive)
Reg.   hablar   41
nublarse *to become cloudy, misty* Reg.   hablar   41
numerar *to number* (transitive) Reg.   hablar   41
nutrir *to nourish* Reg.   vivir   89
nutrirse de *to feed on* Reg.   vivir   89

obedecer *to obey*   parecer   53
objetar *to object* Reg.   hablar   41
obligar a *to oblige to* Reg.   pagar   52
obligarse a *to make oneself do*
something Reg.   hablar   41

obnubilar *to make obscure, befuddled*
Reg.   hablar   41
obnubilarse *to become cloudy (mind,*
ideas) Reg.   hablar   41
obrar *to act (* i.e. *to work); to perform*
*(*e.g. *miracles)* Reg.   hablar   41
obscurecer = **oscurecer**   parecer   53
obscurecerse = **oscurecerse**   parecer   53
obsequiar con *to give something as a*
present to Reg.   hablar   41
observar *to observe* Reg.   hablar   41
obsesionar *to obsess* (transitive) Reg. hablar   41
obsesionarse por *to become obsessed*
about Reg.   hablar   41
obstaculizar *to hinder* Reg.   realizar   65
obstar para que *to stand in the way of*
Reg.   hablar   41
obstinarse en *to insist obstinately on*
Reg.   hablar   41
obstruir *to obstruct*   construir   23
obtener *to obtain*   tener   82
obturar *to stop up, block* Reg.   hablar   41
obviar *to obviate* Reg.   hablar   41
ocasionar *to cause (*e.g. *damage,*
suffering) Reg.   hablar   41
ocluir *to occlude*   construir   23
ocultar *to conceal* Reg.   hablar   41
ocultarse *to hide* (intransitive) Reg. hablar   41
ocupar *to occupy* Reg.   hablar   41
ocuparse de *to look after* Reg.   hablar   41
ocurrir *to happen* Reg.   vivir   89
ocurrirse a *to occur to (*e.g. *idea,*
thought) Reg.   vivir   89
odiar *to hate* Reg.   hablar   41
ofender *to offend* Reg.   comer   22
ofenderse *to take offense/(Brit.) offence*
Reg.   comer   22

ofertar *to sell as a special offer; to offer*
   (for sale) Reg.   hablar   41
oficiar *to officiate* Reg.   hablar   41
ofrecer *to offer*   parecer   53
ofrecerse *to present itself (opportunity,*
   etc.)   parecer   53
ofrendar *to offer up (prayers,*
   sacrifices) Reg.   hablar   41
ofuscar *to blind (passions, rage)* Reg.   sacar   74
oír *to hear*   oír   50
ojear *to eye* Reg.   hablar   41
oler *to smell*   oler   51
olfatear *to sniff out* Reg.   hablar   41
olvidar *to forget* Reg.   hablar   41
olvidarse de *to forget (unintentionally)*
   Reg.   hablar   41
omitir *to omit; to neglect* Reg.   vivir   89
ondear *to wave, ripple (e.g. flag)* Reg.   hablar   41
operar *to operate* Reg.   hablar   41
opinar *to express/hold an opinion* Reg.   hablar   41
oponer *to set up (e.g. a counter-*
   argument, counter-proposal)   poner   58
oponerse a *to oppose*   poner   58
oprimir *to oppress; to squeeze* Reg.   vivir   89
optar por *to opt; **o. a** to apply for* Reg.   hablar   41
optimizar *to optimize* Reg.   realizar   65
ordenar *to put in order; to sort; to*
   ordain; to command Reg.   hablar   41
ordenarse *to be ordained (priest)* Reg.   hablar   41
ordeñar *to milk* Reg.   hablar   41
organizar *to organize* Reg.   realizar   65
orientar *to orient* Reg.   hablar   41
orientarse *to find one's way around* Reg.   hablar   41
originar *to create, give rise to (e.g.*
   conflict) Reg.   hablar   41
originarse *to arise (problems, etc.)* Reg.   hablar   41

orillar *to skirt round (obstacles, problems)* Reg.   hablar   41

orinar *to urinate* Reg.   hablar   41

orlar *to trim with a fringe* Reg.   hablar   41

ornamentar *to adorn* Reg.   hablar   41

orquestar *to orchestrate* Reg.   hablar   41

osar *to dare* (= **atreverse**) Reg.   hablar   41

oscilar *to oscillate* Reg.   hablar   41

oscurecer *to darken* (transitive and intransitive)   parecer   53

oscurecerse *to darken* (intransitive)   parecer   53

osificarse *to ossify* Reg.   sacar   74

ostentar *to show off* (intransitive)*; to hold (an office); to flaunt (wealth)* Reg.   hablar   41

otear *to scan (with the eyes)* Reg.   hablar   41

otorgar *to grant, award* Reg.   pagar   52

ovillarse *to curl up in a ball* (intransitive) Reg.   hablar   41

oxidarse *to rust* Reg.   hablar   41

oxigenar *to bleach (hair)* Reg.   hablar   41

oxigenarse *to bleach one's (own) hair; to get some fresh air* Reg.   hablar   41

pacer *to pasture; to graze*   parecer   53

pacificar *to pacify* Reg.   sacar   74

pacificarse *to calm down* Reg.   sacar   74

pactar *to agree terms for* Reg.   hablar   41

pactarse *to make a pact* Reg.   hablar   41

padecer *to suffer* (transitive and intransitive)   parecer   53

pagar *to pay; to pay for* Reg.   pagar   52

paladear *to relish* Reg.   hablar   41

palear *to shovel* Reg.   hablar   41

paliar *to palliate; to ease* Reg.   hablar   41

palidecer *to turn pale*   parecer   53

palmear *to slap on the back* Reg.   hablar   41

palmotear *to clap;* also = **palmear** Reg.	hablar	41
palpar *to feel (with the hands)* Reg.	hablar	41
palpitar *to throb* Reg.	hablar	41
papelear *to look through papers* Reg.	hablar	41
parafrasear *to paraphrase* Reg.	hablar	41
paralizar *to paralyze* Reg.	realizar	65
paralizarse *to become paralyzed* Reg.	realizar	65
parangonar *to compare* (= **comparar**) Reg.	hablar	41
parapetarse *to take cover* Reg.	hablar	41
parar *to stop* (transitive and intransitive) Reg.	hablar	41
pararse *to stop* (intransitive)*;* (Lat. Am.) *to stand up* Reg.	hablar	41
parcelar *to parcel out* Reg.	hablar	41
parchar *to patch* Reg.	hablar	41
parear a *to match to* Reg.	hablar	41
parecer *to seem*	parecer	53
parecerse a *resemble*	parecer	53
parir *to give birth* Reg.	vivir	89
parodiar *to parody* Reg.	hablar	41
parpadear *to blink* Reg.	hablar	41
parquear (Lat. Am.) *to park* (= **aparcar**) Reg.	hablar	41
parrandear *to go out on a spree* Reg.	hablar	41
participar *to participate; to notify* Reg.	hablar	41
particularizar *to particularize (= to characterize)* Reg.	realizar	65
partir *to split; to depart* Reg.	vivir	89
partirse *to splinter, break* (intransitive) Reg.	vivir	89
pasar *to pass* (consult a dictionary for idiomatic meanings) Reg.	hablar	41
pasarse *to overdo it; to jump (lights, etc.); to spend (time)* Reg.	hablar	41
pasear *to go for a walk; to take for a walk* Reg.	hablar	41

pasearse *to go for a walk* Reg.	hablar	41
pasmar *to stun* Reg.	hablar	41
pasmarse *to be stunned* Reg.	hablar	41
pastar *to graze* Reg.	hablar	41
pasterizar = **pasteurizar** Reg.	realizar	65
pasteurizar *to pasteurize* Reg.	realizar	65
pastorear *to tend (flocks)* Reg.	hablar	41
patalear *to stamp the feet* Reg.	hablar	41
patear *to kick* Reg.	hablar	41
patentar *to patent* Reg.	hablar	41
patentizar *to make evident; to reveal* Reg.	realizar	65
patinar *to skate; to skid* Reg.	hablar	41
patrocinar *to sponsor* Reg.	hablar	41
patronear *to skipper* Reg.	hablar	41
patrullar *to patrol* Reg.	hablar	41
pavimentar *to pave* Reg.	hablar	41
pavonearse *to strut, swagger* Reg.	hablar	41
pecar *to sin* Reg.	sacar	74
pedalear *to pedal* Reg.	hablar	41
pedantear *to be pedantic* Reg.	hablar	41
pedir *to ask; to ask for*	pedir	54
pegar *to hit; to stick* (transitive and intransitive) Reg.	pagar	52
pegarse *to stick* (intransitive; consult a dictionary for idiomatic meanings) Reg.	pagar	52
peinar *to comb; to do someone's hair* Reg.	hablar	41
peinarse *to get one's hair done; to do one's hair* Reg.	hablar	41
pelar *to peel* (transitive) Reg.	hablar	41
pelarse *to peel* (intransitive) Reg.	hablar	41
pelear *to fight; to quarrel* Reg.	hablar	41
pelearse = **pelear** Reg.	hablar	41
peligrar *to be in danger* Reg.	hablar	41
pellizcar *to pinch* Reg.	sacar	74

penalizar *to penalize* Reg.	realizar	65
pender de *to hang from* (= **colgar**) Reg.	comer	22
penetrar *to penetrate* Reg.	hablar	41
pensar *to think; to intend to*	cerrar	18
pensarse *to think something over*	cerrar	18
percatarse de *to notice, realize* Reg.	hablar	41
percibir *to perceive; to receive (wages, etc.)* Reg.	vivir	89
perder *to lose*	perder	55
perderse *to get lost; to miss (program, appointment, etc.)*	perder	55
perdonar *to pardon* Reg.	hablar	41
perdurar *to last a long time* Reg.	hablar	41
perecer *to perish*	parecer	53
peregrinar *to go on a pilgrimage* Reg.	hablar	41
perfeccionar *to perfect* Reg.	hablar	41
perfilar *to shape* Reg.	hablar	41
perfilarse *to be outlined, silhouetted* Reg.	hablar	41
perforar *to perforate* Reg.	hablar	41
perfumar *to perfume* Reg.	hablar	41
pergeñar (archaic) *to sketch* Reg.	hablar	41
perjudicar *to damage; to be harmful to* Reg.	sacar	74
perjurar *to commit perjury; to swear (an oath)* Reg.	hablar	41
permanecer *to remain; to stay*	parecer	53
permitir *to permit, allow* Reg.	vivir	89
permutar *to barter, exchange* Reg.	hablar	41
pernoctar *to spend the night* Reg.	hablar	41
perorar *to make an impassioned speech; to hold forth* Reg.	hablar	41
perpetrar *to perpetrate* Reg.	hablar	41
perpetuarse *to perpetuate*	continuar	25
perseguir *to persecute; to pursue*	seguir	77
perseverar *to persevere* Reg.	hablar	41
persignarse *to cross oneself* Reg.	hablar	41

persistir *to persist* Reg.	vivir	89
personalizar *to personalize* Reg.	realizar	65
personarse *to appear, show up (persons only)* Reg.	hablar	41
personificar *to personify* Reg.	sacar	74
perspirar *to perspire; to sweat* Reg.	hablar	41
persuadir a *to persuade to* Reg.	vivir	89
persuadirse de *to become convinced of* Reg.	vivir	89
pertenecer a *to belong to*	parecer	53
pertrechar *to equip* Reg.	hablar	41
perturbar *to perturb* Reg.	hablar	41
pervertir *to pervert*	sentir	78
pervertirse *to become perverted*	sentir	78
pesar *to weigh; to weigh down* Reg.	hablar	41
pescar *to fish; to catch* Reg.	sacar	74
pestañear *to blink* Reg.	hablar	41
peticionar *to petition* Reg.	hablar	41
petrificarse *to become petrified* Reg.	sacar	74
piar *to chirp*	liar	45
picar *to itch; to sting* Reg.	sacar	74
picarse *to be irritated; to go rotten* Reg.	sacar	74
picotear *to peck* Reg.	hablar	41
pifiar *to get it wrong* (colloquial) Reg.	hablar	41
pillar *to catch* Reg.	hablar	41
pilotar *to pilot* Reg.	hablar	41
pilotear = **pilotar** Reg.	hablar	41
pinchar *to puncture* Reg.	hablar	41
pincharse *to burst* (intransitive) Reg.	hablar	41
pintar *to paint;* **él no pinta** *he doesn't matter* Reg.	hablar	41
pintarrajear *to daub* Reg.	hablar	41
piratear *to pirate* Reg.	hablar	41
piropear *to compliment (a pretty woman)* Reg.	hablar	41
pisar *to step on* Reg.	hablar	41
pisotear *to trample* Reg.	hablar	41

pitar *to blow a whistle; to whistle* Reg.	hablar	41
placer *to please* (= **gustar**)	placer	56
plagiar *to plagiarize* Reg.	hablar	41
planchar *to iron* Reg.	hablar	41
planear *to plan; to glide* Reg.	hablar	41
planificar *to plan* Reg.	sacar	74
plantar *to plant* Reg.	hablar	41
plantear *to set, pose (a problem)* Reg.	hablar	41
plantearse *to arise (problem); to consider (a problem)* Reg.	hablar	41
plañir (archaic) *to lament*	gruñir	39
plasmar *to give form to (*e.g. *ideas)* Reg.	hablar	41
plasmarse *to be expressed (*e.g. *ideas in a work of art)* Reg.	hablar	41
platear *to plate with silver* Reg.	hablar	41
platicar *to converse* (Lat. Am.) Reg.	sacar	74
plegar *to fold*	negar	49
pleitear *to litigate, go to court* Reg.	hablar	41
pluralizar *to pluralize* Reg.	realizar	65
poblar *to populate*	contar	24
poder *to be able; can; may*	poder	57
podrir = **pudrir** Reg.	vivir	89
poetizar *to poetize* Reg.	realizar	65
polarizar *to polarize* Reg.	realizar	65
polemizar *to start a polemic* Reg.	realizar	65
politiquear *to play politics* Reg.	hablar	41
polvorear *to powder* Reg.	hablar	41
ponderar *to praise* Reg.	hablar	41
poner *to put* (consult a dictionary for idiomatic meanings)	poner	58
ponerse *to become; to put on (clothes)*	poner	58
pontificar *to pontificate* Reg.	sacar	74
popularizar *to popularize* Reg.	realizar	65
porfiar en *to persist in*	liar	45
pormenorizar *to tell in detail; to itemize* Reg.	realizar	65

portar *to carry; to bear* Reg.	hablar	41
portarse *to behave* Reg.	hablar	41
posar *to pose; to place; to perch* Reg.	hablar	41
posarse *to perch; to alight (birds, helicopters)* Reg.	hablar	41
poseer *to possess*	poseer	59
posesionarse de *to take possession of* Reg.	hablar	41
posibilitar *to make possible* Reg.	hablar	41
posponer *to postpone*	poner	58
postergar *to pass over (= disregard seniority); to delay* Reg.	pagar	52
postrar *to prostrate* (transitive) Reg.	hablar	41
postrarse *to be prostrated, laid out (person)* Reg.	hablar	41
postular *to postulate* Reg.	hablar	41
potenciar *to boost* Reg.	hablar	41
practicar *to practice/(Brit.) to practise* Reg.	sacar	74

For the conjugation of unlisted verbs beginning with **pre-** see the root verb

precaverse *to take precautions* Reg.	comer	22
preceder *to precede* Reg.	comer	22
preciarse de *to boast of* Reg.	hablar	41
precintar *to seal* Reg.	hablar	41
precipitar *to precipitate, rush* (transitive) Reg.	hablar	41
precipitarse *to rush* (intransitive) Reg.	hablar	41
precisar *to state precisely; to need* Reg.	hablar	41
preconcebir *to preconceive*	pedir	54
preconizar *to advocate* Reg.	realizar	65
predecir *to predict*	maldecir	47
predestinar *to predestine* Reg.	hablar	41
predicar *to preach* Reg.	sacar	74
predisponer *to predispose*	poner	58
predominar *to predominate* Reg.	hablar	41
prefabricar *to prefabricate* Reg.	sacar	74

preferir *to prefer*	sentir	78
prefijar *to prefix* Reg.	hablar	41
pregonar *to proclaim, make public* Reg.	hablar	41
preguntar *to ask* (i.e. *to ask a question*) Reg.	hablar	41
prejuzgar *to prejudge* Reg.	pagar	52
preludiar *to be a foretaste of* Reg.	hablar	41
premeditar *to premeditate* Reg.	hablar	41
premiar *to reward* Reg.	hablar	41
prendarse *to fall for (a person)* Reg.	hablar	41
prender *to catch; to arrest; to pin on; to switch on* Reg.	comer	22
prenderse *to catch fire* Reg.	comer	22
prensar *to press (*e.g. *grapes, olives)* Reg.	hablar	41
preñar *to make pregnant* (familiar for **dejar embarazada**) Reg.	hablar	41
preocupar *to preoccupy* Reg.	hablar	41
preocuparse *to be worried* Reg.	hablar	41
preparar *to prepare* Reg.	hablar	41
prepararse *to get ready; to be imminent* Reg.	hablar	41
preponderar *to prevail* Reg.	hablar	41
presagiar *to presage* Reg.	hablar	41
prescindir de *to do without* Reg.	vivir	89
preseleccionar *to shortlist* Reg.	hablar	41
prescribir *to prescribe*	escribir	37
presenciar *to witness (an event)* Reg.	hablar	41
presentar *to present; to introduce* Reg.	hablar	41
presentarse *to appear (= turn up)* Reg.	hablar	41
presentir *to have a presentiment of*	sentir	78
preservar *to preserve (from damage or danger)* Reg.	hablar	41
presidir *to preside over* Reg.	vivir	89
presionar *to pressure* Reg.	hablar	41
prestar *to lend; to pay (attention)* Reg.	hablar	41

prestarse a *to offer or lend oneself to*
  Reg.   hablar   41
prestigiar *to enhance the prestige of*
  Reg.   hablar   41
presumir *to boast;* **p. de...** *to boast that*
  one is... Reg.   vivir   89
presupuestar *to budget for* Reg.   hablar   41
pretender *to claim; to aspire to* Reg.   comer   22
pretextar *to use a pretext* Reg.   hablar   41
prevalecer *to prevail*   parecer   53
prevalerse de *to take advantage of*   valer   85
prevaricar *to pervert (justice); to use*
  corrupt methods Reg.   sacar   74
prevenir *to prevent*   venir   87
prevenirse contra *to take advance*
  measures against   venir   87
prever *to foresee*   ver   88
primar *to be foremost* Reg.   hablar   41
principiar *to begin* Reg.   hablar   41
pringar *to cover in grease* Reg.   pagar   52
priorizar *to give priority to* Reg.   realizar   65
privar de *to deprive of; to be foremost*
  (feature) Reg.   hablar   41
privilegiar *to privilege* Reg.   hablar   41
probar *to test; to try; to prove*   contar   24
probarse *to try on (clothes)*   contar   24
proceder de *to originate from* Reg.   comer   22
procesar *to try (in court); to process*
  Reg.   hablar   41
proclamar *to proclaim* Reg.   hablar   41
procrastinar *to procrastinate* Reg.   hablar   41
procrear *to breed (*transitive and
  intransitive*)* Reg.   hablar   41
procurar *to try hard to; to obtain* Reg.   hablar   41
procurarse *to acquire for oneself* Reg.   hablar   41
prodigar *to lavish; to squander* Reg.   pagar   52

prodigarse en *to be generous with (praise, compliments)* Reg.	pagar	52
producir *to produce*	producir	60
producirse *to take place; to occur*	producir	60
profanar *to defile* Reg.	hablar	41
proferir *to utter (insults)*	sentir	78
profesar *to profess* Reg.	hablar	41
profetizar *to prophesy* Reg.	realizar	65
profundizar en *to go into details* Reg.	realizar	65
programar *to program* Reg.	hablar	41
progresar *to progress* Reg.	hablar	41
prohibir *to prohibit; to forbid*	prohibir	61
prohijar *to adopt (child, ideas)*	aislar	5
prologar *to write a preface to* Reg.	pagar	52
prolongar *to prolong* Reg.	pagar	52
prolongarse *to stretch (distance, time)* (intransitive) Reg.	pagar	52
promediar *to average* Reg.	hablar	41
prometer *to promise* Reg.	comer	22
promocionar *to promote (sales)* Reg.	hablar	41
promover *to stimulate, encourage (plan)*	mover	48
pronosticar *to forecast* Reg.	sacar	74
pronunciar *to pronounce* Reg.	hablar	41
propagar *to propagate* Reg.	pagar	52
propagarse *to spread* (intransitive) Reg.	pagar	52
propalar *to divulge* Reg.	hablar	41
propasarse *to go too far* Reg.	hablar	41
propender a *to tend to* Reg.	comer	22
propiciar *to propitiate* Reg.	hablar	41
propinar *to give (a blow)* Reg.	hablar	41
proponer *to propose*	poner	58
proponerse *to resolve; to set out to*	poner	58
proporcionar *to provide* Reg.	hablar	41
propugnar *to advocate* Reg.	hablar	41
propulsar *to propel* Reg.	hablar	41
prorrogar *to defer; to postpone* Reg.	pagar	52

prorrumpir en *to burst out in (applause, etc.)* Reg.	vivir	89
proscribir *to proscribe*	escribir	37
proseguir *to continue; to proceed*	seguir	77
prosperar *to prosper* Reg.	hablar	41
prostituir *to prostitute*	construir	23
protagonizar *to take a leading part in (a performance, etc.)* Reg.	realizar	65
proteger *to protect* Reg.	proteger	62
protestar *to protest* Reg.	hablar	41
proveer *to provide*	proveer	63
proveerse *to get supplies*	proveer	63
provocar *to provoke* Reg.	sacar	74
proyectar *to plan* Reg.	hablar	41
psicoanalizar *to psychoanalyze* Reg.	realizar	65
publicar *to publish* Reg.	sacar	74
pudrir *to rot* (past participle **podrido**) Reg.	vivir	89
pugnar *to strive* Reg.	hablar	41
pujar *to strain (= to push with one's muscles)* Reg.	hablar	41
pulir *to polish* Reg.	vivir	89
pulsar *to press (a button, etc.)* Reg.	hablar	41
pulular *to swarm* Reg.	hablar	41
pulverizar *to pulverize* Reg.	realizar	65
puntualizar *to specify in detail* Reg.	realizar	65
puntuar *to punctuate; to grade/(Brit.) mark (examinations, etc.)*	continuar	25
punzar *to prick; to perforate* Reg.	realizar	65
purgar *to purge; to purify* Reg.	pagar	52
purificar *to purify* Reg.	sacar	74
quebrantar *to break down (morale, health)* (transitive) Reg.	hablar	41
quebrar *to snap, break* (transitive)	cerrar	18
quebrarse *to snap, break* (intransitive)	hablar	41

quedar *to remain; to be left* (consult dictionary for idiomatic uses) Reg.	hablar	41
quedarse *to stay* (consult dictionary for idiomatic uses) Reg.	hablar	41
quejarse *to complain* Reg.	hablar	41
quemar *to burn* (transitive) Reg.	hablar	41
quemarse *to burn* (intransitive) Reg.	hablar	41
querellarse *to take legal action* Reg.	hablar	41
querer *to want; to love*	querer	64
quitar *to remove; to take away* Reg.	hablar	41
quitarse *to take off (clothing)* Reg.	hablar	41
rabiar *to rage* Reg.	hablar	41
racionalizar *to rationalize* Reg.	realizar	65
racionar *to ration* Reg.	hablar	41
radiar *to broadcast* Reg.	hablar	41
radicar en *to stem from* Reg.	sacar	74
radicarse *to settle* Reg.	sacar	74
raer *to scrape* (= **raspar**)	caer	17
rajar *to crack* (transitive) Reg.	hablar	41
rajarse *to crack* (intransitive) Reg.	hablar	41
ralentizar *to slow down* (transitive) Reg.	realizar	65
ralentizarse *to slow down* (intransitive) Reg.	realizar	65
rallar *to grate (e.g. cheese)* Reg.	hablar	41
ramificarse *to branch out* Reg.	sacar	74
rapar *to shave* Reg.	hablar	41
raptar *to kidnap* Reg.	hablar	41
rasar *to skim (the surface)* Reg.	hablar	41
rascar *to scratch* Reg.	sacar	74
rasgar *to rip* Reg.	pagar	52
rasguñar *to scratch* (transitive) Reg.	hablar	41
raspar *to scrape* Reg.	hablar	41
rastrear *to track; to trail* Reg.	hablar	41
rastrillar *to rake* Reg.	hablar	41
rasurar *to shave* (Lat. Am.) Reg.	hablar	41
ratificar *to ratify* Reg.	sacar	74

rayar *to scratch, mark;* **r. en** *to border*
  on Reg.   hablar   41
razonar *to reason* Reg.   hablar   41
For the conjugation of unlisted verbs beginning with **re-**,
  see the root verb
reaccionar *to react* Reg.   hablar   41
reacondicionar *to recondition* Reg.   hablar   41
reactivar *to reactivate* Reg.   hablar   41
readaptar *to readapt* Reg.   hablar   41
readmitir *to readmit* Reg.   vivir   89
reafirmar *to reaffirm* Reg.   hablar   41
reajustar *to readjust* Reg.   hablar   41
realinear *to realign* Reg.   hablar   41
realizar *to fulfill/(Brit.) fulfil; to make*
  real; to carry out Reg.   realizar   65
realzar *to emphasize; to highlight* Reg.   realizar   65
reanimar *to revive; to comfort* Reg.   hablar   41
reanimarse *to be revived* Reg.   hablar   41
reanudar *to renew; to resume* Reg.   hablar   41
reaparecer *to reappear*   parecer   53
rearmar *to rearm* Reg.   hablar   41
reavivar *to revive* Reg.   hablar   41
rebajar *to lower (prices); to humiliate*
  Reg.   hablar   41
rebajarse a *to lower oneself to* Reg.   hablar   41
rebanar *to slice* Reg.   hablar   41
rebasar *to overflow; to go beyond*
  (limits) Reg.   hablar   41
rebatir *to refute* Reg.   vivir   89
rebelarse *to rebel* Reg.   hablar   41
reblandecerse *to go soft*   parecer   53
rebobinar *to rewind (tape)* Reg.   hablar   41
rebosar de *to abound in (energy, etc.)*
  Reg.   hablar   41
rebotar *to rebound* Reg.   hablar   41
rebozar *to cover with batter* Reg.   realizar   65
rebrotar *to sprout* Reg.   hablar   41

rebuscar *to rummage* Reg.	sacar	74
rebuznar *to bray* Reg.	hablar	41
recabar *to gather (information)* Reg.	hablar	41
recaer *to relapse*	caer	17
recalcar *to emphasize* Reg.	sacar	74
recalentar *to reheat; to overheat*	cerrar	18
recalentarse *to become overheated*	cerrar	18
recapacitar *to reconsider* Reg.	hablar	41
recapitular *to recapitulate* Reg.	hablar	41
recargar *to charge extra; to recharge* Reg.	pagar	52
recatarse *to be abashed, ashamed* Reg.	hablar	41
recauchutar *to retread (a tire/(Brit.) tyre)* Reg.	hablar	41
recaudar *to collect (taxes, rent)* Reg.	hablar	41
recelar de *to be suspicious of* Reg.	hablar	41
recetar *to prescribe* Reg.	hablar	41
rechazar *to reject* Reg.	realizar	65
rechinar *to squeak (e.g. hinges)* Reg.	hablar	41
rechistar *to winge, complain* Reg.	hablar	41
recibir *to receive* Reg.	vivir	89
recitar *to recite* Reg.	hablar	41
reclamar *to demand (rights, privileges, etc.); to complain* Reg.	hablar	41
reclinar *to rest, lean back* (transitive) Reg.	hablar	41
reclinarse *to lean back* Reg.	hablar	41
recluir *to intern*	construir	23
recluirse *to go into seclusion*	construir	23
reclutar *to recruit* Reg.	hablar	41
recobrar *to recover (e.g. health)* Reg.	hablar	41
recobrarse *to recover (from an illness)* Reg.	hablar	41
recoger *to pick up* Reg.	proteger	62
recogerse *to retire (go to bed); to withdraw* (intransitive)*; to roll up (sleeves)* Reg.	proteger	62

recomendar *to recommend*	cerrar	18
recompensar *to reward* Reg.	hablar	41
reconcentrar en *to concentrate on* Reg.	hablar	41
reconciliar *to reconcile* Reg.	hablar	41
reconciliarse con *to be reconciled with* Reg.	hablar	41
reconfortar *to comfort* Reg.	hablar	41
reconocer *to recognize; to admit (truth, fact)*	parecer	53
reconquistar *to reconquer* Reg.	hablar	41
reconsiderar *to reconsider* Reg.	hablar	41
reconstruir *to rebuild*	construir	23
reconvenir *to reproach*	venir	87
recopilar *to compile (anthologies, etc.)* Reg.	hablar	41
recordar *to remember; to remind*	contar	24
recorrer *to travel all over; to tour* Reg.	comer	22
recortar *to cut out (e.g. an article from a newspaper); to cut (spending)* Reg.	hablar	41
recortarse *to stand out* Reg.	hablar	41
recostar *to lean* (transitive)	contar	24
recostarse *to lie down; to lie back*	contar	24
recrear *to recreate* Reg.	hablar	41
recrearse *to take pleasure* Reg.	hablar	41
recriminar *to recriminate* Reg.	hablar	41
recrudecerse *to grow more intense*	parecer	53
rectificar *to rectify* Reg.	sacar	74
recubrir de *to cover with (e.g. paper, paint)*	cubrir	26
recular *to reverse* (intransitive) Reg.	hablar	41
recuperar *to recover* (transitive) Reg.	hablar	41
recuperarse de *to recover from* (intransitive) Reg.	hablar	41
recurrir *to appeal (a legal decision);* **r. a** *to resort to* Reg.	vivir	89
redactar *to write up (e.g. an article)* Reg.	hablar	41

redimir *to redeem* Reg.	vivir	89
redoblar *to redouble* Reg.	hablar	41
redondear *to round off; to make round* Reg.	hablar	41
reducir *to reduce*	producir	60
redundar en *to result in* Reg.	hablar	41

Verbs beginning with **ree-** may be optionally spelt **re-**

reelegir *to re-elect*	regir	66
reembolsar *to refund* Reg.	hablar	41
reemplazar *to substitute; to replace* Reg.	realizar	65
reencarnarse *to be reincarnated* Reg.	hablar	41
reestructurar *to restructure* Reg.	hablar	41
referir *to tell (story)*	sentir	78
referirse a *to refer to*	sentir	78
refinar *to refine* Reg.	hablar	41
reflejar *to reflect (an image)* Reg.	hablar	41
reflexionar *to reflect (= to think over)* Reg.	hablar	41
reformar *to reform; to renovate (building)* Reg.	hablar	41
reforzar *to reinforce*	almorzar	6
refregar *to scrub hard*	negar	49
refrenar *to restrain; to rein in* Reg.	hablar	41
refrendar *to countersign* Reg.	hablar	41
refrescar *to refresh; to cool* (transitive); *to get cooler* (e.g. *weather*) Reg.	sacar	74
refrigerar *to refrigerate* Reg.	hablar	41
refulgir *to shine brightly* Reg.	rugir	72
refundir *to recast* Reg.	vivir	89
refunfuñar *to grumble* Reg.	hablar	41
refutar *to refute* Reg.	hablar	41
regalar *to give as a present* Reg.	hablar	41
regañar *to scold; to quarrel* Reg.	hablar	41
regar *to water; to irrigate*	negar	49
regatear *to haggle; to bargain* Reg.	hablar	41
regenerar *to regenerate* Reg.	hablar	41

regentar *to manage (a business)* Reg.	hablar	41
regimentar *to regiment*	cerrar	18
regir *to rule; to steer*	regir	66
registrar *to search* (transitive)*; to record* Reg.	hablar	41
regocijarse de *to rejoice at* Reg.	hablar	41
regodearse en/con *to take great pleasure in* Reg.	hablar	41
regresar *to return* Reg.	hablar	41
regular *to regulate* Reg.	hablar	41
regularizar *to regularize* Reg.	realizar	65
regurgitar *to regurgitate* Reg.	hablar	41
rehabilitar *to rehabilitate* Reg.	hablar	41
rehacer *to redo*	hacer	42
rehacerse de *to recover from*	hacer	42
rehilar *to quiver*	aislar	5
rehogar *to toss lightly in oil (cooking)* Reg.	pagar	52
rehuir *to shun, flee from*	rehuir	67
rehusar *to refuse*	aullar	11
reinar *to reign* Reg.	hablar	41
reincidir *to reoffend* Reg.	vivir	89
reincorporarse a *to rejoin (group)* Reg.	hablar	41
reintegrar *to reinstate* Reg.	hablar	41
reintegrarse a *to rejoin; to return to (membership, community)* Reg.	hablar	41
reír = reírse	reír	68
reírse *to laugh*	reír	68
reiterar *to reiterate; to repeat* Reg.	hablar	41
reivindicar *to claim, demand (rights, etc.)* Reg.	sacar	74
reivindicarse *to vindicate oneself* Reg.	sacar	74
rejuvenecer *to reinvigorate*	parecer	53
rejuvenecerse *to become rejuvenated*	parecer	53
relacionar *to relate (= to link together)* Reg.	hablar	41
relajar *to relax* (transitive) Reg.	hablar	41

relajarse to relax (intransitive) Reg.	hablar	41
relampaguear to flash with lightning Reg.	hablar	41
relatar to relate (= to narrate) Reg.	hablar	41
releer to reread	poseer	59
relegar to relegate Reg.	pagar	52
relevar to relieve (e.g. workmate on shift) Reg.	hablar	41
relevarse to take turns; to work in shifts Reg.	hablar	41
relinchar to neigh Reg.	hablar	41
rellenar to refill; to fill up; to stuff Reg.	hablar	41
relucir to shine; to glitter	lucir	46
relumbrar to shine Reg.	hablar	41
remachar to rivet; to hammer home (a point) Reg.	hablar	41
remar to row Reg.	hablar	41
remarcar to stress; to mark again Reg.	sacar	74
rematar to finish off (job); to auction off Reg.	hablar	41
remedar to ape Reg.	hablar	41
remediar to remedy Reg.	hablar	41
rememorar to recall Reg.	hablar	41
remendar to mend; to patch	cerrar	18
remitir to remit; to send (letters, etc.) Reg.	vivir	89
remojar to soak (transitive) Reg.	hablar	41
remolcar to tow Reg.	sacar	74
remontar to surmount Reg.	hablar	41
remorder to cause remorse	mover	48
remover to stir; (Lat. Am.) to remove	mover	48
remozar to rejuvenate, renovate Reg.	realizar	65
remunerar to remunerate Reg.	hablar	41
renacer to be born again; to bloom again	parecer	53
rendir to produce results/profits (consult a dictionary for idiomatic uses)	pedir	54

rendirse *to surrender; to give up*	pedir	54
renegar de *to renounce (principles)*	negar	49
renovar *to renovate; to renew*	contar	24
renquear *to limp* Reg.	hablar	41
renunciar a *to renounce; to resign* Reg.	hablar	41
reñir *to scold; to have a quarrel*	reñir	69
reorganizar *to reorganize* Reg.	realizar	65
reorientar *to reorient* Reg.	realizar	65
reparar *to repair; r. en to notice* Reg.	hablar	41
repartir *to distribute; to share out* Reg.	vivir	89
repasar *to review; to revise* Reg.	hablar	41
repatriar *to repatriate* Reg.	hablar	41
or	liar	45
repeler *to repel* Reg.	comer	22
repetir *to repeat*	pedir	54
repercutir en *to have an impact on* Reg.	vivir	89
repiquetear *to ring out (bells)* Reg.	hablar	41
replantear *to restate (a question)* Reg.	hablar	41
replegar *to fold up; to tuck in*	negar	49
replicar *to answer back* Reg.	sacar	74
repoblar *to repopulate*	contar	24
reponer *to replace*	poner	58
reponerse *to recover* (intransitive)	poner	58
reportar *to bring in (profits, results)* Reg.	hablar	41
reportear (Lat. Am.) *to report (news)* Reg.	hablar	41
reposar *to rest* Reg.	hablar	41
repostar *to refuel*	contar	24
reprender *to scold* Reg.	comer	22
representar *to represent* Reg.	hablar	41
reprimir *to repress* Reg.	vivir	89
reprobar *to reprove*	contar	24
reprochar *to reproach* Reg.	hablar	41
reproducir *to reproduce*	producir	60
reptar *to slither, crawl* Reg.	hablar	41
repudiar *to repudiate* Reg.	hablar	41

repugnar *to disgust* Reg.	hablar	41
repuntar *to recover (prices, economy, etc.)* Reg.	hablar	41
requebrar *to say flattering things to*	cerrar	18
requerir *to require*	sentir	78
requisar *to confiscate* Reg.	hablar	41
resaltar *to stand out* Reg.	hablar	41
resarcir *to compensate; to repay (* e.g. *the effort)* Reg.	zurcir	92
resbalar *to slip* Reg.	hablar	41
resbalarse *to slip (persons)* Reg.	hablar	41
rescatar *to rescue* Reg.	hablar	41
rescindir *to rescind* Reg.	vivir	89
resecar *to dry out* (transitive) Reg.	sacar	74
resecarse *to dry out* (intransitive) Reg.	sacar	74
resentirse de *to be resentful; not to have recovered from*	sentir	78
reseñar *to review (a book, etc.)* Reg.	hablar	41
reservar *to reserve; to put aside* Reg.	hablar	41
resfriarse *to catch cold*	liar	45
resguardar *to protect* Reg.	hablar	41
resguardarse de *to take shelter from* Reg.	hablar	41
residir en *to reside in* Reg.	vivir	89
resignarse a *to resign oneself to* Reg.	hablar	41
resistir *to bear; tolerate; to hold out* Reg.	vivir	89
resistirse a *to resist; to be unwilling to* Reg.	vivir	89
resollar *to breathe hard*	contar	24
resolver *to resolve, solve* (transitive)	volver	90
resolverse a *to make up one's mind to*	volver	90
resonar *to echo*	contar	24
resoplar *to puff* Reg.	hablar	41
respaldar *to back* Reg.	hablar	41
respaldarse *to sit back;* **r. en** *to rely on* Reg.	hablar	41

respectar *to concern* (third person only)
Reg.   hablar   41
respetar *to respect* Reg.   hablar   41
respirar *to breathe* Reg.   hablar   41
resplandecer *to shine* (intransitive)   parecer   53
responder *to answer; to respond* Reg.   comer   22
responsabilizar *to hold to account* Reg.   realizar   65
responsabilizarse de *to take
responsibility for* Reg.   realizar   65
resquebrajar *to crack; to split*
(transitive) Reg.   hablar   41
resquebrajarse *to break up; to split*
(intransitive) Reg.   hablar   41
restablecer *to re-establish; to restore*   parecer   53
restablecerse *to recover* (intransitive)   parecer   53
restañar *to staunch (blood)* Reg.   hablar   41
restar *to subtract; to be left* Reg.   hablar   41
restaurar *to restore (order, political
regime)* Reg.   hablar   41
restituir a *to return (to the rightful
owner)* (transitive)   construir   23
restregar *to rub or scrub hard*   negar   49
restringir *to restrict; to hamper*   rugir   72
resucitar *to bring back to life; to come
back to life* Reg.   hablar   41
resultar *to result; to turn out to be*
(consult dictionary for idiomatic
uses) Reg.   hablar   41
resumir *to summarize* Reg.   vivir   89
resurgir *to resurge; to re-emerge* Reg.   rugir   72
retar *to challenge* Reg.   hablar   41
retardar *to delay; to slow up* (transitive)
Reg.   hablar   41
retardarse *to be late* Reg.   hablar   41
retemblar *to shake; to quiver* Reg.   cerrar   18
retener *to keep back; to retain*   tener   82
retenerse *to restrain oneself*   tener   82

retirar *to take away/out; to draw back* (transitive) Reg.	hablar	41
retirarse *to retire; to withdraw* (intransitive) Reg.	hablar	41
retocar *to touch up (painting, photo)* Reg.	sacar	74
retomar *to take up again* Reg.	hablar	41
retoñar *to sprout* Reg.	hablar	41
retorcer *to twist* (transitive)	cocer	19
retorcerse *to twist, writhe* (intransitive)	cocer	19
retornar *to return* (= **volver**, **regresar**) Reg.	hablar	41
retractarse *to go back (on a previous statement)* Reg.	hablar	41
retraer *to bring back; to pull in*	traer	83
retraerse *to withdraw* (intransitive)	traer	83
retransmitir *to repeat (a radio or TV program)* Reg.	vivir	89
retrasar *to delay* (transitive) Reg.	hablar	41
retrasarse *to be late; to fall behind* Reg.	hablar	41
retratar *to photograph; to make a painting of* Reg.	hablar	41
retribuir *to reward (financially, for one's efforts)*	construir	23
retroceder *to back away; to move back* (intransitive) Reg.	comer	22
retumbar *to rumble* Reg.	hablar	41
reunir *to join together, assemble* (transitive)	reunir	70
reunirse *to gather* (e.g. *for a meeting*) (intransitive)	reunir	70
revalorar = **revalorizar** Reg.	hablar	41
revalorizar *to revalue* Reg.	realizar	65
revelar *to reveal; to develop (a photo)* Reg.	hablar	41
revelarse *to reveal oneself* Reg.	hablar	41
revender *to resell* Reg.	comer	22

reventar *to burst* (transitive and intransitive)	cerrar	18
reverberar *to twinkle, glimmer* Reg.	hablar	41
reverdecer *to grow green again*	parecer	53
reverter *to overflow*	perder	55
revertir a *to revert to*	sentir	78
revestir de *to coat, cover with (a substance)*	pedir	54
revestirse de *to arm oneself with (e.g. courage)*	pedir	54
revisar *to review* Reg.	hablar	41
revitalizar *to revitalize* Reg.	realizar	65
revivir *to revive* (intransitive); *to relive (past experience)* Reg.	vivir	89
revocar *to revoke; to plaster* Reg.	sacar	74
revolcar *to knock to the ground*	trocar	84
revolcarse *to wallow; to roll around* (intransitive)	trocar	84
revolotear *to flutter around* Reg.	hablar	41
revolucionar *to revolutionize* Reg.	hablar	41
revolucionarse *to revolt; to get excited* Reg.	hablar	41
revolver *to stir up; to disorder*	volver	90
revolverse *to twist and turn* (intransitive)	volver	90
rezagarse *to fall behind* Reg.	pagar	52
rezar *to pray* Reg.	realizar	65
rezongar *to grumble* Reg.	pagar	52
rezumar *to ooze* (transitive and intransitive) Reg.	hablar	41
ridiculizar *to ridicule* Reg.	realizar	65
rielar *to twinkle, glisten* Reg.	hablar	41
rifar *to raffle* Reg.	hablar	41
rimar *to rhyme* Reg.	hablar	41
rivalizar en *to compete; to vie in* Reg.	realizar	65
rizar *to curl* (transitive) Reg.	realizar	65
rizarse *to curl* (intransitive) Reg.	realizar	65

robar *to steal* Reg.	hablar	41
robustecer *to strengthen*	parecer	53
robustecerse *to become strong*	parecer	53
rociar *to sprinkle (with liquid)*	liar	45
rodar *to roll* (intransitive)*; to film; to travel (cars, etc.)*	contar	24
rodear *to surround* Reg.	hablar	41
rodearse de *to surround oneself with* Reg.	hablar	41
rodrigar *to prop; to prop up (plants)* Reg.	pagar	52
roer *to gnaw*	roer	71
rogar *to beg*	colgar	20
romper (past participle **roto**) *to break* (transitive)*; to tear up* Reg.	comer	22
romperse (past participle **roto**) *to break* (intransitive) Reg.	comer	22
roncar *to snore* Reg.	sacar	74
rondar *to hover around; to patrol; to lurk* Reg.	hablar	41
ronronear *to purr* Reg.	hablar	41
rotar *to rotate* (transitive and intransitive) Reg.	hablar	41
rotarse *to take turns (according to a rota)* Reg.	hablar	41
rotular *to label* Reg.	hablar	41
rozar *to brush (= to touch lightly)* Reg.	realizar	65
rubicar *to add one's flourish (to a signature)* Reg.	sacar	74
rugir *to bellow; to rumble*	rugir	72
rumiar *to ruminate; to chew the cud* Reg.	hablar	41
rumorear *to rumor/(Brit.) rumour; to spread by rumor* Reg.	hablar	41
runrunear *to purr* Reg.	hablar	41
rutilar *to sparkle; to shine* Reg.	hablar	41

saber *to know; to know how to;* **s. a** *to taste of*   saber   73

saborear *to relish, savor/(Brit.) savour* Reg.   hablar   41

sabotear *to sabotage* Reg.   hablar   41

sacar *to draw out; to pull out* (consult dictionary for idiomatic meanings) Reg.   sacar   74

saciar *to satiate* Reg.   hablar   41

saciarse de *to eat one's fill of* Reg.   hablar   41

sacrificar *to sacrifice* Reg.   sacar   74

sacrificarse *to make a sacrifice (of oneself)* Reg.   sacar   74

sacudir *to jolt, shake* (transitive) Reg.   vivir   89

sacudirse *to shrug off (problem, etc.)* Reg.   vivir   89

sahumar *to perfume with incense*   aislar   5

sajar *to make an incision in; to cut open* Reg.   hablar   41

salar *to salt* Reg.   hablar   41

salir *to leave; to go out; to come out*   salir   75

salirse *to leak (liquids, etc.); to walk out (of meetings, etc.)*   salir   75

salivar *to salivate* Reg.   hablar   41

salmodiar *to sing in a monotone; to sing psalms* Reg.   hablar   41

salpicar de *to splash with* Reg.   sacar   74

salpimentar *to season (* e.g. *with salt and pepper)*   cerrar   18

saltar *to jump* (transitive and intransitive) Reg.   hablar   41

saltarse *to jump (traffic lights); to skip (* i.e. *to miss out)* Reg.   hablar   41

saltear *to sauté; to hold up (* i.e. *to rob)* Reg.   hablar   41

saludar *to greet; to salute* Reg.   hablar   41

salvar *to save (i.e. from danger); to salvage* Reg.	hablar	41
salvarse de *to avoid (death, ignominy, etc.)* Reg.	hablar	41
sanar *to recover; to heal* Reg.	hablar	41
sancionar *to fine; to sanction* Reg.	hablar	41
sanear *to clean up* Reg.	hablar	41
sangrar *to bleed* (transitive and intransitive); *to indent (paragraph)* Reg.	hablar	41
santificar *to sanctify* Reg.	sacar	74
santiguarse *to make the sign of the cross*	averiguar	13
saquear *to loot, pillage* Reg.	hablar	41
satirizar *to satirize* Reg.	realizar	65
satisfacer *to satisfy*	satisfacer	76
satisfacerse *to take satisfaction; to be satisfied*	satisfacer	76
saturar *to saturate* Reg.	hablar	41
sazonar *to season* Reg.	hablar	41
secar *to dry* (transitive) Reg.	sacar	74
secarse *to dry* (intransitive) Reg.	sacar	74
seccionar *to section* Reg.	hablar	41
secretar *to secrete* Reg.	hablar	41
secuestrar *to kidnap* Reg.	hablar	41
secularizar *to secularize* Reg.	realizar	65
secundar *to support (= to back up)* Reg.	hablar	41
sedar *to sedate* Reg.	hablar	41
sedimentarse *to settle (= form a sediment)* Reg.	hablar	41
seducir *to seduce; to charm*	producir	60
segar *to reap*	negar	49
segregar *to segregate; to secrete* Reg.	pagar	52
seguir *to follow; + gerund to continue to*	seguir	77
seguirse de *to follow on from*	seguir	77
sellar *to seal; to stamp* Reg.	hablar	41
sembrar *to sow*	cerrar	18
semejar *to resemble* Reg.	hablar	41

sensacionalizar *to sensationalize* Reg.	realizar	65
sensibilizar *to sensitize* Reg.	realizar	65
sentar *to seat; to suit*	cerrar	18
sentarse *to sit down*	cerrar	18
sentenciar *to sentence* Reg.	hablar	41
sentir *to feel; to regret*	sentir	78
sentirse *to feel*	sentir	78
señalar *to indicate; to point out; to signal* Reg.	hablar	41
señalarse por *to be distinguished by* Reg.	hablar	41
separar *to separate* (transitive) Reg.	hablar	41
separarse *to separate* (intransitive) Reg.	hablar	41
sepultar *to bury* Reg.	hablar	41
ser *to be*	ser	79
serenar *to calm* Reg.	hablar	41
serenarse *to grow calm* Reg.	hablar	41
sermonear *to lecture (= to reprimand)* Reg.	hablar	41
serpentear *to meander* Reg.	hablar	41
serrar *to saw*	cerrar	18
servir *to serve; to be useful*	pedir	54
servirse *to help oneself to*	pedir	54
sesear *to pronounce Spanish c before e or i, and also z, like s* Reg.	hablar	41
sesgar *to bias (data)* Reg.	pagar	52
sicoanalizar = psicoanalizar Reg.	realizar	65
signar *to put a mark on; to sign* Reg.	hablar	41
significar *to mean; to signify* Reg.	sacar	74
significarse *to distinguish oneself* Reg.	sacar	74
silbar *to whistle* Reg.	hablar	41
silenciar *to silence* Reg.	hablar	41
simbolizar *to symbolize* Reg.	realizar	65
simpatizar *to get on well (with others); to be sympathetic to (ideas)* Reg.	realizar	65
simplificar *to simplify* Reg.	sacar	74
simular *to simulate* Reg.	hablar	41

simultanear con *to carry on*		
simultaneously with (transitive) Reg.	hablar	41
sincerarse *to tell the whole truth* Reg.	hablar	41
sincronizar *to synchronize* Reg.	realizar	65
sindicalizarse *to join a union* Reg.	realizar	65
singularizar *to single out* Reg.	realizar	65
singularizarse por *to stand out because*		
of Reg.	realizar	65
sintonizar *to tune (a radio)* Reg.	realizar	65
sirgar *to tow (a boat)* Reg.	pagar	52
sistematizar *to systematize* Reg.	realizar	65
sitiar *to besiege* Reg.	hablar	41
situar *to situate; to locate*	continuar	25
situarse *to be located*	continuar	25
sobar *to grope* Reg.	hablar	41
sobornar *to bribe* Reg.	hablar	41
sobrar *to be more than enough; to be left*		
over Reg.	hablar	41

For the conjugation of unlisted verbs beginning with
   sobre-, see the root verb

sobreactuar *to overact*	continuar	25
sobrecalentar *to overheat*	cerrar	18
sobrecargar *to overload; to overcharge*		
Reg.	pagar	52
sobrecoger *to frighten; to overcome with*		
emotion Reg.	proteger	62
sobrecogerse *to be overcome with*		
emotion Reg.	proteger	62
sobrecompensar *to overcompensate*		
Reg.	hablar	41
sobreentender *to understand (something*		
not made explicit)	perder	55
sobreexcitar *to overexcite* Reg.	hablar	41
sobreexponer *to overexpose*	poner	58
sobrehilar *to overcast (sewing)*	aislar	5
sobrellenar *to overfill* Reg.	hablar	41
sobrellevar *to endure; to suffer* Reg.	hablar	41

sobrepasar *to surpass; to exceed* Reg.	hablar	41
sobrepasarse *to go too far* Reg.	hablar	41
sobreponer *to superimpose*	poner	58
sobreponerse *to get a grip on oneself*	poner	58
sobresalir *to stand out; to excel*	salir	75
sobresaltar *to frighten* Reg.	hablar	41
sobresaltarse *to jump (with fright)* Reg.	hablar	41
sobreseer *to dismiss* (= **despedir**)	poseer	59
sobrevenir *to happen; to take place (usually tragedies, etc.)*	venir	87
sobrevivir *to survive* Reg.	vivir	89
sobrevolar *to fly over; to overfly*	contar	24
socarrar *to singe; to scorch* (transitive) Reg.	hablar	41
socavar *to undermine* Reg.	hablar	41
socializar *to socialize* Reg.	realizar	65
socorrer *to assist; to aid* Reg.	comer	22
sofocar *to suffocate* (transitive) Reg.	sacar	74
sofocarse *to get intensely upset* Reg.	sacar	74
sofreír *to sauté*	reír	68
sofrenar *to restrain* Reg.	hablar	41
solaparse *to overlap* Reg.	hablar	41
solazar *to solace; to console* Reg.	realizar	65
solazarse *to take one's ease* Reg.	realizar	65
soldar *to solder; to weld*	contar	24
soldarse *to fuse together* (intransitive)	contar	24
solear *to sun* Reg.	hablar	41
solemnizar *to solemnize* Reg.	realizar	65
soler *to be accustomed to; to be used to*	soler	80
solicitar *to apply for* Reg.	hablar	41
solidarizar con *to make common cause with* Reg.	realizar	65
solidarizarse con = **solidarizar** Reg.	realizar	65
solidificarse *to solidify* Reg.	sacar	74
soliviantar *to rouse; to incite* Reg.	hablar	41
soliviantarse *to mutiny* Reg.	hablar	41
sollozar *to sob* Reg.	realizar	65

soltar *to untie; to unfasten; to set free;* *to release*	contar	24
soltarse *to become loose; to loosen up*	contar	24
solucionar *to solve* Reg.	hablar	41
solventar *to settle (accounts); to resolve* *(a matter)* Reg.	hablar	41
sombrear *to shade* Reg.	hablar	41
someter *to subdue; to submit* Reg.	comer	22
someterse a *to submit to* Reg.	comer	22
sonar *to sound; to ring*	contar	24
sonarse *to blow one's nose*	contar	24
sondear *to sound; to poll (opinion)* Reg.	hablar	41
sonorizar *to add the sound track (to a* *film)* Reg.	realizar	65
sonreír = **sonreírse**	reír	68
sonreírse *to smile*	reír	68
sonrojarse *to flush; to blush* Reg.	hablar	41
sonsacar *to draw out (a secret)* Reg.	sacar	74
soñar *to dream*	contar	24
sopesar *to weigh up* Reg.	hablar	41
soplar *to blow (wind, etc.); to whisper* Reg.	hablar	41
soportar *to endure; to put up with* Reg.	hablar	41
sorber *to sip* Reg.	comer	22
sorprender *to surprise* Reg.	comer	22
sorprenderse de *to be surprised at* Reg.	comer	22
sortear *to draw lots for; to raffle; to get* *round (a problem)* Reg.	hablar	41
sosegar *to calm*	negar	49
sosegarse *to calm down*	negar	49
soslayar *to dodge, get round (a* *problem)* Reg.	hablar	41
sospechar *to suspect* Reg.	hablar	41
sostener *to support* (e.g. *weight); to* *maintain (an opinion)*	tener	82
soterrar *to bury*	cerrar	18
suavizar *to smooth; to tone down* Reg.	realizar	65

subarrendar *to sublet*	cerrar	18
subastar *to auction* Reg.	hablar	41
subcontratar *to subcontract* Reg.	hablar	41
subdividir *to subdivide* Reg.	vivir	89
subir *to go up; to come up; to raise; to lift; to increase* (transitive and intransitive) Reg.	vivir	89
subirse *to get on (vehicles); to climb* Reg.	vivir	89
sublevar *to incite to rebellion* Reg.	hablar	41
sublevarse *to revolt* Reg.	hablar	41
sublimar *to sublimate* Reg.	hablar	41
subordinar *to subordinate* Reg.	hablar	41
subrayar *to underline; to emphasize* Reg.	hablar	41
subrogar *to subrogate; to substitute* Reg.	pagar	52
subsanar *to correct (an error)* Reg.	hablar	41
subscribir *to subscribe; to endorse; to sign*	escribir	37
subsidiar *to subsidize* Reg.	hablar	41
subsistir *to subsist* Reg.	vivir	89
subtitular *to subtitle* Reg.	hablar	41
subvencionar *to subsidize* Reg.	hablar	41
subvertir *to subvert*	sentir	78
subyacer *to underlie*	yacer	91
subyugar *to subjugate* Reg.	pagar	52
succionar *to suck* Reg.	hablar	41
suceder *to happen* Reg.	comer	22
sucederse *to follow one after the other* Reg.	comer	22
sucumbir *to succumb* Reg.	vivir	89
sudar *to sweat* Reg.	hablar	41
sufragar *to defray (costs)* Reg.	pagar	52
sufrir *to suffer; to undergo* Reg.	vivir	89
sugerir *to suggest*	sentir	78
sugestionar *to put an idea into someone's head* Reg.	hablar	41

sujetar *to fasten; to subject* Reg.	hablar	41
sujetarse a *to hold tight to; to submit to* Reg.	hablar	41
sumar *to add* Reg.	hablar	41
sumarse a *to be additional to* Reg.	hablar	41
sumergir *to submerge* (transitive)	rugir	72
sumergirse *to submerge* (intransitive)	rugir	72
suministrar *to supply* Reg.	hablar	41
sumir en *to plunge into* (*doubt, despair*) (transitive) Reg.	vivir	89
sumirse en *to be plunged into* Reg.	vivir	89
supeditar a *to subordinate to* Reg.	hablar	41
superar *to surpass* Reg.	hablar	41
superponer *to superimpose*	poner	58
suplantar *to supplant* Reg.	hablar	41
suplementar *to supplement* Reg.	hablar	41
suplir *to substitute; to make up for* Reg.	vivir	89
suponer *to suppose; to presuppose*	poner	58
suprimir *to suppress; to do away with; to withdraw* (*bus, train services, etc.*) Reg.	vivir	89
supurar *to fester* Reg.	hablar	41
surgir *to arise* (*problem*)*; to spurt out*	rugir	72
surtir *to produce* (*success*) Reg.	vivir	89
suscitar *to arouse* Reg.	hablar	41
suscribir = **subscribir**	escribir	37
suspender *to suspend; to fail* (*examination*) (transitive and intransitive) Reg.	comer	22
suspirar *to sigh* Reg.	hablar	41
sustanciar *to substantiate* Reg.	hablar	41
sustentar *to maintain* (*an opinion*)*; to support* (*financially*) Reg.	hablar	41
sustituir *to replace, substitute*	construir	23
sustraer *to subtract; to steal*	traer	83
sustraerse a *to get out of* (*a duty, chore*)	traer	83

tabalear *to drum with the fingers* Reg.	hablar	41
tabicar *to wall up* Reg.	sacar	74
tabletear *to rattle* Reg.	hablar	41
tabular *to tabulate* Reg.	hablar	41
tachar *to cross out;* **t. de** *to label someone (e.g. as a liar)* Reg.	hablar	41
taconear *to walk noisily (e.g. wearing high heels)* Reg.	hablar	41
taladrar *to drill* Reg.	hablar	41
talar *to fell (trees)* Reg.	hablar	41
tallar *to carve* Reg.	hablar	41
tambalearse *to stagger* Reg.	hablar	41
tamizar *to sieve, sift* Reg.	realizar	65
tantear *to feel (with the hands) (transitive); to grope* Reg.	hablar	41
tañer *to play (musical instrument); to chime*	tañer	81
tapar *to cover up* Reg.	hablar	41
tapiar *to wall in* Reg.	hablar	41
tapizar *to line (sewing)* Reg.	realizar	65
taponar *to plug* Reg.	hablar	41
taponarse *to get blocked* Reg.	hablar	41
taquigrafiar *to take down in shorthand*	liar	45
tararear *to hum* Reg.	hablar	41
tardar *to be late; to take (time)* Reg.	hablar	41
tartajear *to stutter* Reg.	hablar	41
tartamudear *to stutter* Reg.	hablar	41
tasar *to evaluate; to tax* Reg.	hablar	41
tatuar *to tattoo*	continuar	25
techar *to roof* Reg.	hablar	41
teclear *to type (on a keyboard); to key in* Reg.	hablar	41
tejar *to roof with tiles* Reg.	hablar	41
tejer *to weave* Reg.	comer	22
telefonear *to telephone* Reg.	hablar	41
televisar *to televise* Reg.	hablar	41
temblar *to tremble*	cerrar	18

temer *to fear* Reg.	comer	22
temerse *to fear (= to regret that)* Reg.	comer	22
temperar *to temper* Reg.	hablar	41
templar *to tune; to grow more moderate (temperature)* Reg.	hablar	41
templarse *to grow moderate (temperature)* Reg.	hablar	41
tender *to spread out; to reach out;* **t. a** *to tend to*	perder	55
tenderse *to lie down*	perder	55
tener *to have* (consult a dictionary for idiomatic meanings)	tener	82
tensar *to tense* Reg.	hablar	41
tentar *to tempt; to feel (with the hands)*	cerrar	18
teñir *to dye*	reñir	69
teorizar *to theorize* Reg.	realizar	65
terciar *to mediate* Reg.	hablar	41
terciarse *to crop up (subject)* Reg.	hablar	41
tergiversar *to twist (facts, etc.)* Reg.	hablar	41
terminar *to end; to finish* (transitive and intransitive) Reg.	hablar	41
terminarse *to run out (* i.e. *become exhausted)* Reg.	hablar	41
terraplenar *to bank; to fill (with dirt)* Reg.	hablar	41
tertuliar *to sit around and talk* Reg.	hablar	41
testar *to make a testament or will* Reg.	hablar	41
testimoniar *to testify* Reg.	hablar	41
tildar de *to brand/label as (*e.g. *liar, etc.)* Reg.	hablar	41
timar *to swindle* Reg.	hablar	41
timbrar *to stamp (*e.g. *document)* Reg.	hablar	41
timonear *to steer (boat)* Reg.	hablar	41
tintar *to tint* Reg.	hablar	41
tintinear *to jingle* Reg.	hablar	41
tirar *to pull; to throw away* Reg.	hablar	41
tirarse *to dive; to throw oneself* Reg.	hablar	41

tiritar *to shiver* Reg.	hablar	41
tirotear *to shoot at random* Reg.	hablar	41
titilar *to twinkle* Reg.	hablar	41
titiritar *to shiver* Reg.	hablar	41
titubear *to hesitate; to stutter* Reg.	hablar	41
titular *to give a title to* Reg.	hablar	41
titularse *to be called (books, films)* Reg.	hablar	41
tiznar *to smudge with soot* Reg.	hablar	41
tocar *to touch; to play (musical instrument)* Reg.	sacar	74
tolerar *to tolerate* Reg.	hablar	41
tomar *to take; (Lat. Am.) to drink* Reg.	hablar	41
tonificar *to invigorate* Reg.	sacar	74
tontear *to talk or act foolishly* Reg.	hablar	41
toparse con *to run into (i.e. to meet by chance)* Reg.	hablar	41
topetar = topetear	hablar	41
topetear *to bump into* Reg.	hablar	41
torcer *to twist; to bend* (transitive)	cocer	19
torcerse *to become twisted*	cocer	19
torear *to fight bulls* Reg.	hablar	41
tornar *to return* (= **volver**) Reg.	hablar	41
tornear *to turn (on a lathe)* Reg.	hablar	41
torpedear *to torpedo* Reg.	hablar	41
torrar *to toast, brown* Reg.	hablar	41
torturar *to torture* Reg.	hablar	41
toser *to cough* Reg.	comer	22
tostar *to toast*	contar	24
totalizar *to totalize* Reg.	realizar	65
trabajar *to work* Reg.	hablar	41
trabar *to clasp together; to join; to strike up (*e.g. *friendship)* Reg.	hablar	41
trabarse *to get stuck* Reg.	hablar	41
trabucarse *to become confused; to be mixed up* Reg.	sacar	74
traducir *to translate*	producir	60

traer *to bring*	traer	83
traficar *to trade; to traffic* Reg.	sacar	74
tragar *to swallow* Reg.	pagar	52
tramar *to plot; to devise (a scheme)* Reg.	hablar	41
tramitar *to deal with (formalities)* Reg.	hablar	41
trampear *to cheat* Reg.	hablar	41
tranquilizar *to tranquilize/(Brit.) tranquillize* Reg.	realizar	65

Verbs beginning with **trans-** not listed here may be found under the spelling **tras-**

transbordar *to transfer; to change trains* Reg.	hablar	41
transcender = **trascender**	perder	55
transcribir *to transcribe*	escribir	37
transcurrir *to elapse; to pass (time; intransitive)* Reg.	vivir	89
transferir *to transfer*	sentir	78
transfigurar *to transfigure* Reg.	hablar	41
transformar *to transform* Reg.	hablar	41
transfundir *to transfuse* Reg.	vivir	89
transgredir *to transgress*	abolir	1
transigir *to compromise; to give in*	rugir	72
transitar *to travel around* Reg.	hablar	41
translucirse = **traslucirse**	lucir	46
transmitir *to transmit* Reg.	lucir	46
transpirar *to sweat* Reg.	hablar	41
transponer = **trasponer**	poner	58
transvasar = **trasvasar** Reg.	hablar	41
trapichear *to fence (stolen goods)* Reg.	hablar	41
traquetear *to rattle* Reg.	hablar	41
trascender *to come to light; to transcend*	perder	55
trascribir = **transcribir**	escribir	37
trascurrir = **transcurrir**	vivir	89
trasegar *to shuffle; to decant*	negar	49
trasfundir = **transfundir**	vivir	89
trasgredir = **transgredir**	abolir	1

trashumar *to move to new pastures (seasonally)* Reg.	abolir	1
trasladar *to transfer* (transitive) Reg.	hablar	41
trasladarse *to move (to new premises)* Reg.	hablar	41
traslucirse *to show through (emotions)*	lucir	46
trasnochar *to stay up all night* Reg.	hablar	41
traspapelar *to mislay among other papers* Reg.	hablar	41
traspapelarse *to be mislaid among other papers* Reg.	hablar	41
traspasar *to pierce through; to go beyond; to sell (lease on a property)* Reg.	hablar	41
trasplantar *to transplant* Reg.	hablar	41
trasponer *to surpass; to transpose*	poner	58
trasquilar *to shear* Reg.	hablar	41
trastear *to rummage* Reg.	hablar	41
trastocar *to disorder, shuffle (papers)* Reg.	sacar	74
trastornar *to upset* Reg.	hablar	41
trastornarse *to be upset* Reg.	hablar	41
trastrocar *to alter*	trocar	84
trastrocarse *to become shuffled, disordered*	trocar	84
trasvasar *to decant* Reg.	hablar	41
tratar *to deal with; to treat; to handle;* **t. de** *to try to* Reg.	hablar	41
tratarse de *to be a question of* Reg.	hablar	41
traumatizar *to traumatize* Reg.	realizar	65
trazar *to trace* Reg.	realizar	65
trenzar *to braid* Reg.	realizar	65
trepar *to clamber; to climb* Reg.	hablar	41
treparse a *to climb onto* Reg.	hablar	41
trepidar *to vibrate* Reg.	hablar	41
tributar *to pay (homage, admiration, etc.); to pay taxes* Reg.	hablar	41

trillar *to thresh* Reg.	hablar	41
trinar *to warble* Reg.	hablar	41
triplicar *to triple* (transitive) Reg.	sacar	74
triplicarse *to triple* (intransitive) Reg.	sacar	74
tripular *to man (ships, planes, etc.)* Reg.	hablar	41
triturar *to pulverize; to crush* Reg.	hablar	41
triunfar *to triumph* Reg.	hablar	41
trizarse *to break into pieces* (intransitive) Reg.	realizar	65
trocar *to exchange, barter*	trocar	84
trocarse en = **convertirse en**	trocar	84
trompicar *to stumble* Reg.	sacar	74
tronar *to thunder*	contar	24
tronchar *to snap* (transitive) Reg.	hablar	41
troncharse *to snap* (intransitive) Reg.	hablar	41
tropezar *to stumble*	comenzar	21
troquelar *to strike, mint (i.e. a coin)* Reg.	hablar	41
trozar *to break to pieces; to cut into pieces* Reg.	realizar	65
truhanear *to act like a rascal* Reg.	hablar	41
truncar *to truncate, cut short* Reg.	sacar	74
tumbar *to knock down* Reg.	hablar	41
tumbarse *to lie down* Reg.	hablar	41
turbar *to disturb* Reg.	hablar	41
turbarse *to be disturbed, embarrassed* Reg.	hablar	41
turnarse *to take turns* Reg.	hablar	41
tutear *to address someone using the familiar pronoun **tú*** Reg.	hablar	41
ubicar *to place; to locate* (esp. Lat. Am.) Reg.	sacar	74
ufanarse de *to boast about* Reg.	hablar	41
ultimar *to finalize* Reg.	hablar	41
ultrajar *to offend; to insult* Reg.	hablar	41

ulular *to hoot* Reg.	hablar	41
uncir *to yoke* Reg.	zurcir	92
ungir *to anoint*	rugir	72
unificar *to unify* Reg.	sacar	74
unificarse *to become unified* Reg.	sacar	74
unir *to join together* (transitive) Reg.	vivir	89
unirse *to join together* (intransitive) Reg.	hablar	41
untar de *to smear with* Reg.	hablar	41
untarse *to become smeared* Reg.	hablar	41
urbanizar *to develop (land)* Reg.	realizar	65
urdir *to plot; to scheme* Reg.	vivir	89
urgir *to be urgent; to drive on (*e.g. *ambition)*	rugir	72
usar *to use* Reg.	hablar	41
usurpar *to usurp* Reg.	hablar	41
utilizar *to utilize* Reg.	realizar	65
vacar *to be vacant; to be idle* Reg.	sacar	74
vaciar *to empty* (transitive)	liar	45
vaciarse *to empty* (intransitive)	liar	45
vacilar *to vacillate* Reg.	hablar	41
vacunar *to vaccinate* Reg.	hablar	41
vadear *to ford; to overcome* Reg.	hablar	41
vagabundear *to loaf around* Reg.	hablar	41
vagar *to wander; to drift* Reg.	pagar	52
vaguear *to loaf, laze about* Reg.	hablar	41
valer *to be worth; to be valid*	valer	85
valerse de *to take advantage of; to use*	valer	85
vallar *to fence* Reg.	hablar	41
valorar en *to value at (amount)* Reg.	hablar	41
valorizar = **valorar** Reg.	realizar	65
valorizarse *to appreciate (in value)* Reg.	realizar	65
vanagloriarse *to boast* Reg.	hablar	41
vaporizar *to vaporize; to atomize* Reg.	realizar	65
vapulear *to beat, whip* Reg.	hablar	41

varar *to beach (a boat)* Reg.	hablar	41
varear *to knock down (olives, nuts)* Reg.	hablar	41
variar *to vary*	liar	45
vaticinar *to forecast* Reg.	hablar	41
vedar *to prohibit* (= **prohibir**) Reg.	hablar	41
vegetar *to vegetate* Reg.	hablar	41
vejar *to vex; to treat badly* Reg.	hablar	41
velar *to keep a vigil; to stay up all night;* **v. por** *to care for* Reg.	hablar	41
vencer *to defeat* Reg.	vencer	86
vendar *to bandage* Reg.	hablar	41
vender *to sell* Reg.	comer	22
vendimiar *to harvest* Reg.	hablar	41
venerar *to revere; to worship* Reg.	hablar	41
vengar *to avenge* Reg.	pagar	52
vengarse de *to take revenge for* Reg.	pagar	52
venir *to come* (consult a dictionary for idiomatic meanings)	venir	87
venirse de *to come away from, leave a place*	venir	87
ventilar *to ventilate* Reg.	hablar	41
ventiscar *to drift (snow); to blow a blizzard* Reg.	sacar	74
ver *to see*	ver	88
verse *to see oneself; to be seen* (consult a dictionary for idiomatic meanings)	ver	88
veranear *to summer* Reg.	hablar	41
verdear *to turn green; to show its greenness* Reg.	hablar	41
verificar *to verify; to check; to carry out* Reg.	sacar	74
verificarse *to take place; to occur* Reg.	sacar	74
versar sobre *to deal with (*as in *this book 'deals with'...)* Reg.	hablar	41
versificar *to versify* Reg.	sacar	74
verter *to pour out*	perder	55

vestir *to dress; to wear*	pedir	54
vestirse *to get dressed*	pedir	54
vetar *to veto* Reg.	hablar	41
viajar *to travel* Reg.	hablar	41
vibrar *to vibrate* Reg.	hablar	41
viciar *to vitiate; to become degenerate* *(person)* Reg.	hablar	41
viciarse *to get into bad habits*	hablar	41
vidriar *to glaze* Reg.	hablar	41
vigorizar *to invigorate* Reg.	realizar	65
vilipendiar *to vilify* Reg.	hablar	41
vincular *to link* Reg.	hablar	41
vindicar *to vindicate* Reg.	sacar	74
violar *to violate; to rape* Reg.	hablar	41
violentar *to do violence to; to force* *(doors, etc.)* Reg.	hablar	41
virar *to veer* Reg.	hablar	41
visar *to grant a visa; to endorse* Reg.	hablar	41
visitar *to visit* Reg.	hablar	41
vislumbrar *to glimpse* Reg.	hablar	41
visualizar *to visualize; to display* (e.g. *on computer screen)* Reg.	realizar	65
vitalizar *to vitalize* Reg.	realizar	65
vituperar *to vituperate* Reg.	hablar	41
vivaquear *to bivouac* Reg.	hablar	41
vivir *to live* Reg.	vivir	89
vocalizar *to vocalize* Reg.	realizar	65
vocear *to shout* Reg.	hablar	41
vociferar *to shout; to announce* *boastfully* Reg.	hablar	41
volar *to fly; to blow up* (i.e. *with* *explosives)*	contar	24
volatilizar *to make volatile* Reg.	realizar	65
volatilizarse *to vanish into thin air* Reg.	realizar	65
volcar *to tip over; to overturn*	trocar	84
volcarse *to be knocked over; to overturn* *(intransitive)*	trocar	84

voltear *to turn over* (transitive) Reg.	hablar	41
volver *to return* (intransitive); *to turn over* (transitive)	volver	90
volverse *to become; to turn round* (intransitive); *to turn back* (intransitive)	volver	90
vomitar *to vomit* Reg.	hablar	41
votar *to vote* Reg.	hablar	41
vulcanizar *to vulcanize* Reg.	realizar	65
vulgarizar *to popularize* Reg.	realizar	65
vulnerar *to wound* Reg.	hablar	41
yacer *to lie (i.e. be lying down)*	yacer	91
yuxtaponer *to juxtapose*	poner	58
zafarse de *to get out of (an obligation)* Reg.	hablar	41
zaherir *to wound (emotionally)*	sentir	78
zambullirse *to dive* (= **tirarse al agua**)	bullir	15
zamparse *to gobble down (food)* Reg.	hablar	41
zanganear *to loaf; to idle* Reg.	hablar	41
zangolotear *to jiggle* (transitive) Reg.	hablar	41
zangolotearse *to jiggle or shake about* (intransitive) Reg.	hablar	41
zanjar *to settle (a problem, debt)* Reg.	hablar	41
zapatear *to tap with the feet; to tap dance* Reg.	hablar	41
zarandear *to shake hard* Reg.	hablar	41
zarandearse *to be shaken about* Reg.	hablar	41
zarpar *to set sail* Reg.	hablar	41
zigzaguear *to zigzag* Reg.	hablar	41
zozobrar *to founder* Reg.	hablar	41
zumbar *to buzz* (intransitive); *to thrash* Reg.	hablar	41
zurcir *to darn* Reg.	zurcir	92
zurrar *to spank* Reg.	hablar	41
zurriagar *to whip* Reg.	pagar	52

TABLES OF MODEL VERBS

The following three sets of forms are not shown in the tables

(1) Compound Tenses, since they all formed the same way in Spanish, i.e. by adding the past participle (shown in the tables) to the appropriate tense of the verb **haber** (no. 40). There are no exceptions: unlike French, Italian and German, Spanish has no compound tenses conjugated with the verb *to be*.

The compound tenses include:

- Perfect Indicative, corresponding roughly to the English *I have done, I have seen*. It is formed from the present indicative of **haber** plus the past participle, e.g. from **hablar**:

he hablado *I have spoken*	**hemos hablado**
has hablado *you have spoken*	**habéis hablado**
ha hablado *etc.*	**han hablado**

- The Pluperfect, a common tense corresponding to the English *I had done, I had said, I had gone*, etc. It is formed from the imperfect indicative of **haber** plus the past participle, e.g.

había hablado *I had spoken*	**habíamos hablado**
habías hablado *you had spoken*	**habíais hablado**
había hablado *etc.*	**habían hablado**

- The Conditional Perfect, commonly found in conditional tenses like **si hubieras tenido más dinero, *lo habrías comprado** if you'd had more money, **you would have bought it***. It therefore corresponds to the English *I would have done, I would have said, he would have gone*, etc. It is formed from the imperfect indicative or, optionally, the **-ra** subjunctive of **haber** plus the past participle, e.g.

  habría/hubiera hablado *I would have spoken*
  habrías/hubieras hablado *you would have spoken*

habría/hubiera hablado *etc.*
habríamos/hubiéramos hablado
habríais/hubierais hablado
habrían/hubieran hablado

- The Perfect Subjunctive, a fairly common form which has no exact English translation. It is the subjunctive form of the perfect indicative, and occurs in phrases like **no creo que lo haya hecho** *I don't think that he did it*, **sin que te hayamos visto** *without us seeing you*. It is formed from the present subjunctive of **haber** plus the past participle, e.g.

haya hablado	**hayamos hablado**
hayas hablado	**hayáis hablado**
haya hablado	**hayan hablado**

- The Pluperfect Subjunctive, which has no exact English equivalent. It is found in phrases like **antes de que hubieran llegado** *before they had arrived*, **era poco probable que se hubiera dado cuenta** *it was unlikely that he had realized*. It is formed from the imperfect subjunctive, **-ra** or **-se** form, of **haber** plus the past participle, e.g.

hubiera/hubiese hablado
hubieras/hubieses hablado
hubiera/hubiese hablado
hubiéramos/hubiésemos hablado
hubierais/hubieseis hablado
hubieran/hubiesen hablado

- The Anterior Preterit (**pretérito anterior**). This tense is virtually extinct in spoken Spanish and is unusual in written language. It means the same as the pluperfect indicative, i.e. *I had seen, etc.* and is usually replaced by the preterit tense, e.g. **cuando hubo terminado** is normally said **cuando terminó** *when he finished*. It is formed from the preterit of **haber** plus the past participle:

hube hablado	**hubimos hablado**
hubiste hablado	**hubisteis hablado**
hubo hablado	**hubieran hablado**

(2) The Future Subjunctive. This is obsolete and is only found nowadays in legal or other very formal documents. In ordinary language the imperfect subjunctive replaces it. It is formed by replacing the last **a** in the **-ra** imperfect subjunctive by an **e**, e.g.

hablare	**habláremos**
hablares	**hablareis**
hablare	**hablaren**

(3) Continuous forms, e.g. **estoy hablando** *I am speaking,* **estamos poniendo** *we are putting,* etc. These are always formed by combining the correct form of **estar** (no.38) with the gerund, which is shown in the verb tables. The following forms are possible.

Indicative

Present	**estoy hablando**, etc.	*I am speaking*
Imperfect	**estaba hablando**, etc.	*I was speaking*
Preterit	**estuve hablando**, etc.	*I spoke (for a certain time)*
Perfect	**he estado**, etc. **hablando**	*I have been speaking*
Pluperfect	**había estado**, etc. **hablando**	*I had been speaking*
Future	**estaré hablando**, etc.	*I will be speaking*
Conditional	**estaria hablando**, etc.	*I would be speaking*
Future Perfect	**habré estado**, etc. **hablando**	*I will have been speaking*
Conditional Perfect	**habría estado**, etc. **hablando**	*I would have been speaking*

Subjunctive (no exact English translations)

Present	**esté hablando**, etc.
Imperfect	**estuviera/estuviese hablando**, etc.

Perfect   **haya estado hablando**, etc.
Future Perfect   **hubiera/hubiese estado hablando**, etc.

Note: The meaning of these various continuous tenses is usually self-evident to English-speakers, with the following two exceptions:

The present continuous can never refer to the future in Spanish: *I am going to Florida tomorrow* is **mañana voy a Florida**, never *'mañana estoy yendo'*.

The preterit continuous has no clear English equivalent. It refers to an action that went on for a certain time in the past, and then finished. Compare **hablé con ella** *I talked to her* and **estuve hablando con ella** *I spent a certain time talking to her, I had a talk with her.*

1 Abolir *to abolish*

Gerund **aboliendo**   *Past Participle* **abolido**

Imperative   (*the* **tú** *form is not used*) **abolid**
    (*the* **ustedes** *forms are not used*)

PRESENT *not used, not used, not used,* **abolimos, abolís,** *not used*

PRETERIT **abolí, aboliste, abolió, abolimos, abolisteis, abolieron**

IMPERFECT **abolía, abolías, abolía, abolíamos, abolíais, abolían**

FUTURE **aboliré, abolirás, abolirá, aboliremos, aboliréis, abolirán**

CONDITIONAL **aboliría, abolirías, aboliría, aboliríamos, aboliríais, abolirían**

PRESENT SUBJUNCTIVE *not used*

IMPERFECT SUBJUNCTIVE (**-ra**) **aboliera, abolieras, aboliera, aboliéramos, abolierais, abolieran**

IMPERFECT SUBJUNCTIVE (**-se**) **aboliese, abolieses, aboliese, aboliésemos, abolieseis, aboliesen**

This is a so-called 'defective' verb. These verbs have the peculiarity that the only forms allowed are those whose ending begins with **i**. There is only one other defective verb in common use, **agredir** *to assault,* although **garantir** is sometimes still used in Latin America for **garantizar** *to guarantee.* There is a tendency nowadays also to use forms of these verbs whose ending begins with **e**, e.g. **abole** *he abolishes.*

  The other verbs of this type listed in this book are virtually unused nowadays, only their past participle being found (e.g. **aguerrido** *battle-hardened*).

2 Abrir *to open*

Gerund **abriendo**   *Past Participle* **abierto**

Imperative   **abre abrid**
                      abra abran

PRESENT **abro, abres, abre, abrimos, abrís, abren**

PRETERIT **abrí, abriste, abrió, abrimos, abristeis, abrieron**

IMPERFECT **abría, abrías, abría, abríamos, abríais, abrían**

FUTURE **abriré, abrirás, abrirá, abriremos, abriréis, abrirán**

CONDITIONAL **abriría, abrirías, abriría, abriríamos, abriríais, abrirían**

PRESENT SUBJUNCTIVE **abra, abras, abra, abramos, abráis, abran**

IMPERFECT SUBJUNCTIVE (**-ra**) **abriera, abrieras, abriera, abriéramos, abrierais, abrieran**

IMPERFECT SUBJUNCTIVE (**-se**) **abriese, abrieses, abriese, abriésemos, abrieseis, abriesen**

This is a regular **-ir** verb except for the irregular past participle **abierto**. **Reabrir** *to reopen* and **entreabrir** *to half-open* are conjugated the same way.

3 Adquirir *to acquire*

Gerund **adquiriendo** *Past Participle* **adquirido**

Imperative **adquiere adquirid**
adquiera adquieran

PRESENT **adquiero, adquieres, adquiere, adquirimos, adquirís, adquieren**

PRETERIT **adquirí, adquiriste, adquirió, adquirimos, adquiristeis, adquirieron**

IMPERFECT **adquiría, adquirías, adquiría, adquiríamos, adquiríais, adquirían**

FUTURE **adquiriré, adquirirás, adquirirá, adquiriremos, adquiriréis, adquirirán**

CONDITIONAL **adquiriría, adquirirías, adquiriría, adquiriríamos, adquiriríais, adquirirían**

PRESENT SUBJUNCTIVE **adquiera, adquieras, adquiera, adquiramos, adquiráis, adquieran**

IMPERFECT SUBJUNCTIVE (**-ra**) **adquiriera, adquirieras, adquiriera, adquiriéramos, adquirierais, adquirieran**

IMPERFECT SUBJUNCTIVE (**-se**) **adquiriese, adquirieses, adquiriese, adquiriésemos, adquirieseis, adquiriesen**

In older Spanish this verb was **adquerir**, which explains the unusual change **i** > **ie** when stressed. The only other verb conjugated like it is the rare and literary **inquirir** *to enquire*.

4 Agorar *to prophesy*

Gerund **agorando**   *Past Participle* **agorado**

Imperative   **agüera agorad**
                 agüere agüeren

PRESENT **agüero, agüeras, agüera, agoramos, agoráis, agüeran**

PRETERIT **agoré, agoraste, agoró, agoramos, agorasteis, agoraron**

IMPERFECT **agoraba, agorabas, agoraba, agorábamos, agorabais, agoraban**

FUTURE **agoraré, agorarás, agorará, agoraremos, agoraréis, agorarán**

CONDITIONAL **agoraría, agorarías, agoraría, agoraríamos, agoraríais, agorarían**

PRESENT SUBJUNCTIVE **agüere, agüeres, agüere, agoremos, agoréis, agüeren**

IMPERFECT SUBJUNCTIVE (**-ra**) **agorara, agoraras, agorara, agoráramos, agorarais, agoraran**

IMPERFECT SUBJUNCTIVE (**-se**) **agorase, agorases, agorase, agorásemos, agoraseis, agorasen**

An archaic verb, **augurar** being the normal ways of expressing *to prophesy*. It is a radical-changing verb conjugated exactly like **contar** (no. 24) save for the dieresis over the **u** to show that this vowel is not silent.

5 Aislar *to isolate; to insulate*

Gerund **aislando**   *Past Participle* **aislado**

Imperative   **aísla aislad**
                aísle aíslen

PRESENT **aíslo, aíslas, aísla, aislamos, aisláis, aíslan**

PRETERIT **aislé, aislaste, aisló, aislamos, aislasteis, aislaron**

IMPERFECT **aislaba, aislabas, aislaba, aislábamos, aislabais, aislaban**

FUTURE **aislaré, aislarás, aislará, aislaremos, aislaréis, aislarán**

CONDITIONAL **aislaría, aislarías, aislaría, aislaríamos, aislaríais, aislarían**

PRESENT SUBJUNCTIVE **aísle, aísles, aísle, aislemos, aisléis, aíslen**

IMPERFECT SUBJUNCTIVE (-ra) **aislara, aislaras, aislara, aisláramos, aislarais, aislaran**

IMPERFECT SUBJUNCTIVE (-se) **aislase, aislases, aislase, aislásemos, aislaseis, aislasen**

This is a regular -**ar** verb except for the accent written on **i** when the latter is stressed. This accent was introduced by the spelling reforms of 1959 and even today many people omit it. There are a few other verbs similarly affected; an **h** between the vowel and the **i** does not make the accent unnecessary. The following are occasionally found:

ahitarse de *to gorge on, to stuff oneself* (i.e. **atiborrarse de**)

amohinarse *to sulk* (i.e. **enfurruñarse**)

rehilar *to quiver* (i.e. **temblar**) accented form **rehílo**, etc.

6 Almorzar *to have lunch*

Gerund **almorzando**   *Past Participle* **almorzado**

Imperative   **almuerza almorzad**
                      almuerce almuercen

PRESENT **almuerzo, almuerzas, almuerza, almorzamos, almorzáis, almuerzan**

PRETERIT **almorcé, almorzaste, almorzó, almorzamos, almorzasteis, almorzaron**

IMPERFECT **almorzaba, almorzabas, almorzaba, almorzábamos, almorzabais, almorzaban**

FUTURE **almorzaré, almorzarás, almorzará, almorzaremos, almorzaréis, almorzarán**

CONDITIONAL **almorzaría, almorzarías, almorzaría, almorzaríamos, almorzaríais, almorzarían**

PRESENT SUBJUNCTIVE **almuerce, almuerces, almuerce, almorcemos, almorcéis, almuercen**

IMPERFECT SUBJUNCTIVE (**-ra**) **almorzara, almorzaras, almorzara, almorzáramos, almorzarais, almorzaran**

IMPERFECT SUBJUNCTIVE (**-se**) **almorzase, almorzases, almorzase, almorzásemos, almorzaseis, almorzasen**

A radical-changing verb conjugated like **contar** (no. 24) except for the predictable **z > c** before **e.** Other common verbs conjugated in the same way are:

esforzar *to encourage; to push (a person into trying harder)*
esforzarse por *to try hard to*
forzar *to force*
reforzar *to strengthen*

7 Andar *to walk; to go about*

Gerund **andando**   *Past Participle* **andado**

Imperative   **anda andad**
                      ande anden

PRESENT **ando, andas, anda, andamos, andáis, andan**

PRETERIT **anduve, anduviste, anduvo, anduvimos, anduvisteis, anduvieron**

IMPERFECT **andaba, andabas, andaba, andábamos, andabais, andaban**

FUTURE **andaré, andarás, andará, andaremos, andaréis, andarán**

CONDITIONAL **andaría, andarías, andaría, andaríamos, andaríais, andarían**

PRESENT SUBJUNCTIVE **ande, andes, ande, andemos, andéis, anden**

IMPERFECT SUBJUNCTIVE **(-ra) anduviera, anduvieras, anduviera, anduviéramos, anduvierais, anduvieran**

IMPERFECT SUBJUNCTIVE **(-se) anduviese, anduvieses, anduviese, anduviésemos, anduvieseis, anduviesen**

Irregular verb in constant use. It is in fact a regular **-ar** verb except for the preterit and imperfect subjunctive forms in **-uv-**. The preterit uses the irregular preterit endings and is completely unexpected: Spanish-speaking children have to be reminded to say **anduve** and not 'andé'. **Andar** has numerous other meanings and idiomatic uses that should be sought in a dictionary.

The only other verb conjugated like it is **desandar** *to retrace steps*, which is rarely seen and then usually only in the infinitive form.

8 Arcaizar *to make archaic*

Gerund **arcaizando**   *Past Participle* **arcaizado**

Imperative   **arcaíza arcaizad**

arcaíce arcaícen

PRESENT **arcaízo, arcaízas, arcaíza, arcaizamos, arcaizáis, arcaízan**

PRETERIT **arcaicé, arcaizaste, arcaizó, arcaizamos, arcaizasteis, arcaizaron**

IMPERFECT **arcaizaba, arcaizabas, arcaizaba, arcaizábamos, arcaizabais, arcaizaban**

FUTURE **arcaizaré, arcaizarás, arcaizará, arcaizaremos, arcaizaréis, arcaizarán**

CONDITIONAL **arcaizaría, arcaizarías, arcaizaría, arcaizaríamos, arcaizaríais, arcaizarían**

PRESENT SUBJUNCTIVE **arcaíce, arcaíces, arcaíce, arcaicemos, arcaicéis, arcaícen**

IMPERFECT SUBJUNCTIVE (**-ra**) **arcaizara, arcaizaras, arcaizara, arcaizáramos, arcaizarais, arcaizaran**

IMPERFECT SUBJUNCTIVE (**-se**) **arcaizase, arcaizases, arcaizase, arcaizásemos, arcaizaseis, arcaizasen**

This verb is conjugated exactly like **aislar** (no. 5), and is therefore a regular **-ar** verb except for the spelling change **z** > **c** before **e** and the accent on the stressed **í** (introduced in 1959). It is a rare verb, and verbs conjugated like it are not very common, e.g.

enraizar *to take root* (i.e. **echar raíces**)

europeizar *to Europeanise*, stressed form **europeíza**, etc.

homogeneizar *to homogenise*

judaizar *to Judaise*

9 Argüir *to argue a point*

Gerund **arguyendo**   *Past Participle* **argüido**

Imperative	**arguye argüid**
	arguya arguyan

PRESENT **arguyo, arguyes, arguye, argüimos, argüís, arguyen**

PRETERIT **argüí, argüiste, arguyó, argüimos, argüisteis, arguyeron**

IMPERFECT **argüía, argüías, argüía, argüíamos, argüíais, argüían**

FUTURE **argüiré, argüirás, argüirá, argüiremos, argüiréis, argüirán**

CONDITIONAL **argüiría, argüirías, argüiría, argüiríamos, argüiríais, argüirían**

PRESENT SUBJUNCTIVE **arguya, arguyas, arguya, arguyamos, arguyáis, arguyan**

IMPERFECT SUBJUNCTIVE **(-ra) arguyera, arguyeras, arguyera, arguyéramos, arguyerais, arguyeran**

IMPERFECT SUBJUNCTIVE **(-se) arguyese, arguyeses, arguyese, arguyésemos, arguyeseis, arguyesen**

This verb is conjugated exactly like **construir** (no. 23), except that a dieresis appears in the combination **üi** to show that the **u** is not silent. The regular verb **argumentar** has almost the same meaning and is increasingly common. Both verbs mean *to argue that*. *To have an argument* is **discutir**.

No other verbs are conjugated like **argüir**, but many are conjugated like **construir**.

10 Asir *to grasp/seize*

Gerund **asiendo**   *Past Participle* **asido**

Imperative   **ase asid**

(asga asgan)

PRESENT **(asgo), ases, ase, asimos, asís, asen**
PRETERIT **así, asiste, asió, asimos, asisteis, asieron**
IMPERFECT **asía, asías, asía, asíamos, asíais, asían**
FUTURE **asiré, asirás, asirá, asiremos, asiréis, asirán**
CONDITIONAL **asiría, asirías, asiría, asiríamos, asiríais, asirían**
PRESENT SUBJUNCTIVE **(asga), (asgas), (asga), (asgamos), (asgáis), (asgan)**
IMPERFECT SUBJUNCTIVE **(-ra) asiera, asieras, asiera, asiéramos, asierais, asieran**
IMPERFECT SUBJUNCTIVE **(-se) asiese, asieses, asiese, asiésemos, asieseis, asiesen**

This verb rarely used and the forms containing a **g** are always avoided. The idea of *seize, grasp* is nowadays usually expressed by the regular verb **agarrar**.

Desasirse de *to free oneself from someone's clutches* is conjugated in the same way, but it is also rare; **librarse de** (regular) expresses the same idea.

11 Aullar *to howl*

Gerund **aullando**   *Past Participle* **aullado**

Imperative   **aúlla aullad**

          aúlle aúllen

Present **aúllo, aúllas, aúlla, aullamos, aulláis, aúllan**

PRETERIT **aullé, aullaste, aulló, aullamos, aullasteis, aullaron**

IMPERFECT **aullaba, aullabas, aullaba, aullábamos, aullabais, aullaban**

FUTURE **aullaré, aullarás, aullará, aullaremos, aullaréis, aullarán**

CONDITIONAL **aullaría, aullarías, aullaría, aullaríamos, aullaríais, aullarían**

PRESENT *Subjunctive* **aúlle, aúlles, aúlle, aullemos, aulléis, aúllen**

IMPERFECT SUBJUNCTIVE (**-ra**) **aullara, aullaras, aullara, aulláramos, aullarais, aullaran**

IMPERFECT SUBJUNCTIVE (**-se**) **aullase, aullases, aullase, aullásemos, aullaseis, aullasen**

A regular -ar verb except for the accent on the stressed **ú**. This accent has been required since the spelling reforms of 1959. A few other verbs are similarly affected, of which the only ones likely to be occasionally encountered are:

ahumar *to smoke (meat, etc.)*, stressed form **ahúmo**, etc. To smoke a cigarette is **fumar**.

desahuciar *to evict* (usually **desalojar**), stressed form **desahúcio**, etc.

rehusar *to refuse* (transitive, usually **rechazar**), stressed form **rehúso**, etc.

12 Avergonzar   *to shame*

Gerund **avergonzando**   *Past Participle* **avergonzado**

Imperative   **avergüenza avergonzad**
                      avergüence avergüencen

PRESENT **avergüenzo, avergüenzas, avergüenza,
avergonzamos, avergonzáis, avergüenzan**

PRETERIT **avergoncé, avergonzaste, avergonzó,
avergonzamos, avergonzasteis, avergonzaron**

IMPERFECT **avergonzaba, avergonzabas, avergonzaba,
avergonzábamos, avergonzabais, avergonzaban**

FUTURE **avergonzaré, avergonzarás, avergonzará,
avergonzaremos, avergonzaréis, avergonzarán**

CONDITIONAL **avergonzaría, avergonzarías, avergonzaría,
avergonzaríamos, avergonzaríais, avergonzarían**

PRESENT SUBJUNCTIVE **avergüence, avergüences,
avergüence, avergoncemos, avergoncéis, avergüencen**

IMPERFECT SUBJUNCTIVE (**-ra**) **avergonzara, avergonzaras,
avergonzara, avergonzáramos, avergonzarais,
avergonzaran**

IMPERFECT SUBJUNCTIVE (**-se**) **avergonzase, avergonzases,
avergonzase, avergonzásemos, avergonzaseis,
avergonzasen**

Conjugated like **almorzar** (no. 6), except for the dieresis on
the **üe** to show that the **u** is not silent. Note the regular
spelling change **z** > **c** before **e**. **Avergonzarse** *to be ashamed* is
conjugated in the same way. So is **desvergonzarse** *to act in a
shameless manner*, but it is rare.

13 Averiguar *to ascertain*

Gerund **averiguando**   *Past Participle* **averiguado**

Imperative   **averigua averiguad**
               averigüe averigüen

PRESENT **averiguo, averiguas, averigua, averiguamos, averiguáis, averiguan**

PRETERIT **averigüé, averiguaste, averiguó, averiguamos, averiguasteis, averiguaron**

IMPERFECT **averiguaba, averiguabas, averiguaba, averiguábamos, averiguabais, averiguaban**

FUTURE **averiguaré, averiguarás, averiguará, averiguaremos, averiguaréis, averiguarán**

CONDITIONAL **averiguaría, averiguarías, averiguaría, averiguaríamos, averiguaríais, averiguarían**

PRESENT SUBJUNCTIVE **averigüe, averigües, averigüe, averigüemos, averigüéis, averigüen**

IMPERFECT SUBJUNCTIVE (**-ra**) **averiguara, averiguaras, averiguara, averiguáramos, averiguarais, averiguaran**

IMPERFECT SUBJUNCTIVE (**-se**) **averiguase, averiguases, averiguase, averiguásemos, averiguaseis, averiguasen**

A regular -**ar** verb, except that a dieresis is used to show that **u** is not silent. The **u** is never stressed (contrast **continuar**, no. 25).

Verbs ending in -**cuar**, e.g. **evacuar** *to evacuate*, are conjugated in the same way (at least in Spain), but without the dieresis. But conjugation like **continuar** (no. 25) is considered correct in much of Latin America and is common in Spain.

14 Balbucir *to stammer*

Gerund **balbuciendo**   *Past Participle* **balbucido**

Imperative   **balbuce balbucid**
                          not used

PRESENT NOT USED, **balbuces, balbuce, balbucimos,
   balbucís, balbucen**

PRETERIT **balbucí, balbuciste, balbució, balbucimos,
   balbucisteis, balbucieron**

IMPERFECT **balbucía, balbucías, balbucía, balbucíamos,
   balbucíais, balbucían**

FUTURE **balbuciré, balbucirás, balbucirá, balbuciremos,
   balbuciréis, balbucirán**

CONDITIONAL **balbuciría, balbucirías, balbuciría,
   balbuciríamos, balbuciríais, balbucirían**

PRESENT SUBJUNCTIVE *not used*

IMPERFECT SUBJUNCTIVE **(-ra) balbuciera, balbucieras,
   balbuciera, balbuciéramos, balbucierais, balbucieran**

IMPERFECT SUBJUNCTIVE **(-se) balbuciese, balbucieses,
   balbuciese, balbuciésemos, balbucieseis, balbuciesen**

Balbucir has the unique peculiarity that no form containing
a **z** occurs. It is virtually obsolete, although third-person
forms are still seen in literary styles. **Balbucear** means the
same, is a regular **-ar** verb and is more common.

15 Bullir *to seethe (intransitive)*

Gerund **bullendo**   *Past Participle* **bullido**

Imperative   **bulle bullid**
                      bulla bullan

PRESENT **bullo, bulles, bulle, bullimos, bullís, bullen**

PRETERIT **bullí, bulliste, bulló, bullimos, bullisteis, bulleron**

IMPERFECT **bullía, bullías, bullía, bullíamos, bullíais, bullían**

FUTURE **bulliré, bullirás, bullirá, bulliremos, bulliréis, bullirán**

CONDITIONAL **bulliría, bullirías, bulliría, bulliríamos, bulliríais, bullirían**

PRESENT SUBJUNCTIVE **bulla, bullas, bulla, bullamos, bulláis, bullan**

IMPERFECT SUBJUNCTIVE **(-ra) bullera, bulleras, bullera, bulléramos, bullerais, bulleran**

IMPERFECT SUBJUNCTIVE **(-se) bullese, bulleses, bullese, bullésemos, bulleseis, bullesen**

A regular **-ir** verb affected by the standard spelling rule that **ió > ó** and **ie > e** after **ll** (because the latter already contains a palatal sound). Similarly affected are:

engulir *to gulp down*
escabullirse *to skive off, to slip away*
mullir *to fluff up (a pillow)*
zambullirse *to dive (into the water)*

16 Caber *to fit (intransitive)*

Gerund **cabiendo**   *Past Participle* **cabido**

| *Imperative* | **cabe cabed** |
| | **quepa quepan** |

PRESENT **quepo, cabes, cabe, cabemos, cabéis, caben**
PRETERIT **cupe, cupiste, cupo, cupimos, cupisteis, cupieron**
IMPERFECT **cabía, cabías, cabía, cabíamos, cabíais, cabían**
FUTURE **cabré, cabrás, cabrá, cabremos, cabréis, cabrán**
CONDITIONAL **cabría, cabrías, cabría, cabríamos, cabríais, cabrían**
PRESENT SUBJUNCTIVE **quepa, quepas, quepa, quepamos, quepáis, quepan**
IMPERFECT SUBJUNCTIVE (**-ra**) **cupiera, cupieras, cupiera, cupiéramos, cupierais, cupieran**
IMPERFECT SUBJUNCTIVE (**-se**) **cupiese, cupieses, cupiese, cupiésemos, cupieseis, cupiesen**

Extremely irregular: Spanish-speaking children constantly make the mistake of saying 'cabo' for **quepo**. Usage:

Esto no cabe aquí *this doesn't fit here*
Tú no cabes *there's no room for you*
¿Quepo yo? *is there any room for me?*

17 Caer *to fall*

Gerund **cayendo**   *Past Participle* **caído**

Imperative   **cae caed**

caiga caigan

PRESENT **caigo, caes, cae, caemos, caéis, caen**
PRETERIT **caí, caíste, cayó, caímos, caísteis, cayeron**
IMPERFECT **caía, caías, caía, caíamos, caíais, caían**
FUTURE **caeré, caerás, caerá, caeremos, caeréis, caerán**
CONDITIONAL **caería, caerías, caería, caeríamos, caeríais, caerían**
PRESENT SUBJUNCTIVE **caiga, caigas, caiga, caigamos, caigáis, caigan**
IMPERFECT SUBJUNCTIVE (**-ra**) **cayera, cayeras, cayera, cayéramos, cayerais, cayeran**
IMPERFECT SUBJUNCTIVE (**-se**) **cayese, cayeses, cayese, cayésemos, cayeseis, cayesen**

The appearance of **g** in some forms constitutes the main irregularity. The preterit is regular. Other verbs similarly conjugated are:

caerse *to fall down/over*
decaer *to decay* (economically, morally; not *to rot*, which is **pudrir**)
raer *to scrape* (rare, usually **raspar, fregar**)
recaer *to relapse*

18 Cerrar *to shut/close*

Gerund **cerrando**   *Past Participle* **cerrado**

Imperative   **cierra cerrad**

                    cierre cierren

PRESENT **cierro, cierras, cierra, cerramos, cerráis, cierran**

PRETERIT **cerré, cerraste, cerró, cerramos, cerrasteis, cerraron**

IMPERFECT **cerraba, cerrabas, cerraba, cerrábamos, cerrabais, cerraban**

FUTURE **cerraré, cerrarás, cerrará, cerraremos, cerraréis, cerrarán**

CONDITIONAL **cerraría, cerrarías, cerraría, cerraríamos, cerraríais, cerrarían**

PRESENT SUBJUNCTIVE **cierre, cierres, cierre, cerremos, cerréis, cierren**

IMPERFECT SUBJUNCTIVE (**-ra**) **cerrara, cerraras, cerrara, cerráramos, cerrarais, cerraran**

IMPERFECT SUBJUNCTIVE (**-se**) **cerrase, cerrases, cerrase, cerrásemos, cerraseis, cerrasen**

A frequently-encountered type of radical changing verb: **e> ie** when stressed. Common verbs of this sort are:

acertar *to get right*	**helar** *to freeze*
apretar *to squeeze*	**nevar** *to snow*
atravesar *to cross*	**pensar** *to think*
calentar *to heat*	**quebrar** *to snap*
confesar *to confess*	**recomendar** *to recommend*
despertar *to wake up*	**sentarse** *to sit*
enterrar *to bury*	

Verbs ending in **-egar** are similar, but show spelling changes. See **negar**.(no. 49).

19 Cocer *to cook; to boil*

Gerund **cociendo**   *Past Participle* **cocido**

Imperative   **cuece coced**

cueza cuezan

PRESENT **cuezo, cueces, cuece, cocemos, cocéis, cuecen**
PRETERIT **cocí, cociste, coció, cocimos, cocisteis, cocieron**
IMPERFECT **cocía, cocías, cocía, cocíamos, cocíais, cocían**
FUTURE **coceré, cocerás, cocerá, coceremos, coceréis, cocerán**
CONDITIONAL **cocería, cocerías, cocería, coceríamos, coceríais, cocerían**
PRESENT SUBJUNCTIVE **cueza, cuezas, cueza, cozamos, cozáis, cuezan**
IMPERFECT SUBJUNCTIVE **(-ra) cociera, cocieras, cociera, cociéramos, cocierais, cocieran**
IMPERFECT SUBJUNCTIVE **(-se) cociese, cocieses, cociese, cociésemos, cocieseis, cociesen**

Conjugated exactly like **mover** (no. 48), but with the spelling change **c** > **z** before **a** or **o**. Other verbs similarly conjugated are:

escocer *to sting*, *to smart* (usually **picar**)
retorcerse *to writhe*
torcer *to twist* (transitive)

20 Colgar *to hang up*

Gerund **colgando**   *Past Participle* **colgado**

| *Imperative* | **cuelga colgad** |
| | **cuelgue cuelguen** |

PRESENT **cuelgo, cuelgas, cuelga, colgamos, colgáis, cuelgan**

PRETERIT **colgué, colgaste, colgó, colgamos, colgasteis, colgaron**

IMPERFECT **colgaba, colgabas, colgaba, colgábamos, colgabais, colgaban**

FUTURE **colgaré, colgarás, colgará, colgaremos, colgaréis, colgarán**

CONDITIONAL **colgaría, colgarías, colgaría, colgaríamos, colgaríais, colgarían**

PRESENT SUBJUNCTIVE **cuelgue, cuelgues, cuelgue, colguemos, colguéis, cuelguen**

IMPERFECT SUBJUNCTIVE (**-ra**) **colgara, colgaras, colgara, colgáramos, colgarais, colgaran**

IMPERFECT SUBJUNCTIVE (**-se**) **colgase, colgases, colgase, colgásemos, colgaseis, colgasen**

Conjugated like **contar** (no. 24: **o** > **ue** when stressed), but with the predictable insertion of a silent **u** before **e** to keep the **g** hard. Similar verbs:

descolgar *to take down*

rogar *to request*

21 Comenzar *to begin*

Gerund **comenzando**   *Past Participle* **comenzado**

Imperative   **comienza comenzad**

                  comience comiencen

PRESENT **comienzo, comienzas, comienza, comenzamos, comenzáis, comienzan**

PRETERIT **comencé, comenzaste, comenzó, comenzamos, comenzasteis, comenzaron**

IMPERFECT **comenzaba, comenzabas, comenzaba, comenzábamos, comenzabais, comenzaban**

FUTURE **comenzaré, comenzarás, comenzará, comenzaremos, comenzaréis, comenzarán**

CONDITIONAL **comenzaría, comenzarías, comenzaría, comenzaríamos, comenzaríais, comenzarían**

PRESENT SUBJUNCTIVE **comience, comiences, comience, comencemos, comencéis, comiencen**

IMPERFECT SUBJUNCTIVE (**-ra**) **comenzara, comenzaras, comenzara, comenzáramos, comenzarais, comenzaran**

IMPERFECT SUBJUNCTIVE (**-se**) **comenzase, comenzases, comenzase, comenzásemos, comenzaseis, comenzasen**

Conjugated like **cerrar** (no. 18: **e** > **ie** when stressed), but with the predictable spelling change **z** > **c** before **e**. Similar verbs:

empezar *to begin*

tropezar *to stumble*

22 Comer *to eat*

Gerund **comiendo**   *Past Participle* **comido**

Imperative   **come comed**

                         coma coman

PRESENT **como, comes, come, comemos, coméis, comen**

PRETERIT **comí, comiste, comió, comimos, comisteis, comieron**

IMPERFECT **comía, comías, comía, comíamos, comíais, comían**

FUTURE **comeré, comerás, comerá, comeremos, comeréis, comerán**

CONDITIONAL **comería, comerías, comería, comeríamos, comeríais, comerían**

PRESENT SUBJUNCTIVE **coma, comas, coma, comamos, comáis, coman**

IMPERFECT SUBJUNCTIVE **(-ra) comiera, comieras, comiera, comiéramos, comierais, comieran**

IMPERFECT SUBJUNCTIVE **(-se) comiese, comieses, comiese, comiésemos, comieseis, comiesen**

Completely regular, which makes it a convenient model for the **-er** conjugation.

Verbs whose infinitive ends in **-cer** (numerous) should be sought in the list as they may show irregularities. The majority are conjugated like **parecer** (no. 53), but a few are conjugated like **vencer** (no. 86) or **cocer** (no. 19).

For infinitives ending in **-ger** see **proteger** (no. 62), which has predictable spelling changes.

Verbs ending in **-tender** are conjugated like **perder** (no. 55), with the exception of **pretender** *to claim*, which is like **comer**.

23 Construir *to build*

Gerund **construyendo**   *Past Participle* **construido**

Imperative   **construye construid**
construya construyan

PRESENT **construyo, construyes, construye, construimos, construís, construyen**

PRETERIT **construí, construiste, construyó, construimos, construisteis, construyeron**

IMPERFECT **construía, construías, construía, construíamos, construíais, construían**

FUTURE **construiré, construirás, construirá, construiremos, construiréis, construirán**

CONDITIONAL **construiría, construirías, construiría, construiríamos, construiríais, construirían**

PRESENT SUBJUNCTIVE **construya, construyas, construya, construyamos, construyáis, construyan**

IMPERFECT SUBJUNCTIVE (**-ra**) **construyera, construyeras, construyera, construyéramos, construyerais, construyeran**

IMPERFECT SUBJUNCTIVE (**-se**) **construyese, construyeses, construyese, construyésemos, construyeseis, construyesen**

A regular **-ir** verb but for the **y** inserted between **u** and **o** or **a**. The past participle does not have an accent. Similar common verbs are:

atribuir *to attribute*   **huir** *to flee*
concluir *to conclude*   **incluir** *to include*
contribuir *to contribute*   **influir** *to influence*
destruir *to destroy*   **intuir** *to intuit*
distribuir *to distribute*   **substituir** *to substitute*
excluir *to exclude*

24 Contar   *to count; to tell a story*

Gerund **contando**   *Past Participle* **contado**

Imperative   **cuenta contad**

          cuente cuenten

PRESENT **cuento, cuentas, cuenta, contamos, contáis, cuentan**

PRETERIT **conté, contaste, contó, contamos, contasteis, contaron**

IMPERFECT **contaba, contabas, contaba, contábamos, contabais, contaban**

FUTURE **contaré, contarás, contará, contaremos, contaréis, contarán**

CONDITIONAL **contaría, contarías, contaría, contaríamos, contaríais, contarían**

PRESENT SUBJUNCTIVE **cuente, cuentes, cuente, contemos, contéis, cuenten**

IMPERFECT SUBJUNCTIVE **(-ra) contara, contaras, contara, contáramos, contarais, contaran**

IMPERFECT SUBJUNCTIVE **(-se) contase, contases, contase, contásemos, contaseis, contasen**

A common type of radical changing **-ar** verb in which stressed **o** > **ue**. Similar common verbs:

acordarse de *to remember*	**desaprobar** *to approve*
acostarse *to go to bed*	**encontrar** *to find*
apostar *to bet*	**mostrar** *to show*
aprobar *to approve; to pass an exam*	**probar** *to prove; to try out*
colarse *to slip through*	**recordar** *to recall*
costar *to cost*	**rodar** *to roll*
demostrar *to demonstrate (a fact)*	**soltar** *to let go*
	soñar *to dream*
	volar *to fly*

25 Continuar *to continue*

Gerund **continuando**   *Past Participle* **continuado**

Imperative   **continúa continuad**
                     continúe continúen

PRESENT **continúo, continúas, continúa, continuamos, continuáis, continúan**

PRETERIT **continué, continuaste, continuó, continuamos, continuasteis, continuaron**

IMPERFECT **continuaba, continuabas, continuaba, continuábamos, continuabais, continuaban**

FUTURE **continuaré, continuarás, continuará, continuaremos, continuaréis, continuarán**

CONDITIONAL **continuaría, continuarías, continuaría, continuaríamos, continuaríais, continuarían**

PRESENT SUBJUNCTIVE **continúe, continúes, continúe, continuemos, continuéis, continúen**

IMPERFECT SUBJUNCTIVE (**-ra**) **continuara, continuaras, continuara, continuáramos, continuarais, continuaran**

IMPERFECT SUBJUNCTIVE (**-se**) **continuase, continuases, continuase, continuásemos, continuaseis, continuasen**

This is a regular **-ar** verb, but the **u** is stressed, unlike **averiguar** (no. 13). There are forty similar verbs in the list, the most commonly encountered being:

acentuar *to accentuate*	**insinuar** *to insinuate*
actuar *to act*	**perpetuarse** *to be*
devaluar *to devalue*	*perpetuated*
efectuar *to effect*	**puntuar** *to punctuate;*
exceptuar *to except*	*to grade*
fluctuar *to fluctuate*	**situar** *to situate*
graduar *to graduate; to grade*	

26 Cubrir *to cover*

Gerund **cubriendo**   *Past Participle* **cubierto**

Imperative   **cubre cubrid**

                     cubra cubran

PRESENT **cubro, cubres, cubre, cubrimos, cubrís, cubren**

PRETERIT **cubrí, cubriste, cubrió, cubrimos, cubristeis, cubrieron**

IMPERFECT **cubría, cubrías, cubría, cubríamos, cubríais, cubrían**

FUTURE **cubriré, cubrirás, cubrirá, cubriremos, cubriréis, cubrirán**

CONDITIONAL **cubriría, cubrirías, cubriría, cubriríamos, cubriríais, cubrirían**

PRESENT SUBJUNCTIVE **cubra, cubras, cubra, cubramos, cubráis, cubran**

IMPERFECT SUBJUNCTIVE (**-ra**) **cubriera, cubrieras, cubriera, cubriéramos, cubrierais, cubrieran**

IMPERFECT SUBJUNCTIVE (**-se**) **cubriese, cubrieses, cubriese, cubriésemos, cubrieseis, cubriesen**

A regular -**ir** verb except for the past participle ending in -**ierto**. Similar verbs are:

descubrir *to discover*
encubrir *to cover up (facts)*
recubrir *to cover; to line (e.g. with material)*

27 Dar *to give*

Gerund **dando**   *Past Participle* **dado**

Imperative   **da dad**

                      dé den

PRESENT **doy, das, da, damos, dais, dan**
PRETERIT **di, diste, dio** *(no accent!)*, **dimos, disteis, dieron**
IMPERFECT **daba, dabas, daba, dábamos, dabais, daban**
FUTURE **daré, darás, dará, daremos, daréis, darán**
CONDITIONAL **daría, darías, daría, daríamos, daríais, darían**
PRESENT SUBJUNCTIVE **dé, des, dé, demos, deis, den**
IMPERFECT SUBJUNCTIVE **(-ra) diera, dieras, diera, diéramos, dierais, dieran**
IMPERFECT SUBJUNCTIVE **(-se) diese, dieses, diese, diésemos, dieseis, diesen**

Irregular verb, the main irregularities being the unexpected form **doy** and the fact that, although it is an **-ar** verb, the preterit and the imperfect subjunctives are conjugated as for **-er** verbs. Note that the preterit forms have no accents: the spelling **dió** for **dio** was abolished in 1959. The accent on the present subjunctive **dé** merely serves to distinguish it from the preposition **de** *of*.

There are no other similar verbs in everyday use.

28 Decir *to say*

Gerund **diciendo** *Past Participle* **dicho**

Imperative   **di decid**

                   diga digan

PRESENT **digo, dices, dice, decimos, decís, dicen**

PRETERIT **dije, dijiste, dijo, dijimos, dijisteis, dijeron**

IMPERFECT **decía, decías, decía, decíamos, decíais, decían**

FUTURE **diré, dirás, dirá, diremos, diréis, dirán**

CONDITIONAL **diría, dirías, diría, diríamos, diríais, dirían**

PRESENT SUBJUNCTIVE **diga, digas, diga, digamos, digáis, digan**

IMPERFECT SUBJUNCTIVE **(-ra) dijera, dijeras, dijera, dijéramos, dijerais, dijeran**

IMPERFECT SUBJUNCTIVE **(-se) dijese, dijeses, dijese, dijésemos, dijeseis, dijesen**

Irregular verb. The preterit and imperfect subjunctive endings have a typical feature of irregular verbs: **-ie** becomes **e** when it follows **j**: **dijeron, dijera, dijese**, not *'dijieron'*, etc. Similar verbs:

contradecir *to contradict*

desdecirse de *to go back on* (a promise)

   Predecir *to predict* is usually conjugated like **maldecir** (no. 47).

29 Delinquir *to act delinquently*

Gerund **delinquiendo**   *Past Participle* **delinquido**

Imperative   **delinque delinquid**
                     delinca delincan

PRESENT **delinco, delinques, delinque, delinquimos, delinquís, delinquen**

PRETERIT **delinquí, delinquiste, delinquió, delinquimos, delinquisteis, delinquieron**

IMPERFECT **delinquía, delinquías, delinquía, delinquíamos, delinquíais, delinquían**

FUTURE **delinquiré, delinquirás, delinquirá, delinquiremos, delinquiréis, delinquirán**

CONDITIONAL **delinquiría, delinquirías, delinquiría, delinquiríamos, delinquiríais, delinquirían**

PRESENT SUBJUNCTIVE **delinca, delincas, delinca, delincamos, delincáis, delincan**

IMPERFECT SUBJUNCTIVE **(-ra) delinquiera, delinquieras, delinquiera, delinquiéramos, delinquierais, delinquieran**

IMPERFECT SUBJUNCTIVE **(-se) delinquiese, delinquieses, delinquiese, delinquiésemos, delinquieseis, delinquiesen**

A regular -**ir** verb, except for the predictable spelling change **qu** > **c** before **a** or **o**. This verb is confined to very literary styles and is rarely seen, except occasionally in the infinitive form. No similar verbs are in everyday use in the modern language.

30 Desosar *to bone*

Gerund **desosando**   *Past Participle* **desosado**

Imperative   **deshuesa desosad**

 deshuese deshuesen

PRESENT **deshueso, deshuesas, deshuesa, desosamos, desosáis, deshuesan**

PRETERIT **desosé, desosaste, desosó, desosamos, desosasteis, desosaron**

IMPERFECT **desosaba, desosabas, desosaba, desosábamos, desosabais, desosaban**

FUTURE **desosaré, desosarás, desosará, desosaremos, desosaréis, desosarán**

CONDITIONAL **desosaría, desosarías, desosaría, desosaríamos, desosaríais, desosarían**

PRESENT SUBJUNCTIVE **deshuese, deshueses, deshuese, desosemos, desoséis, deshuesen**

IMPERFECT SUBJUNCTIVE **(-ra) desosara, desosaras, desosara, desosáramos, desosarais, desosaran**

IMPERFECT SUBJUNCTIVE **(-se) desosase, desosases, desosase, desosásemos, desosaseis, desosasen**

An archaic verb, conjugated like **contar** (no. 24), except for the predictable inclusion of **h** before **ue** when this diphthong begins a syllable. **Oler** *to smell* displays the same phenomenon. **Desosar** is nowadays replaced by the regular **deshuesar**.

31 Desvaír *to cause to fade (colors, etc.)*

Gerund **desvayendo**	*Past Participle* **desvaído**

Imperative   (*the* **tú** *form is not used*) **desvaíd**
   (*the* **ustedes** *forms are not used*)

PRESENT *not used, not used, not used,* **desvaímos, desvaís,** *not used*

PRETERIT **desvaí, desvaíste, desvayó, desvaímos, desvaísteis, desvayeron**

IMPERFECT **desvaía, desvaías, desvaía, desvaíamos, desvaíais, desvaían**

FUTURE **desvairé, desvairás, desvairá, desvairemos, desvairéis, desvairán**

CONDITIONAL **desvairía, desvairías, desvairía, desvairíamos, desvairíais, desvairían**

PRESENT SUBJUNCTIVE *not used*

IMPERFECT SUBJUNCTIVE (**-ra**) **desvayera, desvayeras, desvayera, desvayéramos, desvayerais, desvayeran**

IMPERFECT SUBJUNCTIVE (**-se**) **desvayese, desvayeses, desvayese, desvayésemos, desvayeseis, desvayesen**

A rare type of defective verb, similar to **abolir** (no. 1) in that only forms whose endings begin with **i** (or, in this case, **y**) are found. This verb is nowadays seen only in its participle form **desvaído** *faded, washed-out*: **desteñir** is the usual word for *to fade*, applied to colors/(Brit.) colours. **Embaír** *to swindle*, *to cheat* is conjugated in the same way, but it is virtually extinct, being replaced by the regular verb **estafar**.

32 Discernir *to discern*

Gerund **discerniendo**   *Past Participle* **discernido**

Imperative   **discierne discernid**

discierna disciernan

PRESENT **discierno, disciernes, discierne, discernimos, discernís, disciernen**

PRETERIT **discerní, discerniste, discernió, discernimos, discernisteis, discernieron**

IMPERFECT **discernía, discernías, discernía, discerníamos, discerníais, discernían**

FUTURE **discerniré, discernirá, discernirá, discerniremos, discerniréis, discernirán**

CONDITIONAL **discerniría, discernirías, discerniría, discerniríamos, discerniríais, discernirían**

PRESENT SUBJUNCTIVE **discierna, disciernas, discierna, discernamos, discernáis, disciernan**

IMPERFECT SUBJUNCTIVE (**-ra**) **discerniera, discernieras, discerniera, discerniéramos, discernierais, discernieran**

IMPERFECT SUBJUNCTIVE (**-se**) **discerniese, discernieses, discerniese, discerniésemos, discernieseis, discerniesen**

This is a radical changing **-ir** verb which shows the common replacement of stressed **e** by **ie**. Such verbs are in fact very uncommon in the **-ir** conjugation (but common in the other two conjugations). Most radical-changing **-ir** verbs are like **sentir** (no. 78), which has the added complication **e > i** in the third-person preterit. Similar to **discernir** are

cernir *to sieve,* usually replaced by **cerner**.
cernirse *to loom*, usually replaced by **cernerse**
concernir *to concern* (third-person only)

33 Distinguir *to distinguish*

Gerund **distinguiendo**   *Past Participle* **distinguido**

Imperative   **distingue distinguid**
distinga distingan

PRESENT **distingo, distingues, distingue, distinguimos, distinguís, distinguen**

PRETERIT **distinguí, distinguiste, distinguió, distinguimos, distinguisteis, distinguieron**

IMPERFECT **distinguía, distinguías, distinguía, distinguíamos, distinguíais, distinguían**

FUTURE **distinguiré, distinguirás, distinguirá, distinguiremos, distinguiréis, distinguirán**

CONDITIONAL **distinguiría, distinguirías, distinguiría, distinguiríamos, distinguiríais, distinguirían**

PRESENT SUBJUNCTIVE **distinga, distingas, distinga, distingamos, distingáis, distingan**

IMPERFECT SUBJUNCTIVE (**-ra**) **distinguiera, distinguieras, distinguiera, distinguiéramos, distinguierais, distinguieran**

IMPERFECT SUBJUNCTIVE (**-se**) **distinguiese, distinguieses, distinguiese, distinguiésemos, distinguieseis, distinguiesen**

A regular **-ir** verb which shows the spelling change **gu > g** before **a** or **o**, the **g** being hard throughout. Only **extinguir** *to extinguish* is conjugated like it, this verb being literary and usually replaced in everyday speech by **apagar**.

34 Dormir *to sleep*

Gerund **durmiendo**   *Past Participle* **dormido**

Imperative   **duerme dormid**
                      duerma duerman

PRESENT **duermo, duermes, duerme, dormimos, dormís, duermen**

PRETERIT **dormí, dormiste, durmió, dormimos, dormisteis, durmieron**

IMPERFECT **dormía, dormías, dormía, dormíamos, dormíais, dormían**

FUTURE **dormiré, dormirás, dormirá, dormiremos, dormiréis, dormirán**

CONDITIONAL **dormiría, dormirías, dormiría, dormiríamos, dormiríais, dormirían**

PRESENT SUBJUNCTIVE **duerma, duermas, duerma, durmamos, durmáis, duerman**

IMPERFECT SUBJUNCTIVE (**-ra**) **durmiera, durmieras, durmiera, durmiéramos, durmierais, durmieran**

IMPERFECT SUBJUNCTIVE (**-se**) **durmiese, durmieses, durmiese, durmiésemos, durmieseis, durmiesen**

A special type of radical changing verb showing the changes stressed **o** > **ue** and unstressed **o** > **u** in certain forms of the preterit and present subjunctive, and throughout the imperfect subjunctive. **Dormirse** *to go to sleep* and **morir** (or **morirse)** *to die* are conjugated the same way; the latter has an irregular past participle, **muerto.** All these verbs are in common use.

35 Erguir *to prick up (ears)* **(transitive)**

Gerund **irguiendo**   *Past Participle* **erguido**

Imperative   **yergue (irgue) erguid**
yerga (irga) yergan (irgan)

PRESENT **yergo, yergues, yergue, erguimos, erguís, yerguen
(irgo, irgues, irgue, erguimos, erguís, irguen)**

PRETERIT **erguí, erguiste, irguió, erguimos, erguisteis,
irguieron**

IMPERFECT **erguía, erguías, erguía, erguíamos, erguíais,
erguían**

FUTURE **erguiré, erguirás, erguirá, erguiremos, erguiréis,
erguirán**

CONDITIONAL **erguiría, erguirías, erguiría, erguiríamos,
erguiríais, erguirían**

PRESENT SUBJUNCTIVE **yerga, yergas, yerga, yergamos,
yergáis, yergan (irga, irgas, irga, irgamos, irgáis, irgan)**

IMPERFECT SUBJUNCTIVE (-ra) **irguiera, irguieras, irguiera,
irguiéramos, irguierais, irguieran**

IMPERFECT SUBJUNCTIVE (-se) **irguiese, irguieses, irguiese,
irguiésemos, irguieseis, irguiesen**

Conjugated like **sentir** (no. 78) with the regular spelling change **ie** > **ye** when this occurs at the beginning of a word, and the loss of silent **u** before **o** or **a**. The bracketed forms are optional variants. There are no other exactly similar verbs apart from **erguirse** *to rear up, to sit up straight*.

36 Errar *to wander, err*

Gerund **errando**   *Past Participle* **errado**

Imperative   **yerra errad**

yerre yerren

PRESENT **yerro, yerras, yerra, erramos, erráis, yerran**

PRETERIT **erré, erraste, erró, erramos, errasteis, erraron**

IMPERFECT **erraba, errabas, erraba, errábamos, errabais, erraban**

FUTURE **erraré, errarás, errará, erraremos, erraréis, errarán**

CONDITIONAL **erraría, errarías, erraría, erraríamos, erraríais, errarían**

PRESENT SUBJUNCTIVE **yerre, yerres, yerre, erremos, erréis, yerren**

IMPERFECT SUBJUNCTIVE (**-ra**) **errara, erraras, errara, erráramos, errarais, erraran**

IMPERFECT SUBJUNCTIVE (**-se**) **errase, errases, errase, errásemos, erraseis, errasen**

Conjugated like **cerrar** (no.18: **e** > **ie** when stressed) but with the predictable, spelling change **ie** > **ye** at the beginning of a word. In some Latin-American countries it is conjugated regularly, **erro, erra**, etc.

37 Escribir *to write*

Gerund **escribiendo**	*Past Participle* **escrito**

Imperative	**escribe escribid**
	escriba escriban

PRESENT **escribo, escribes, escribe, escribimos, escribís, escriben**

PRETERIT **escribí, escribiste, escribió, escribimos, escribisteis, escribieron**

IMPERFECT **escribía, escribías, escribía, escribíamos, escribíais, escribían**

FUTURE **escribiré, escribirás, escribirá, escribiremos, escribiréis, escribirán**

CONDITIONAL **escribiría, escribirías, escribiría, escribiríamos, escribiríais, escribirían**

PRESENT SUBJUNCTIVE **escriba, escribas, escriba, escribamos, escribáis, escriban**

IMPERFECT SUBJUNCTIVE (**-ra**) **escribiera, escribieras, escribiera, escribiéramos, escribierais, escribieran**

IMPERFECT SUBJUNCTIVE (**-se**) **escribiese, escribieses, escribiese, escribiésemos, escribieseis, escribiesen**

Regular -**ir** verb except for the past participle ending in -**ito**. The following have the same peculiarity:

circunscribir *to circumscribe*
describir *to describe*
inscribirse *to enroll/*(Brit.) *enrol*
prescribir *to prescribe*
proscribir *to proscribe*
subscribir *to subscribe*
transcribir *to transcribe*

38 Estar *to be*

Gerund **estando**   *Past Participle* **estado**

Imperative   **está** or **estate estad** or **estaos**

              esté or **estese estén** or **estense**

PRESENT **estoy, estás, está, estamos, estáis, están**

PRETERIT **estuve, estuviste, estuvo, estuvimos, estuvisteis, estuvieron**

IMPERFECT **estaba, estabas, estaba, estábamos, estabais, estaban**

FUTURE **estaré, estarás, estará, estaremos, estaréis, estarán**

CONDITIONAL **estaría, estarías, estaría, estaríamos, estaríais, estarían**

PRESENT SUBJUNCTIVE **esté, estés, esté, estemos, estéis, estén**

IMPERFECT SUBJUNCTIVE **(-ra) estuviera, estuvieras, estuviera, estuviéramos, estuvierais, estuvieran**

IMPERFECT SUBJUNCTIVE **(-se) estuviese, estuvieses, estuviese, estuviésemos, estuvieseis, estuviesen**

Irregular verb of very common occurrence. Note that the pronominal ('reflexive') forms are often used for the imperative: **¡estate quieto!** *sit still!*. By the rules of Spanish spelling, the forms **estate**, **estese** and **estense** should have no accent, but they are often written and printed **estáte**, **estése** and **esténse**.

Estar is used with the gerund to form the Continuous of verbs, e.g. **estoy hablando** *I'm (in the middle of) talking*, etc.

Any good grammar of Spanish will explain the crucial difference of meaning between this verb and **ser**, which also means *to be*.

39 Gruñir *to growl*

Gerund **gruñendo**   *Past Participle* **gruñido**

Imperative   **gruñe gruñid**
               gruña gruñan

PRESENT   gruño, gruñes, gruñe, gruñimos, gruñís, gruñen

PRETERIT   gruñí, gruñiste, gruñó, gruñimos, gruñisteis, gruñeron

IMPERFECT   gruñía, gruñías, gruñía, gruñíamos, gruñíais, gruñían

FUTURE   gruñiré, gruñirás, gruñirá, gruñiremos, gruñiréis, gruñirán

CONDITIONAL   gruñiría, gruñirías, gruñiría, gruñiríamos, gruñiríais, gruñirían

PRESENT SUBJUNCTIVE   gruña, gruñas, gruña, gruñamos, gruñáis, gruñan

IMPERFECT SUBJUNCTIVE (-ra)   gruñera, gruñeras, gruñera, gruñéramos, gruñerais, gruñeran

IMPERFECT SUBJUNCTIVE (-se)   gruñese, gruñeses, gruñese, gruñésemos, gruñeseis, gruñesen

---

A regular -**ir** verb showing the predictable replacement of **ió** by **ó** and **ie** by **e** after a palatal consonant (**ñ**). **Bruñir** *to polish* and **plañir** *to lament* are similarly conjugated, although neither is in common use. Verbs like **reñir** (no. 69) show tho same spelling change, but are radical changing verbs.

40 Haber (auxiliary verb or *there is/there are*)

Gerund **habiendo**   *Past Participle* **habido**

Imperative   *not used*

PRESENT **he, has, ha (hay), hemos, habéis, han**

PRETERIT **hube, hubiste, hubo, hubimos, hubisteis, hubieron**

IMPERFECT **había, habías, había, habíamos, habíais, habían**

FUTURE **habré, habrás, habrá, habremos, habréis, habrán**

CONDITIONAL **habría, habrías, habría, habríamos, habríais, habrían**

PRESENT SUBJUNCTIVE **haya, hayas, haya, hayamos, hayáis, hayan**

IMPERFECT SUBJUNCTIVE **(-ra) hubiera, hubieras, hubiera, hubiéramos, hubierais, hubieran**

IMPERFECT SUBJUNCTIVE **(-se) hubiese, hubieses, hubiese, hubiésemos, hubieseis, hubiesen**

Irregular verb, in constant use.

Haber is the auxiliary verb used to make compound tenses (perfect, pluperfect, future perfect, conditional perfect, etc.). This is the only auxiliary used for this purpose: there is no Spanish equivalent of the French or Italian verbs conjugated with the auxiliary *to be*.

Haber is also used in the third person only to mean *there is/there are*. When it has this meaning, the present indicative form is **hay**. When it is used with this meaning it should always be singular: **había muchos** = *there were a lot of them*. However, Latin Americans and Catalans constantly use the plural (i.e. **habían muchos**), although this is banned from the written language.

41 Hablar *to speak, talk*

Gerund **hablando**   *Past Participle* **hablado**

Imperative   **habla hablad**
  hable hablen

PRESENT **hablo, hablas, habla, hablamos, habláis, hablan**

PRETERIT **hablé, hablaste, habló, hablamos, hablasteis, hablaron**

IMPERFECT **hablaba, hablabas, hablaba, hablábamos, hablabais, hablaban**

FUTURE **hablaré, hablarás, hablará, hablaremos, hablaréis, hablarán**

CONDITIONAL **hablaría, hablarías, hablaría, hablaríamos, hablaríais, hablarían**

PRESENT SUBJUNCTIVE **hable, hables, hable, hablemos, habléis, hablen**

IMPERFECT SUBJUNCTIVE **(-ra) hablara, hablaras, hablara, habláramos, hablarais, hablaran**

IMPERFECT SUBJUNCTIVE **(-se) hablase, hablases, hablase, hablásemos, hablaseis, hablasen**

A completely regular -**ar** verb and typical of the most common type of Spanish verb (72% of the verbs in the Directory of Verbs follow this pattern if we include verbs like **pagar**, **realizar** and **sacar**, which are of the same type but show predictable spelling changes).

Verbs whose infinitive ends in -**ear** are conjugated like **hablar**. The **e** of the stem is never written with an accent, e.g. **pasear** *to go for a walk, to take for a walk*:

Present Indicative	Present Subjunctive
paseo paseamos	**pasee paseemos**
paseas paseáis	**pasees paseéis**
pasea pasean	**pasee paseen**

42 Hacer *to do; to make*

Gerund **haciendo**   *Past Participle* **hecho**

Imperative   **haz haced**

                     haga hagan

PRESENT **hago, haces, hace, hacemos, hacéis, hacen**
PRETERIT **hice, hiciste, hizo, hicimos, hicisteis, hicieron**
IMPERFECT **hacía, hacías, hacía, hacíamos, hacíais, hacían**
FUTURE **haré, harás, hará, haremos, haréis, harán**
CONDITIONAL **haría, harías, haría, haríamos, haríais, harían**

Present Subjunctive **haga, hagas, haga, hagamos, hagáis, hagan**

IMPERFECT SUBJUNCTIVE **(-ra) hiciera, hicieras, hiciera, hiciéramos, hicierais, hicieran**
IMPERFECT SUBJUNCTIVE **(-se) hiciese, hicieses, hiciese, hiciésemos, hicieseis, hiciesen**

Irregular verb, in frequent use and having many idiomatic meanings. The following less common verbs are conjugated in the same way:

contrahacer *to counterfeit*
deshacer *to undo*
deshacerse *to become loose, undone*
rehacer *to re-do*

43 Ir *to go*

Gerund **yendo**	*Past Participle* **ido**

Imperative	**ve id**
	vaya vayan

PRESENT **voy, vas, va, vamos, vais, van**
PRETERIT **fui, fuiste, fue, fuimos, fuisteis, fueron**
IMPERFECT **iba, ibas, iba, íbamos, ibais, iban**
FUTURE **iré, irás, irá, iremos, iréis, irán**
CONDITIONAL **iría, irías, iría, iríamos, iríais, irían**
PRESENT SUBJUNCTIVE **vaya, vayas, vaya, vayamos, vayáis, vayan**
IMPERFECT SUBJUNCTIVE (**-ra**) **fuera, fueras, fuera, fuéramos, fuerais, fueran**
IMPERFECT SUBJUNCTIVE (**-se**) **fuese, fueses, fuese, fuésemos, fueseis, fuesen**

Irregular verb, in frequent use and having many idiomatic meanings. The preterit and the imperfect subjunctive are the same as **ser** *to be*. Apart from **irse** *to go away*, no other verb follows this pattern.

44 Jugar *to play*

Gerund **jugando**   *Past Participle* **jugado**

Imperative   **juega jugad**

juegue jueguen

PRESENT **juego, juegas, juega, jugamos, jugáis, juegan**

PRETERIT **jugué, jugaste, jugó, jugamos, jugasteis, jugaron**

IMPERFECT **jugaba, jugabas, jugaba, jugábamos, jugabais, jugaban**

FUTURE **jugaré, jugarás, jugará, jugaremos, jugaréis, jugarán**

CONDITIONAL **jugaría, jugarías, jugaría, jugaríamos, jugaríais, jugarían**

PRESENT SUBJUNCTIVE **juegue, juegues, juegue, juguemos, juguéis, jueguen**

IMPERFECT SUBJUNCTIVE (**-ra**) **jugara, jugaras, jugara, jugáramos, jugarais, jugaran**

IMPERFECT SUBJUNCTIVE (**-se**) **jugase, jugases, jugase, jugásemos, jugaseis, jugasen**

This verb is unique in that stressed **u** changes to **ue**.

45 Liar *to tie up, tie in a bundle*

Gerund **liando**   *Past Participle* **liado**

Imperative   **lía liad**
                 líe líen

PRESENT **lío, lías, lía, liamos, liáis, lían**
PRETERIT **lié, liaste, lió, liamos, liasteis, liaron**
IMPERFECT **liaba, liabas, liaba, liábamos, liabais, liaban**
FUTURE **liaré, liarás, liará, liaremos, liaréis, liarán**
CONDITIONAL **liaría, liarías, liaría, liaríamos, liaríais,
    liarían**
PRESENT SUBJUNCTIVE **líe, líes, líe, liemos, liéis, líen**
IMPERFECT SUBJUNCTIVE (**-ra**) **liara, liaras, liara, liáramos,
    liarais, liaran**
IMPERFECT SUBJUNCTIVE (**-se**) **liase, liases, liase, liásemos,
    liaseis, liasen**

The endings are those of a regular **-ar** verb, but verbs like
liar are unusual in that the **i** may be stressed and then has an
accent. Compare **cambiar** *to change*: **cambio, cambias,
cambia, cambiamos, cambiáis, cambian**. Similar common
verbs:

ampliar *to extend, enlarge*	**fiar** *to sell on credit*
ansiar *to long for*	**fiarse de** *to trust*
averiarse *to break down*	**fotografiar** *to photograph*
criar *to breed*	**guiar** *to guide*
desafiar *to challenge*	**vaciar** *to empty*
enviar *to send*	**variar** *to vary*

46 Lucir *to show off (transitive)*

Gerund **luciendo**   *Past Participle* **lucido**

Imperative   **luce lucid**

luzca luzcan

PRESENT **luzco, luces, luce, lucimos, lucís, lucen**
PRETERIT **lucí, luciste, lució, lucimos, lucisteis, lucieron**
IMPERFECT **lucía, lucías, lucía, lucíamos, lucíais, lucían**
FUTURE **luciré, lucirás, lucirá, luciremos, luciréis, lucirán**
CONDITIONAL **luciría, lucirías, luciría, luciríamos, luciríais, lucirían**
PRESENT SUBJUNCTIVE **luzca, luzcas, luzca, luzcamos, luzcáis, luzcan**
IMPERFECT SUBJUNCTIVE (**-ra**) **luciera, lucieras, luciera, luciéramos, lucierais, lucieran**
IMPERFECT SUBJUNCTIVE (**-se**) **luciese, lucieses, luciese, luciésemos, lucieseis, luciesen**

Shows the common replacement of **c** by **zc** before **a** or **o**. However, this sound change is much more common in the **-er** conjugation, and only four verbs in current use are like **lucir**:

deslucir *to tarnish (*e.g. *reputations*; transitive*)*
deslucirse *to become tarnished*
relucir *to glow*
traslucirse *to show through* (emotions)

47 Maldecir *to curse*

Gerund **maldiciendo**   *Past Participle* **maldecido**

Imperative   **maldice maldecid**
                      maldiga maldigan

PRESENT **maldigo, maldices, maldice, maldecimos, maldecís, maldicen**

PRETERIT **maldije, maldijiste, maldijo, maldijimos, maldijisteis, maldijeron**

IMPERFECT **maldecía, maldecías, maldecía, maldecíamos, maldecíais, maldecían**

FUTURE **maldeciré, maldecirás, maldecirá, maldeciremos, maldeciréis, maldecirán**

CONDITIONAL **maldeciría, maldecirías, maldeciría, maldeciríamos, maldeciríais, maldecirían**

PRESENT SUBJUNCTIVE **maldiga, maldigas, maldiga, maldigamos, maldigáis, maldigan**

IMPERFECT SUBJUNCTIVE (**-ra**) **maldijera, maldijeras, maldijera, maldijéramos, maldijerais, maldijeran**

IMPERFECT SUBJUNCTIVE (**-se**) **maldijese, maldijeses, maldijese, maldijésemos, maldijeseis, maldijesen**

Conjugated in part like **decir** (no. 28), but with regular future, conditional and imperative forms. **Bendecir** *to bless* is conjugated the same way.

Predecir *to predict* is also normally conjugated like **maldecir**, but alternative future and conditional forms are occasionally found based on **decir**, e.g. **prediré, prediría,** etc.

48 Mover *to move*

Gerund **moviendo**   *Past Participle* **movido**

Imperative   **mueve moved**

                    mueva muevan

PRESENT **muevo, mueves, mueve, movemos, movéis, mueven**

PRETERIT **moví, moviste, movió, movimos, movisteis, movieron**

IMPERFECT **movía, movías, movía, movíamos, movíais, movían**

FUTURE **moveré, moverás, moverá, moveremos, moveréis, moverán**

CONDITIONAL **movería, moverías, movería, moveríamos, moveríais, moverían**

PRESENT SUBJUNCTIVE **mueva, muevas, mueva, movamos, mováis, muevan**

IMPERFECT SUBJUNCTIVE (**-ra**) **moviera, movieras, moviera, moviéramos, movierais, movieran**

IMPERFECT SUBJUNCTIVE (**-ra**) **moviese, movieses, moviese, moviésemos, movieseis, moviesen**

A type of radical changing **-er** verb showing the change **o** to **ue** when stressed. The most common are:

conmover *to move*   **morder** *to bite*
 (emotionally)   **promover** *to encourage*
conmoverse *to be moved*   **remorder** *to cause remorse*
 (emotionally)   **remover** *to stir up; to*
demoler *to demolish*   *remove* (latter meaning in
doler *to hurt*   Latin America only)
llover *to rain*

Verbs like **cocer** (no. 19) are similar but for spelling changes.

49 Negar *to deny*

Gerund **negando**   *Past Participle* **negado**

| *Imperative* | **niega negad** |
| | **niegue nieguen** |

PRESENT **niego, niegas, niega, negamos, negáis, niegan**

PRETERIT **negué, negaste, negó, negamos, negasteis, negaron**

IMPERFECT **negaba, negabas, negaba, negábamos, negabais, negaban**

FUTURE **negaré, negarás, negará, negaremos, negaréis, negarán**

CONDITIONAL **negaría, negarías, negaría, negaríamos, negaríais, negarían**

PRESENT SUBJUNCTIVE **niegue, niegues, niegue, neguemos, neguéis, nieguen**

IMPERFECT SUBJUNCTIVE (**-ra**) **negara, negaras, negara, negáramos, negarais, negaran**

IMPERFECT SUBJUNCTIVE (**-se**) **negase, negases, negase, negásemos, negaseis, negasen**

Identical to **cerrar** (no. 18: **e** > **ie** when stressed), but with the spelling change **g** > **gu** before **e** or **i** because the **g** is always hard. Common verbs of this sort are:

cegar *to blind*	**plegar** *to fold up*
denegar *to turn down (a request)*	**refregar** *to scrub hard*
	regar *to water*
desasosegarse *to become restless, troubled*	**renegar de** *to renounce (beliefs)*
desplegar *to unfold*	**restregar** *to rub*
fregar *to scrub; to wash up*	**segar** *to harvest*
negarse a *to refuse to*	**sosegar** *to calm*

50 Oír *to hear*

Gerund **oyendo**   *Past Participle* **oído**

Imperative   **oye oíd**

          oiga oigan

PRESENT **oigo, oyes, oye, oímos, oís, oyen**

PRETERIT **oí, oíste, oyó, oímos, oísteis, oyeron**

IMPERFECT **oía, oías, oía, oíamos, oíais, oían**

FUTURE **oiré, oirás, oirá, oiremos, oiréis, oirán**

CONDITIONAL **oiría, oirías, oiría, oiríamos, oiríais, oirían**

PRESENT SUBJUNCTIVE **oiga, oigas, oiga, oigamos, oigáis, oigan**

IMPERFECT SUBJUNCTIVE (-ra) **oyera, oyeras, oyera, oyéramos, oyerais, oyeran**

IMPERFECT SUBJUNCTIVE (-se) **oyese, oyeses, oyese, oyésemos, oyeseis, oyesen**

Irregular verb. **Desoír** *to turn a deaf ear to* is conjugated the same way, but is confined to literary usage.

51 Oler *to smell*

Gerund **oliendo**   *Past Participle* **olido**

Imperative   **huele oled**
                 huela huelan

PRESENT **huelo, hueles, huele, olemos, oléis, huelen**
PRETERIT **olí, oliste, olió, olimos, olisteis, olieron**
IMPERFECT **olía, olías, olía, olíamos, olíais, olían**
FUTURE **oleré, olerás, olerá, oleremos, oleréis, olerán**
CONDITIONAL **olería, olerías, olería, oleríamos, oleríais,
olerían**
PRESENT SUBJUNCTIVE **huela, huelas, huela, olamos, oláis,
huelan**
IMPERFECT SUBJUNCTIVE (**-ra**) **oliera, olieras, oliera,
oliéramos, olierais, olieran**
IMPERFECT SUBJUNCTIVE (**-se**) **oliese, olieses, oliese,
oliésemos, olieseis, oliesen**

Conjugated the same way as **mover** (no. 48), but with the
predictable addition of **h** when the diphthong **ue** occurs at
the beginning of a word. There are no other similar verbs.

52 Pagar *to pay*

Gerund **pagando**   *Past Participle* **pagado**

Imperative   **paga pagad**

                   pague paguen

PRESENT **pago, pagas, paga, pagamos, pagáis, pagan**

PRETERIT **pagué, pagaste, pagó, pagamos, pagasteis, pagaron**

IMPERFECT **pagaba, pagabas, pagaba, pagábamos, pagabais, pagaban**

FUTURE **pagaré, pagarás, pagará, pagaremos, pagaréis, pagarán**

CONDITIONAL **pagaría, pagarías, pagaría, pagaríamos, pagaríais, pagarían**

PRESENT SUBJUNCTIVE **pague, pagues, pague, paguemos, paguéis, paguen**

IMPERFECT SUBJUNCTIVE (**-ra**) **pagara, pagaras, pagara, pagáramos, pagarais, pagaran**

IMPERFECT SUBJUNCTIVE (**-se**) **pagase, pagases, pagase, pagásemos, pagaseis, pagasen**

Regular **-ar** verb showing the predictable spelling change **g** > **gu** before **e**. A common type: over 180 similar verbs appear in the Directory of Verbs.

53 Parecer *to seem*

Gerund **pareciendo**   *Past Participle* **parecido**

Imperative   **parece pareced**

parezca parezcan

PRESENT **parezco, pareces, parece, parecemos, parecéis, parecen**

PRETERIT **parecí, pareciste, pareció, parecimos, parecisteis, parecieron**

IMPERFECT **parecía, parecías, parecía, parecíamos, parecíais, parecían**

FUTURE **pareceré, parecerás, parecerá, pareceremos, pareceréis, parecerán**

CONDITIONAL **parecería, parecerías, parecería, pareceríamos, pareceríais, parecerían**

PRESENT SUBJUNCTIVE **parezca, parezcas, parezca, parezcamos, parezcáis, parezcan**

IMPERFECT SUBJUNCTIVE (**-ra**) **pareciera, parecieras, pareciera, pareciéramos, parecierais, parecieran**

IMPERFECT SUBJUNCTIVE (**-se**) **pareciese, parecieses, pareciese, pareciésemos, parecieseis, pareciesen**

Regular except for the change **c** > **zc** before **a** or **o**. The immense majority of verbs whose infinitive ends in **-cer** conjugate like this. Only a few show the more predictable change **c** > **z**; these are listed under **vencer** (no. 86).

54 Pedir *to ask for*

Gerund **pidiendo**   *Past Participle* **pedido**

Imperative   **pide pedid**

pida pidan

PRESENT **pido, pides, pide, pedimos, pedís, piden**

PRETERIT **pedí, pediste, pidió, pedimos, pedisteis, pidieron**

IMPERFECT **pedía, pedías, pedía, pedíamos, pedíais, pedían**

FUTURE **pediré, pedirás, pedirá, pediremos, pediréis, pedirán**

CONDITIONAL **pediría, pedirías, pediría, pediríamos, pediríais, pedirían**

PRESENT SUBJUNCTIVE **pida, pidas, pida, pidamos, pidáis, pidan**

IMPERFECT SUBJUNCTIVE (**-ra**) **pidiera, pidieras, pidiera, pidiéramos, pidierais, pidieran**

IMPERFECT SUBJUNCTIVE (**-se**) **pidiese, pidieses, pidiese, pidiésemos, pidieseis, pidiesen**

Radical changing verb in which **e** > **i** in various forms. This type is not uncommon and certain verbs, e.g. **regir** (66), **reír** (no. 68) and **reñir** (no. 69), are conjugated the same way but for slight spelling changes. Common verbs conjugated like **pedir** are:

competir *to compete*
concebir *to conceive*
derretir *to melt* (transitive)
derretirse *to melt* (intransitive)
despedir *to fire (from a job)*
despedirse de *to say goodbye to*
expedir *to issue (a document)*

gemir *to groan*
impedir *to prevent*
invertir *to invest*
medir *to measure*
rendir *to yield*
rendirse *to surrender*
repetir *to repeat*
servir *to serve*
vestirse *to get dressed*

55 Perder *to lose*

Gerund **perdiendo**   *Past Participle* **perdido**

Imperative   **pierde perded**
                      pierda pierdan

PRESENT **perdo, pierdes, pierde, perdemos, perdéis, pierden**

PRETERIT **perdí, perdiste, perdió, perdimos, perdisteis, perdieron**

IMPERFECT **perdía, perdías, perdía, perdíamos, perdíais, perdían**

FUTURE **perderé, perderás, perderá, perderemos, perderéis, perderán**

CONDITIONAL **perdería, perderías, perdería, perderíamos, perderíais, perderían**

PRESENT SUBJUNCTIVE **pierda, pierdas, pierda, perdamos, perdáis, pierdan**

IMPERFECT SUBJUNCTIVE **(-ra) perdiera, perdieras, perdiera, perdiéramos, perdierais, perdieran**

IMPERFECT SUBJUNCTIVE **(-se) perdiese, perdieses, perdiese, perdiésemos, perdieseis, perdiesen**

Radical changing verb showing the common change stressed **e** > **ie**. The following are common:

ascender *to promote (* i.e.
to a better position at work)
atender *to attend (* i.e.
to pay attention)
cernerse sobre *to loom over*
defender *to defend*
encender *to light*

entender *to understand*
*(*note: **comprender**, same
meaning, is less common
and is regular*)*
extenderse *to stretch*
(intransitive, i.e. plains,
stretches of land)
tender a *to tend to*
verter *to pour out*

56 Placer *to please*

Gerund **placiendo**   *Past Participle* **placido**

Imperative   **place placed**

plazca (plega) plazcan (plegan)

PRESENT **plazco, places, place, placemos, placéis, placen**

PRETERIT **plací, placiste, plació (plugo), placimos, placisteis, placieron (pluguieron)**

IMPERFECT **placía, placías, placía, placíamos, placíais, placían**

FUTURE **placeré, placerás, placerá, placeremos, placeréis, placerán**

CONDITIONAL **placería, placerías, placería, placeríamos, placeríais, placerían**

PRESENT SUBJUNCTIVE **plazca, plazcas, plazca, plazcamos, plazcáis, plazcan**
(plega, plegas, plega, plegamos, plegáis, plegan)

IMPERFECT SUBJUNCTIVE (-ra) **placiera, placieras, placiera, placiéramos, placierais, placieran**
(pluguiera, pluguieras, pluguiera, pluguiéramos, pluguierais, pluguieran)

IMPERFECT SUBJUNCTIVE (-se*)* **placiese, placieses, placiese, placiésemos, placieseis, placiesen**
(pluguiese, pluguieses, pluguiese, pluguiésemos, pluguieseis, pluguiesen)

This is conjugated the same way as **parecer** (no. 53) and would not need separate mention but for the existence of the bracketed alternative forms, which are found only in archaic written styles.

Placer is a rare and literary verb, occasionally still seen in third-person forms in phrases like **haz lo que te plazca** *do what you like*. **Gustar** (regular) means the same thing.

57 Poder *to be able*

Gerund **pudiendo**   *Past Participle* **podido**

Imperative   *not used*

PRESENT **puedo, puedes, puede, podemos, podéis, pueden**

PRETERIT **pude, pudiste, pudo, pudimos, pudisteis, pudieron**

IMPERFECT **podía, podías, podía, podíamos, podíais, podían**

FUTURE **podré, podrás, podrá, podremos, podréis, podrán**

CONDITIONAL **podría, podrías, podría, podríamos, podríais, podrían**

PRESENT SUBJUNCTIVE **pueda, puedas, pueda, podamos, podáis, puedan**

IMPERFECT SUBJUNCTIVE (**-ra**) **pudiera, pudieras, pudiera, pudiéramos, pudierais, pudieran**

IMPERFECT SUBJUNCTIVE (**-se**) **pudiese, pudieses, pudiese, pudiésemos, pudieseis, pudiesen**

Irregular verb, in constant use. No other verbs are conjugated like it.

58 Poner *to put*

Gerund **poniendo**   *Past Participle* **puesto**

Imperative   **pon poned**

                     ponga pongan

PRESENT **pongo, pones, pone, ponemos, ponéis, ponen**

PRETERIT **puse, pusiste, puso, pusimos, pusisteis, pusieron**

IMPERFECT **ponía, ponías, ponía, poníamos, poníais, ponían**

FUTURE **pondré, pondrás, pondrá, pondremos, pondréis, pondrán**

CONDITIONAL **pondría, pondrías, pondría, pondríamos, pondríais, pondrían**

PRESENT SUBJUNCTIVE **ponga, pongas, ponga, pongamos, pongáis, pongan**

IMPERFECT SUBJUNCTIVE (**-ra**) **pusiera, pusieras, pusiera, pusiéramos, pusierais, pusieran**

IMPERFECT SUBJUNCTIVE **pusiese, pusieses, pusiese, pusiésemos, pusieseis, pusiesen**

Irregular verb, in constant use. **Poner** means *to put*, **meter** (regular) has the more restricted meaning of *to put into*. **Ponerse** *to become, to put on clothes* is also important. There are several compounds of **poner** all conjugated in the same way. The following are not uncommon:

componer *to fix; to compose*
componerse de *to be composed of*
descomponerse *to decay; to fall apart*
disponer de *to dispose of* (i.e. *to possess*)
exponer *to expose*
oponerse a *to oppose*
posponer *to postpone*
predisponer *to predispose*
proponer *to propose*
suponer *to suppose*

The final vowel of the **tú** imperative of these compound forms requires an accent: **pospón**, **propón**, etc.

59 Poseer *to possess*

Gerund **poseyendo**   *Past Participle* **poseído**

| *Imperative* | **posee poseed** |
| | **posea posean** |

PRESENT **poseo, posees, posee, poseemos, poseéis, poseen**

PRETERIT **poseí, poseíste, poseyó, poseímos, poseísteis, poseyeron**

IMPERFECT **poseía, poseías, poseía, poseíamos, poseíais, poseían**

FUTURE **poseeré, poseerás, poseerá, poseeremos, poseeréis, poseerán**

CONDITIONAL **poseería, poseerías, poseería, poseeríamos, poseeríais, poseerían**

PRESENT SUBJUNCTIVE **posea, poseas, posea, poseamos, poseáis, posean**

IMPERFECT SUBJUNCTIVE (**-ra**) **poseyera, poseyeras, poseyera, poseyéramos, poseyerais, poseyeran**

IMPERFECT SUBJUNCTIVE (**-se**) **poseyese, poseyeses, poseyese, poseyésemos, poseyeseis, poseyesen**

A regular -**er** verb, showing the common spelling change **i** > **y** when the former vowel is pronounced *y*. Note the accent in the past participle: contrast the -**uido** of verbs like **construir** (no. 23), which has no accent. The following common verbs are conjugated the same way:

creer *to believe*
leer *to read*
releer *to re-read*

For **proveer** *to supply* and **desproveer** *to deprive* see **proveer** (no. 63).

60 Producir *to produce*

Gerund **produciendo**   *Past Participle* **producido**

Imperative   **produce producid**

produzca produzcan

PRESENT **produzco, produces, produce, producimos, producís, producen**

PRETERIT **produje, produjiste, produjo, produjimos, produjisteis, produjeron**

IMPERFECT **producía, producías, producía, producíamos, producíais, producían**

FUTURE **produciré, producirás, producirá, produciremos, produciréis, producirán**

CONDITIONAL **produciría, producirías, produciría, produciríamos, produciríais, producirían**

PRESENT SUBJUNCTIVE **produzca, produzcas, produzca, produzcamos, produzcáis, produzcan**

IMPERFECT SUBJUNCTIVE **(-ra) produjera, produjeras, produjera, produjéramos, produjerais, produjeran**

IMPERFECT SUBJUNCTIVE **(-se) produjese, produjeses, produjese, produjésemos, produjeseis, produjesen**

Irregular verb, showing the common change **c > zc** before **a** or **o**, and also having a highly irregular preterit stem ending in **-uj**. Note also **-eron, -era, -ese,** etc. in the preterit for the predicted **-ieron, -iera,** etc. All verbs ending in **-ducir** are conjugated the same way. The most common are:

conducir *to drive*   **reproducir** *to reproduce*
deducir *to deduce*   **seducir** *to seduce; to charm*
introducir en *to insert into*   **traducir** *to translate*
reducir *to reduce*

61 Prohibir *to prohibit*

Gerund **prohibiendo**   *Past Participle* **prohibido**

Imperative   **prohíbe prohibid**
              prohíba prohíban

PRESENT **prohíbo, prohíbes, prohíbe, prohibimos, prohibís, prohíben**

PRETERIT **prohibí, prohibiste, prohibió, prohibimos, prohibisteis, prohibieron**

IMPERFECT **prohibía, prohibías, prohibía, prohibíamos, prohibíais, prohibían**

FUTURE **prohibiré, prohibirás, prohibirá, prohibiremos, prohibiréis, prohibirán**

CONDITIONAL **prohibiría, prohibirías, prohibiría, prohibiríamos, prohibiríais, prohibirían**

PRESENT SUBJUNCTIVE **prohíba, prohíbas, prohíba, prohibamos, prohibáis, prohíban**

IMPERFECT SUBJUNCTIVE (**-ra**) **prohibiera, prohibieras, prohibiera, prohibiéramos, prohibierais, prohibieran**

IMPERFECT SUBJUNCTIVE (**-se**) **prohibiese, prohibieses, prohibiese, prohibiésemos, prohibieseis, prohibiesen**

A regular **-ir** verb, unusual only for the appearance of the accent on **i** when this is stressed. The accent was introduced in the spelling reforms of 1959 and even today it does not always appear in printed texts, especially Latin-American ones. **Cohibir** *to inhibit* is conjugated the same way.

62 Proteger *to protect*

Gerund **protegiendo**   *Past Participle* **protegido**

Imperative   **protege proteged**

                    proteja protejan

PRESENT **protejo**, **proteges**, **protege**, **protegemos**, **protegéis**, **protegen**

PRETERIT **protegí**, **protegiste**, **protegió**, **protegimos**, **protegisteis**, **protegieron**

IMPERFECT **protegía**, **protegías**, **protegía**, **protegíamos**, **protegíais**, **protegían**

FUTURE **protegeré**, **protegerás**, **protegerá**, **protegeremos**, **protegeréis**, **protegerán**

CONDITIONAL **protegería**, **protegerías**, **protegería**, **protegeríamos**, **protegeríais**, **protegerían**

PRESENT SUBJUNCTIVE **proteja**, **protejas**, **proteja**, **protejamos**, **protejáis**, **protejan**

IMPERFECT SUBJUNCTIVE (**-ra**) **protegiera**, **protegieras**, **protegiera**, **protegiéramos**, **protegierais**, **protegieran**

IMPERFECT SUBJUNCTIVE (**-se**) **protegiese**, **protegieses**, **protegiese**, **protegiésemos**, **protegieseis**, **protegiesen**

A regular **-er** verb showing the predictable spelling change **g** > **j** before **o, a**.

63 Proveer *to supply*

Gerund **proveyendo**   *Past Participle* **provisto (proveído)**

Imperative   **provee proveed**

provea provean

PRESENT **proveo, provees, provee, proveemos, proveéis, proveen**

PRETERIT **proveí, proveíste, proveyó, proveímos, proveísteis, proveyeron**

IMPERFECT **proveía, proveías, proveía, proveíamos, proveíais, proveían**

FUTURE **proveeré, proveerás, proveerá, proveeremos, proveeréis, proveerán**

CONDITIONAL **proveería, proveerías, proveería, proveeríamos, proveeríais, proveerían**

PRESENT SUBJUNCTIVE **provea, proveas, provea, proveamos, proveáis, provean**

IMPERFECT SUBJUNCTIVE (**-ra**) **proveyera, proveyeras, proveyera, proveyéramos, proveyerais, proveyeran**

IMPERFECT SUBJUNCTIVE (**-se**) **proveyese, proveyeses, proveyese, proveyésemos, proveyeseis, proveyesen**

Conjugated like **poseer** (no. 59) except for the irregular past participle **provisto**. **Desproveer de** *to deprive of* is conjugated the same way, but it is rarely used in its finite forms (the phrase **desprovisto de** *devoid of*, *lacking in* is, however, common).

The alternative past participle is used only in compound tenses.

64 Querer *to want; to love*

Gerund **queriendo**   *Past Participle* **querido**

Imperative   **quiere quered**

quiera quieran

PRESENT **quiero, quieres, quiere, queremos, queréis, quieren**

PRETERIT **quise, quisiste, quiso, quisimos, quisisteis, quisieron**

IMPERFECT **quería, querías, quería, queríamos, queríais, querían**

FUTURE **querré, querrás, querrá, querremos, querréis, querrán**

CONDITIONAL **querría, querrías, querría, querríamos, querríais, querrían**

PRESENT SUBJUNCTIVE **quiera, quieras, quiera, queramos, queráis, quieran**

IMPERFECT SUBJUNCTIVE (**-ra**) **quisiera, quisieras, quisiera, quisiéramos, quisierais, quisieran**

IMPERFECT SUBJUNCTIVE (**-se**) **quisiese, quisieses, quisiese, quisiésemos, quisieseis, quisiesen**

Irregular verb, in constant use. **Malquerer** *to dislike* and **bienquerer** *to like well* are conjugated the same way, but neither is in common use.

65 Realizar *to carry out; to make real*

Gerund **realizando**   *Past Participle* **realizado**

Imperative   **realiza realizad**
                     realice realicen

PRESENT **realizo, realizas, realiza, realizamos, realizáis, realizan**

PRETERIT **realicé, realizaste, realizó, realizamos, realizasteis, realizaron**

IMPERFECT **realizaba, realizabas, realizaba, realizábamos, realizabais, realizaban**

FUTURE **realizaré, realizarás, realizará, realizaremos, realizaréis, realizarán**

CONDITIONAL **realizaría, realizarías, realizaría, realizaríamos, realizaríais, realizarían**

PRESENT SUBJUNCTIVE **realice, realices, realice, realicemos, realicéis, realicen**

IMPERFECT SUBJUNCTIVE (**-ra**) **realizara, realizaras, realizara, realizáramos, realizarais, realizaran**

IMPERFECT SUBJUNCTIVE (**-se**) **realizase, realizases, realizase, realizásemos, realizaseis, realizasen**

A regular **-ar** verb displaying the usual spelling change **z > c** before **e**. A common type: the Directory of Verbs contains 370 examples.

66 Regir *to govern, direct*

Gerund **rigiendo**   *Past Participle* **regido**

Imperative   **rige regid**
                      rija rijan

PRESENT **rijo, riges, rige, regimos, regís, rigen**
PRETERIT **regí, registe, rigió, regimos, registeis, rigieron**
IMPERFECT **regía, regías, regía, regíamos, regíais, regían**
FUTURE **regiré, regirás, regirá, regiremos, regiréis, regirán**
CONDITIONAL **regiría, regirías, regiría, regiríamos,**
  regiríais, regirían
PRESENT SUBJUNCTIVE **rija, rijas, rija, rijamos, rijáis, rijan**
IMPERFECT SUBJUNCTIVE **(-ra)** **rigiera, rigieras, rigiera,**
  rigiéramos, rigierais, rigieran
IMPERFECT SUBJUNCTIVE **(-se)** **rigiese, rigieses, rigiese,**
  rigiésemos, rigieseis, rigiesen

Conjugated like **pedir** (no.54) but with the regular spelling change **g** > **j** before **o** or **a**. The following common verbs are conjugated the same way:

colegir *to infer (= to deduce)*
corregir *to correct*
elegir *to elect; to choose*
reelegir (alternative spelling **relegir**) *to re-elect*

67 Rehuir *to shy away from*

Gerund **rehuyendo**	*Past Participle* **rehuido**

Imperative **rehúye rehuid**
rehúya rehúyan

PRESENT **rehúyo, rehúyes, rehúye, rehuimos, rehuís, rehúyen**

PRETERIT **rehuí, rehuiste, rehuyó, rehuimos, rehuisteis, rehuyeron**

IMPERFECT **rehuía, rehuías, rehuía, rehuíamos, rehuíais, rehuían**

FUTURE **rehuiré, rehuirás, rehuirá, rehuiremos, rehuiréis, rehuirán**

CONDITIONAL **rehuiría, rehuirías, rehuiría, rehuiríamos, rehuiríais, rehuirían**

PRESENT SUBJUNCTIVE **rehúya, rehúyas, rehúya, rehuyamos, rehuyáis, rehúyan**

IMPERFECT SUBJUNCTIVE **(-ra) rehuyera, rehuyeras, rehuyera, rehuyéramos, rehuyerais, rehuyeran**

IMPERFECT SUBJUNCTIVE **(-se) rehuyese, rehuyeses, rehuyese, rehuyésemos, rehuyeseis, rehuyesen**

Conjugated like **construir** (no. 23) except for the accent on the stressed **u**, which was adopted in the spelling changes of 1959.

68 Reír *to laugh*

Gerund **riendo**   *Past Participle* **reído**

Imperative   **ríe reíd**
                      ría rían

PRESENT **río, ríes, ríe, reímos, reís, ríen**

PRETERIT **reí, reíste, rió, reímos, reísteis, rieron**

IMPERFECT **reía, reías, reía, reíamos, reíais, reían**

FUTURE **reiré, reirás, reirá, reiremos, reiréis, reirán**

CONDITIONAL **reiría, reirías, reiría, reiríamos, reiríais, reirían**

PRESENT SUBJUNCTIVE **ría, rías, ría, riamos, riáis, rían**

IMPERFECT SUBJUNCTIVE **(-ra) riera, rieras, riera, riéramos, rierais, rieran**

IMPERFECT SUBJUNCTIVE **(-se) riese, rieses, riese, riésemos, rieseis, riesen**

Conjugated like **pedir** (no. 54), although the absence of the consonant between the **e** and the **i** conceals this fact. Verbs like this one are the only verbs that have an accent in the infinitive. The following common verbs are conjugated in the same way:

desleír *to dissolve* (transitive)

desleírse *to dissolve* (intransitive)

freír *to fry* (past part. **frito**)

reírse *to laugh* (more frequent than *reír*)

sofreír *to sauté* (past part. **sofrito**)

sonreír *to smile*

69 Reñir *to scold*

Gerund **riñendo**   *Past Participle* **reñido**

| *Imperative* | **riñe reñid** |
| | **riña riñan** |

PRESENT **riño, riñes, riñe, reñimos, reñís, riñen**

PRETERIT **reñí, reñiste, riñó, reñimos, reñisteis, riñeron**

IMPERFECT **reñía, reñías, reñía, reñíamos, reñíais, reñían**

FUTURE **reñiré, reñirás, reñirá, reñiremos, reñiréis, reñirán**

CONDITIONAL **reñiría, reñirías, reñiría, reñiríamos, reñiríais, reñirían**

PRESENT SUBJUNCTIVE **riña, riñas, riña, riñamos, riñáis, riñan**

IMPERFECT SUBJUNCTIVE **(-ra) riñera, riñeras, riñera, riñéramos, riñerais, riñeran**

IMPERFECT SUBJUNCTIVE **(-se) riñese, riñeses, riñese, riñésemos, riñeseis, riñesen**

Conjugated like **pedir** (no. 54) except for the predictable replacement of **ió** by **ó** and **ie** by **e** after **ñ**. The following verbs are conjugated the same way:

ceñirse a *to stick close to (a topic)*

desteñir *to fade; to lose colour/*(Brit.) *colour*

teñir *to dye*

70 Reunir *to bring together*

Gerund **reuniendo**   *Past Participle* **reunido**

Imperative   **reúne reunid**

reúna reúnan

PRESENT **reúno, reúnes, reúne, reunimos, reunís, reúnen**

PRETERIT **reuní, reuniste, reunió, reunimos, reunisteis, reunieron**

IMPERFECT **reunía, reunías, reunía, reuníamos, reuníais, reunían**

FUTURE **reuniré, reunirás, reunirá, reuniremos, reuniréis, reunirán**

CONDITIONAL **reuniría, reunirías, reuniría, reuniríamos, reuniríais, reunirían**

PRESENT SUBJUNCTIVE **reúna, reúnas, reúna, reunamos, reunáis, reúnan**

IMPERFECT SUBJUNCTIVE **(-ra) reuniera, reunieras, reuniera, reuniéramos, reunierais, reunieran**

IMPERFECT SUBJUNCTIVE **(-se) reuniese, reunieses, reuniese, reuniésemos, reunieseis, reuniesen**

Regular -**ir** verb except for the appearance of the accent on the stressed **u**. The accent was introduced with the spelling reforms of 1959. **Reunirse** *to meet together* has the same forms.

71 Roer *to gnaw*

Gerund **royendo**   *Past Participle* **roído**

Imperative   **roe roed**

roa (roiga, roya) roan (roigan, royan)

PRESENT **roo (roigo, royo), roes, roe, roemos, roéis, roen**

PRETERIT **roí, roíste, royó, roímos, roísteis, royeron**

IMPERFECT **roía, roías, roía, roíamos, roíais, roían**

FUTURE **roeré, roerás, roerá, roeremos, roeréis, roerán**

CONDITIONAL **roería, roerías, roería, roeríamos, roeríais, roerían**

PRESENT SUBJUNCTIVE **roa, roas, roa, roamos, roáis, roan
(roiga, roigas, roiga, roigamos, roigáis, roigan)
(roya, royas, roya, royamos, royáis, royan)**

IMPERFECT SUBJUNCTIVE **(-ra) royera, royeras, royera,
royéramos, royerais, royeran**

IMPERFECT SUBJUNCTIVE **(-se) royese, royeses, royese,
royésemos, royeseis, royesen**

The alternative forms in brackets are much less common.
Corroer *to corrode* is conjugated in the same way.

72 Rugir *to roar*

Gerund **rugiendo** *Past Participle* **rugido**

Imperative **ruge rugid**
ruja rujan

PRESENT **rujo, ruges, ruge, rugimos, rugís, rugen**
PRETERIT **rugí, rugiste, rugió, rugimos, rugisteis, rugieron**
IMPERFECT **rugía, rugías, rugía, rugíamos, rugíais, rugían**
FUTURE **rugiré, rugirás, rugirá, rugiremos, rugiréis, rugirán**
CONDITIONAL **rugiría, rugirías, rugiría, rugiríamos,**
rugiríais, rugirían
PRESENT SUBJUNCTIVE **ruja, rujas, ruja, rujamos, rujáis,**
rujan
IMPERFECT SUBJUNCTIVE **(-ra)> rugiera, rugieras, rugiera,**
rugiéramos, rugierais, rugieran
IMPERFECT SUBJUNCTIVE **(-se) rugiese, rugieses, rugiese,**
rugiésemos, rugieseis, rugiesen

Regular -**ir** verb except for the spelling change **g** > **j** before **o**
or **a**. Some of the following verbs are commonly found:

afligir *to afflict*
convergir *to converge*
dirigir *to direct; to steer*
dirigirse a *to address; to make for*
exigir *to demand*
fingir *to pretend*
infligir *to inflict*

restringir *to restrict; to constrain*
resurgir *to arise again*
sumergir *to submerge (transitive)*
sumergirse *to submerge (intransitive)*
surgir *to arise*
transigir *to yield; to compromise*

73 Saber *to know*

Gerund **sabiendo**   *Past Participle* **sabido**

Imperative   **sabe sabed**
                              sepa sepan

PRESENT sé, sabes, sabe, sabemos, sabéis, saben
PRETERIT supe, supiste, supo, supimos, supisteis, supieron
IMPERFECT sabía, sabías, sabía, sabíamos, sabíais, sabían
FUTURE sabré, sabrás, sabrá, sabremos, sabréis, sabrán
CONDITIONAL sabría, sabrías, sabría, sabríamos, sabríais,
  sabrían
PRESENT SUBJUNCTIVE sepa, sepas, sepa, sepamos, sepáis,
  sepan
IMPERFECT SUBJUNCTIVE (-ra) supiera, supieras, supiera,
  supiéramos, supierais, supieran
IMPERFECT SUBJUNCTIVE (-se) supiese, supieses, supiese,
  supiésemos, supieseis, supiesen

Irregular verb in constant use.

74 Sacar *to take out, extract*

Gerund **sacando**   *Past Participle* **sacado**

Imperative   **saca sacad**

saque saquen

PRESENT **saco, sacas, saca, sacamos, sacáis, sacan**

PRETERIT **saqué, sacaste, sacó, sacamos, sacasteis, sacaron**

IMPERFECT **sacaba, sacabas, sacaba, sacábamos, sacabais, sacaban**

FUTURE **sacaré, sacarás, sacará, sacaremos, sacaréis, sacarán**

CONDITIONAL **sacaría, sacarías, sacaría, sacaríamos, sacaríais, sacarían**

PRESENT SUBJUNCTIVE **saque, saques, saque, saquemos, saquéis, saquen**

IMPERFECT SUBJUNCTIVE (**-ra**) **sacara, sacaras, sacara, sacáramos, sacarais, sacaran**

IMPERFECT SUBJUNCTIVE (**-se**) **sacase, sacases, sacase, sacásemos, sacaseis, sacasen**

Regular **-ar** verb showing the predictable spelling change **c** > **qu** before **e**. There are 260 examples in the Directory of Verbs

75 Salir *to go out, leave*

Gerund **saliendo**   *Past Participle* **salido**

Imperative   **sal salid**

salga salgan

PRESENT **salgo, sales, sale, salimos, salís, salen**

PRETERIT **salí, saliste, salió, salimos, salisteis, salieron**

IMPERFECT **salía, salías, salía, salíamos, salíais, salían**

FUTURE **saldré, saldrás, saldrá, saldremos, saldréis, saldrán**

CONDITIONAL **saldría, saldrías, saldría, saldríamos, saldríais, saldrían**

PRESENT SUBJUNCTIVE **salga, salgas, salga, salgamos, salgáis, salgan**

IMPERFECT SUBJUNCTIVE **(-ra) saliera, salieras, saliera, saliéramos, salierais, salieran**

IMPERFECT SUBJUNCTIVE **(-se) saliese, salieses, saliese, saliésemos, salieseis, saliesen**

Irregular verb in constant use. **Sobresalir** *to be outstanding* is conjugated the same way.

76 Satisfacer *to satisfy*

Gerund **satisfaciendo**   *Past Participle* **satisfecho**

Imperative   **satisfaz** *(or* **satisface***)* **satisfaced**
                        satisfaga satisfagan

PRESENT **satisfago, satisfaces, satisface, satisfacemos, satisfacéis, satisfacen**

PRETERIT **satisfice, satisficiste, satisfizo, satisficimos, satisficisteis, satisficieron**

IMPERFECT **satisfacía, satisfacías, satisfacía, satisfacíamos, satisfacíais, satisfacían**

FUTURE **satisfaré, satisfarás, satisfará, satisfaremos, satisfaréis, satisfarán**

CONDITIONAL **satisfaría, satisfarías, satisfaría, satisfaríamos, satisfaríais, satisfarían**

PRESENT SUBJUNCTIVE **satisfaga, satisfagas, satisfaga, satisfagamos, satisfagáis, satisfagan**

IMPERFECT SUBJUNCTIVE **(-ra) satisficiera, satisficieras, satisficiera, satisficiéramos, satisficierais, satisficieran**

IMPERFECT SUBJUNCTIVE **(-se) satisficiese, satisficieses, satisficiese, satisficiésemos, satisficieseis, satisficiesen**

Irregular verb, similar in conjugation to **hacer** (no. 42). **Licuefacerse** *to liquefy* (intransitive) is conjugated the same way, but it is not in common use, **licuarse** being more usual.

77 Seguir *to follow*

Gerund **siguiendo**   *Past Participle* **seguido**

Imperative   **sigue seguid**

          siga sigan

PRESENT **sigo, sigues, sigue, seguimos, seguís, siguen**

PRETERIT **seguí, seguiste, siguió, seguimos, seguisteis, siguieron**

IMPERFECT **seguía, seguías, seguía, seguíamos, seguíais, seguían**

FUTURE **seguiré, seguirás, seguirá, seguiremos, seguiréis, seguirán**

CONDITIONAL **seguiría, seguirías, seguiría, seguiríamos, seguiríais, seguirían**

PRESENT SUBJUNCTIVE **siga, sigas, siga, sigamos, sigáis, sigan**

IMPERFECT SUBJUNCTIVE **(-ra)> siguiera, siguieras, siguiera, siguiéramos, siguierais, siguieran**

IMPERFECT SUBJUNCTIVE **(-se) siguiese, siguieses, siguiese, siguiésemos, siguieseis, siguiesen**

Radical-changing verb conjugated like **pedir** (no. 54) but with the spelling change **gu > g** before **a** or **o**. The following common verbs are conjugated the same way:

conseguir *to obtain*
perseguir *to persecute*
proseguir *to proceed with*

78 Sentir *to feel*

Gerund **sintiendo**   *Past Participle* **sentido**

Imperative   **siente sentid**
                sienta sientan

PRESENT **siento, sientes, siente, sentimos, sentís, sienten**

PRETERIT **sentí, sentiste, sintió, sentimos, sentisteis, sintieron**

IMPERFECT **sentía, sentías, sentía, sentíamos, sentíais, sentían**

FUTURE **sentiré, sentirás, sentirá, sentiremos, sentiréis, sentirán**

CONDITIONAL **sentiría, sentirías, sentiría, sentiríamos, sentiríais, sentirían**

PRESENT SUBJUNCTIVE **sienta, sientas, sienta, sintamos, sintáis, sientan**

IMPERFECT SUBJUNCTIVE (**-ra**) **sintiera, sintieras, sintiera, sintiéramos, sintierais, sintieran**

IMPERFECT SUBJUNCTIVE (**-se**) **sintiese, sintieses, sintiese, sintiésemos, sintieseis, sintiesen**

Radical changing verb showing the common change stressed **e > ie**, and also unstressed **e** to **i** in certain forms. The following common verbs are conjugated in the same way:

advertir *to warn*	**interferir** *to interfere*
arrepentirse de *to repent*	**invertir** *to reverse (order*
consentir *to consent*	*of things); to invest*
convertirse en *to change into*	**mentir** *to lie*
diferir *to differ*	**preferir** *to prefer*
divertir *to amuse*	**referirse a** *to refer to*
herir *to wound*	**sugerir** *to suggest*
hervir *to boil*	**transferir** *to transfer*

79 Ser *to be*

Gerund **siendo**   *Past Participle* **sido**

Imperative   **sé sed**

     sea sean

PRESENT **soy, eres, es, somos, sois, son**

PRETERIT **fui** *(no accent!)*, **fuiste, fue** *(no accent!)*, **fuimos, fuisteis, fueron**

IMPERFECT **era, eras, era, éramos, erais, eran**

FUTURE **seré, serás, será, seremos, seréis, serán**

CONDITIONAL **sería, serías, sería, seríamos, seríais, serían**

PRESENT SUBJUNCTIVE **sea, seas, sea, seamos, seáis, sean**

IMPERFECT SUBJUNCTIVE **(-ra) fuera, fueras, fuera, fuéramos, fuerais, fueran**

IMPERFECT SUBJUNCTIVE **(-se) fuese, fueses, fuese, fuésemos, fueseis, fuesen**

Irregular verb in constant use. The preterit forms have no accents: the spellings **fuí** and **fué** were abolished in 1959.

80 Soler *to be accustomed to*

Gerund **soliendo**   *Past Participle* **solido**

Imperative   *not used*

PRESENT **suelo, sueles, suele, solemos, soléis, suelen**
PRETERIT **solí, soliste, solió, solimos, solisteis, solieron**
IMPERFECT **solía, solías, solía, solíamos, solíais, solían**
FUTURE *not used*
CONDITIONAL *not used*
PRESENT SUBJUNCTIVE **suela, suelas, suela, solamos, soláis,
  suelan**
IMPERFECT SUBJUNCTIVE **(-ra) soliera, solieras, soliera,
  soliéramos, solierais, solieran**
IMPERFECT SUBJUNCTIVE **(-se) soliese, solieses, soliese,
  soliésemos, solieseis, soliesen**

Conjugated like **mover** (no. 48) except that certain forms are
not used. The pluperfect and pluperfect conditional are also
not used, but the perfect indicative does occur.

81 Tañer *to chime; to pluck (an instrument)*

Gerund **tañendo**   *Past Participle* **tañido**

Imperative   **tañe tañed**

                taña tañan

PRESENT **taño, tañes, tañe, tañemos, tañéis, tañen**

PRETERIT **tañí, tañiste, tañó, tañimos, tañisteis, tañeron**

IMPERFECT **tañía, tañías, tañía, tañíamos, tañíais, tañían**

FUTURE **tañeré, tañerás, tañerá, tañeremos, tañeréis, tañerán**

CONDITIONAL **tañería, tañerías, tañería, tañeríamos, tañeríais, tañerían**

PRESENT SUBJUNCTIVE **taña, tañas, taña, tañamos, tañáis, tañan**

IMPERFECT SUBJUNCTIVE (**-ra**) **tañera, tañeras, tañera, tañéramos, tañerais, tañeran**

IMPERFECT SUBJUNCTIVE (**-se**) **tañese, tañeses, tañese, tañésemos, tañeseis, tañesen**

Regular **-er** verb showing the usual change **ie** > **e** and **ió** > **o** after **ñ**. **Atañer** *to concern* is conjugated the same way but it is not much used, **concernir** being more usual.

82 Tener *to have*

Gerund **teniendo**   *Past Participle* **tenido**

Imperative   **ten tened**
                tenga tengan

PRESENT   **tengo, tienes, tiene, tenemos, tenéis, tienen**

PRETERIT   **tuve, tuviste, tuvo, tuvimos, tuvisteis, tuvieron**

IMPERFECT   **tenía, tenías, tenía, teníamos, teníais, tenían**

FUTURE   **tendré, tendrás, tendrá, tendremos, tendréis, tendrán**

CONDITIONAL   **tendría, tendrías, tendría, tendríamos, tendríais, tendrían**

PRESENT SUBJUNCTIVE   **tenga, tengas, tenga, tengamos, tengáis, tengan**

IMPERFECT SUBJUNCTIVE **(-ra) tuviera, tuvieras, tuviera, tuviéramos, tuvierais, tuvieran**

IMPERFECT SUBJUNCTIVE **(-se) tuviese, tuvieses, tuviese, tuviésemos, tuvieseis, tuviesen**

Irregular verb in constant use. The following compounds are similar and all are in current use:

abstenerse de *to abstain from*
atenerse a *to abide by*
contener *to contain*
detener *to detain*
detenerse *to halt*
entretener *to hold up (*i.e. *delay someone)*

mantener *to maintain (*i.e. *to look after, support financially)*
obtener *to obtain*
retener *to retain*
sostener *to maintain (an argument); to prop up*

The **tú** imperative of these compound verbs requires an accent on the final vowel: **detén**, **retén**, etc.

83 Traer *to bring*

Gerund **trayendo** *Past Participle* **traído**

Imperative **trae traed**
traiga traigan

PRESENT **traigo, traes, trae, traemos, traéis, traen**
PRETERIT **traje, trajiste, trajo, trajimos, trajisteis, trajeron**
IMPERFECT **traía, traías, traía, traíamos, traíais, traían**
FUTURE **traeré, traerás, traerá, traeremos, traeréis, traerán**
CONDITIONAL **traería, traerías, traería, traeríamos,**
traeríais, traerían
PRESENT SUBJUNCTIVE **traiga, traigas, traiga, traigamos,**
traigáis, traigan
IMPERFECT SUBJUNCTIVE **(-ra) trajera, trajeras, trajera,**
trajéramos, trajerais, trajeran
IMPERFECT SUBJUNCTIVE **(-se) trajese, trajeses, trajese,**
trajésemos, trajeseis, trajesen

Irregular verb in constant use. Note the replacement of **ie** by **e** after **j**, normal in irregular verbs that have -**j**- in the preterit. The following similar verbs are found:

abstraer *to abstract*
abstraerse de *to become oblivious to*
atraer *to attract*
contraer *to contract*
distraer *to distract*
distraerse *to be distracted*
sustraer *to steal* (usually **robar**)

84 Trocar *to swap*

Gerund **trocando**   *Past Participle* **trocado**

Imperative   **trueca trocad**

trueque truequen

PRESENT **trueco, truecas, trueca, trocamos, trocáis, truecan**

PRETERIT **troqué, trocaste, trocó, trocamos, trocasteis, trocaron**

IMPERFECT **trocaba, trocabas, trocaba, trocábamos, trocabais, trocaban**

FUTURE **trocaré, trocarás, trocará, trocaremos, trocaréis, trocarán**

CONDITIONAL **trocaría, trocarías, trocaría, trocaríamos, trocaríais, trocarían**

PRESENT SUBJUNCTIVE **trueque, trueques, trueque, troquemos, troquéis, truequen**

IMPERFECT SUBJUNCTIVE (**-ra**) **trocara, trocaras, trocara, trocáramos, trocarais, trocaran**

IMPERFECT SUBJUNCTIVE (**-se**) **trocase, trocases, trocase, trocásemos, trocaseis, trocasen**

Conjugated like **contar** (no. 24) but with the predictable spelling change stressed **c** > **qu** before **e**. **Trastrocar** *to alter* is conjugated the same way. **Trastocar** *to disorder, muddle up* is constantly confused with it, but is in fact regular (like **sacar**, no. 74). **Derrocar** *to topple* used to be conjugated like **trocar** but nowadays usually follows the pattern of **sacar**.

85 Valer *to be worth; to be useful, valuable*

Gerund **valiendo**   *Past Participle* **valido**

Imperative   **vale valed**

valga valgan

PRESENT **valgo, vales, vale, valemos, valéis, valen**

PRETERIT **valí, valiste, valió, valimos, valisteis, valieron**

IMPERFECT **valía, valías, valía, valíamos, valíais, valían**

FUTURE **valdré, valdrás, valdrá, valdremos, valdréis, valdrán**

CONDITIONAL **valdría, valdrías, valdría, valdríamos, valdríais, valdrían**

PRESENT SUBJUNCTIVE **valga, valgas, valga, valgamos, valgáis, valgan**

IMPERFECT SUBJUNCTIVE (-ra) **valiera, valieras, valiera, valiéramos, valierais, valieran**

IMPERFECT SUBJUNCTIVE (-se) **valiese, valieses, valiese, valiésemos, valieseis, valiesen**

Irregular (because of the unexpected **g**). The following verbs are conjugated the same way:

equivaler a *to be equivalent to*

prevalerse de *to take advantage of* (literary: usually **aprovecharse de**)

valerse de *to avail oneself of*

86 Vencer *to defeat*

Gerund **venciendo**   *Past Participle* **vencido**

Imperative   **vence venced**

             venza venzan

PRESENT **venzo, vences, vence, vencemos, vencéis, vencen**

PRETERIT **vencí, venciste, venció, vencimos, vencisteis, vencieron**

IMPERFECT **vencía, vencías, vencía, vencíamos, vencíais, vencían**

FUTURE **venceré, vencerás, vencerá, venceremos, venceréis, vencerán**

CONDITIONAL **vencería, vencerías, vencería, venceríamos, venceríais, vencerían**

PRESENT SUBJUNCTIVE **venza, venzas, venza, venzamos, venzáis, venzan**

IMPERFECT SUBJUNCTIVE (**-ra**) **venciera, vencieras, venciera, venciéramos, vencierais, vencieran**

IMPERFECT SUBJUNCTIVE (**-se**) **venciese, vencieses, venciese, venciésemos, vencieseis, venciesen**

Regular **-er** verb with the spelling change **c** > **z** before **o** and **a**. The majority of verbs ending in **-cer** are in fact conjugated like **parecer** (no. 46); only a few are conjugated like **vencer**, e.g.

convencer *to convince*
ejercer *to exercise (a profession)*
mecer *to sway* (transitive)
mecerse *to sway* (intransitive)

   Torcer *to twist*, **retorcerse** *to writhe*, **escocer** *to sting* and **cocer** *to cook* are conjugated like **cocer** (no. 19)

87 Venir *to come*

Gerund **viniendo** *Past Participle* **venido**

| *Imperative* | **ven venid** |
| | **venga vengan** |

PRESENT **vengo, vienes, viene, venimos, venís, vienen**

PRETERIT **vine, viniste, vino, vinimos, vinisteis, vinieron**

IMPERFECT **venía, venías, venía, veníamos, veníais, venían**

FUTURE **vendré, vendrás, vendrá, vendremos, vendréis, vendrán**

CONDITIONAL **vendría, vendrías, vendría, vendríamos, vendríais, vendrían**

PRESENT SUBJUNCTIVE **venga, vengas, venga, vengamos, vengáis, vengan**

IMPERFECT SUBJUNCTIVE (**-ra**) **viniera, vinieras, viniera, viniéramos, vinierais, vinieran**

IMPERFECT SUBJUNCTIVE (**-se**) **viniese, vinieses, viniese, viniésemos, vinieseis, viniesen**

Irregular verb in constant use. The following compounds of **venir** follow the same pattern:

avenirse en *to agree on* (literary)	**intervenir en** *to take part in*
contravenir *to contravene*	**prevenir** *to prevent*
convenir en *to agree on*	**reconvenir** *to reproach*
desavenirse *to fall out* (e.g. friends)	**sobrevenir** *to occur* (usually disasters)
devenir *to become*	

(philosophical language only: usually **ponerse**, **hacerse** or **volverse**)

The **tú** imperative of the compounds has an accent, e.g. **prevén**, although the imperative of the compounds is hardly ever used.

88 Ver *to see*

Gerund **viendo**   *Past Participle* **visto**

Imperative   **ve ved**

                    vea vean

PRESENT **veo, ves, ve, vemos, veis, ven**

PRETERIT **vi, viste, vio** *(no accent!)*, **vimos, visteis, vieron**

IMPERFECT **veía, veías, veía, veíamos, veíais, veían**

FUTURE **veré, verás, verá, veremos, veréis, verán**

CONDITIONAL **vería, verías, vería, veríamos, veríais, verían**

PRESENT SUBJUNCTIVE **vea, veas, veas, veamos, veáis, vean**

IMPERFECT SUBJUNCTIVE (**-ra**) **viera, vieras, viera, viéramos, vierais, vieran**

IMPERFECT SUBJUNCTIVE (**-se**) **viese, vieses, viese, viésemos, vieseis, viesen**

Irregular verb, but only insofar as the **e** survives unexpectedly in certain forms (e.g. **veo**, not 'vo', **veía**, not 'vía', etc.). The following common compounds occur, all conjugated like **ver:**

entrever *to glimpse*   **prever** *to foresee*

The third-person present indicative of these compounds requires an accent: **prevé, prevén, entrevé, entrevén.** So does the **tú** imperative (if it is ever used): **prevé, entrevé.**

The third-person singular of the preterit of the compounds also requires an accent: **entrevió, previó.** The accent on the third-person singular preterit of the simple form of **ver** was removed in 1959.

89 Vivir *to live*

Gerund **viviendo**   *Past Participle* **vivido**

Imperative   **vive vivid**

viva vivan

PRESENT **vivo, vives, vive, vivimos, vivís, viven**

PRETERIT **viví, viviste, vivió, vivimos, vivisteis, vivieron**

IMPERFECT **vivía, vivías, vivía, vivíamos, vivíais, vivían**

FUTURE **viviré, vivirás, vivirá, viviremos, viviréis, vivirán**

CONDITIONAL **viviría, vivirías, viviría, viviríamos, viviríais, vivirían**

PRESENT SUBJUNCTIVE **viva, vivas, viva, vivamos, viváis, vivan**

IMPERFECT SUBJUNCTIVE **(-ra) viviera, vivieras, viviera, viviéramos, vivierais, vivieran**

IMPERFECT SUBJUNCTIVE **(-se) viviese, vivieses, viviese, viviésemos, vivieseis, viviesen**

A completely regular **-ir** verb which serves as a good model for the **-ir** conjugation.

90 Volver *to come back*

Gerund **volviendo**   *Past Participle* **vuelto**

Imperative   **vuelve volved**

vuelva vuelvan

PRESENT **vuelvo, vuelves, vuelve, volvemos, volvéis, vuelven**

PRETERIT **volví, volviste, volvió, volvimos, volvisteis, volvieron**

IMPERFECT **volvía, volvías, volvía, volvíamos, volvíais, volvían**

FUTURE **volveré, volverás, volverá, volveremos, volveréis, volverán**

CONDITIONAL **volvería, volverías, volvería, volveríamos, volveríais, volverían**

PRESENT SUBJUNCTIVE **vuelva, vuelvas, vuelva, volvamos, volváis, vuelvan**

IMPERFECT SUBJUNCTIVE **(-ra) volviera, volvieras, volviera, volviéramos, volvierais, volvieran**

IMPERFECT SUBJUNCTIVE **(-se) volviese, volvieses, volviese, volviésemos, volvieseis, volviesen**

Conjugated exactly like **mover** (no. 48) except for the irregular past participle **vuelto**. All verbs ending in -**olver** are conjugated this way, the following being commonly found:

absolver *to absolve*

desenvolverse *to develop* (intransitive)

disolver *to dissolve*

envolver *to wrap up*

resolver *to resolve*

revolver *to stir up*

volverse *to become; to turn back;* **v. a** *to turn to*

91 Yacer (Am.) *to lay;* (Brit.) *to lie (as in 'he lay there', 'here lie the mortal remains of', etc.)*

Gerund **yaciendo**   *Past Participle* **yacido**

Imperative   **yace (yaz) yaced**
                 yazca (yazga, yaga) yazcan (yazgan, yagan)

PRESENT **yazco (yazgo, yago), yaces, yace, yacemos, yacéis, yacen**

PRETERIT **yací, yaciste, yació, yacimos, yacisteis, yacieron**

IMPERFECT **yacía, yacías, yacía, yacíamos, yacíais, yacían**

FUTURE **yaceré, yacerás, yacerá, yaceremos, yaceréis, yacerán**

CONDITIONAL **yacería, yacerías, yacería, yaceríamos, yaceríais, yacerían**

PRESENT SUBJUNCTIVE **yazca, yazcas, yazca, yazcamos, yazcáis, yazcan**
(yazga, yazgas, yazga, yazgamos, yazgáis, yazgan)
(yaga, yagas, yaga, yagamos, yagáis, yagan)

IMPERFECT SUBJUNCTIVE **(-ra) yaciera, yacieras, yaciera, yaciéramos, yacierais, yacieran**

IMPERFECT SUBJUNCTIVE **(-se) yaciese, yacieses, yaciese, yaciésemos, yacieseis, yaciesen**

Usually conjugated like **parecer** (no. 46). This verb not used in everyday speech, being confined to very formal literary styles. **Echarse**, **tumbarse**, **acostarse** or **descansar** are various ways of expressing the same idea.

The bracketed alternative forms are even rarer.

92 Zurcir *to darn*

Gerund **zurciendo**   *Past Participle* **zurcido**

Imperative   **zurce zurcid**

zurza zurzan

PRESENT **zurzo, zurces, zurce, zurcimos, zurcís, zurcen**

PRETERIT **zurcí, zurciste, zurció, zurcimos, zurcisteis, zurcieron**

IMPERFECT **zurcía, zurcías, zurcía, zurcíamos, zurcíais, zurcían**

FUTURE **zurciré, zurcirás, zurcirá, zurciremos, zurciréis, zurcirán**

CONDITIONAL **zurciría, zurcirías, zurciría, zurciríamos, zurciríais, zurcirían**

PRESENT SUBJUNCTIVE **zurza, zurzas, zurza, zurzamos, zurzáis, zurzan**

IMPERFECT SUBJUNCTIVE (**-ra**) **zurciera, zurcieras, zurciera, zurciéramos, zurcierais, zurcieran**

IMPERFECT SUBJUNCTIVE (**-se**) **zurciese, zurcieses, zurciese, zurciésemos, zurcieseis, zurciesen**

Regular **-ir** verb with the spelling change **c > z**. This is not a common type, most verbs ending in **-cir** having some other type of irregularity as well. Similar verbs :

esparcir *to scatter, strew*
esparcirse *to be scattered*
fruncir *to pucker* (the eyebrows)
resarcir *to compensate* (effort)

Sequoyah

GRANT FOREMAN

UNIVERSITY OF OKLAHOMA PRESS

NORMAN

By Grant Foreman
(published by the University of Oklahoma Press)

Advancing the Frontier, 1830–1860
Down the Texas Road
The Five Civilized Tribes
Fort Gibson: A Brief History
A History of Oklahoma
Indian Removal: The Emigration of the Five Civilized Tribes of Indians
Indians and Pioneers: The Story of the American Southwest Before 1830
Marcy and the Gold Seekers: The Journal of Captain R. B. Marcy
Muskogee: The Biography of an Oklahoma Town
(editor) *A Traveler in Indian Territory,* by Ethan Allen Hitchcock
(editor) *Adventure on Red River,* by Captain Randolph B. Marcy
(editor) *A Pathfinder in the Southwest,* by Lieutenant A. W. Whipple
Sequoyah

345263

INTERNATIONAL STANDARD BOOK NUMBERS:
0–8061–0069–9 (cloth); 0–8061–1056–2 (paper)

LIBRARY OF CONGRESS CATALOG CARD NUMBER: 38–27481

Sequoyah is Volume 16 in *The Civilization of the American Indian Series.*

ILLUSTRATIONS

ODE TO SEQUOYAH

(By Alex Posey, Creek Indian Poet)

The names of Watie and Boudinot—
    The valiant warrior and gifted sage—
And other Cherokees, may be forgot,
    But thy name shall descend to every age;
The mysteries enshrouding Cadmus' name
Cannot obscure thy claim to fame.

The people's language cannot perish—nay,
    When from the face of this great continent
Inevitable doom hath swept away
    The last memorial—the last fragment
Of tribes,—some scholar learned shall pore
Upon thy letters, seeking lore.
Some bard shall lift a voice in praise of thee,
    In moving numbers tell the world how men
Scoffed thee, hissed thee, charged with lunacy!
    And who could not give 'nough honor when
At length, in spite of jeers, of want and need,
Thy genius shaped a dream into a deed.

By cloud-capped summits in the boundless west,
    Or mighty river rolling to the sea,
Where'er thy footsteps led thee on that quest,
    Unknown, rest thee, illustrious Cherokee.

SEQUOYAH

George Guess (Sequoyah)

Sequoyah

SEQUOYAH is celebrated as an illiterate Indian genius who, solely from the resources of his mind, endowed a whole tribe with learning; the only man in history to conceive and perfect in its entirety an alphabet or syllabary.

He was born in the Cherokee village of Tuskegee in Tennessee, near Fort Loudon on the Tennessee River, about five miles from the sacred or capital town of Echota. Little is known of his early life, though it is well established that he grew up in the tribe unacquainted with English or civilized arts. He was a craftsman in silver work, an ingenious natural mechanic, whose inventive powers had scope for development in consequence of an affliction to one of his legs that rendered him a cripple for life. In young manhood he removed from the Overhills towns to Willstown in the present State of Alabama.

Sequoyah, whose English name was George Guess, was a soldier in the War of 1812 against the hostile Creek Indians. He served as a private in the company of Mounted and Foot Cherokees commanded by the Cherokee, Capt. John McLamore, and forming part of Col. Gideon Morgan Jr.'s Regiment of Cherokee Indians.

He volunteered at Turkeytown October 7, 1813, less than a month before his regiment under Morgan and Maj. John Lowrey participated in an attack on the town of Tallaschatche. Sequoyah's three months service ended January 6, 1814, but he reenlisted three weeks later. March 27, 1814, his regiment took part in the famous Battle of the Horseshoe that inflicted a decisive defeat on the Creeks. Fifteen days afterward, with the war practically over, Sequoyah was discharged at Hillabee.

These facts are established by the records in the United States war department and in the pension office, including the affidavit of Sequoyah's widow Sally, to whom he was married in 1815, and who, in 1855 at the age of sixty-six, invoked the record of her deceased husband's service in support of her claim for bounty land, authorized by a recent act of congress. In this proceeding, supporting affidavits were made by the Cherokees, Chief John Ross, who also fought at the Battle of the Horseshoe, John Drew, Archibald Campbell and Going Back, who knew of Sequoyah's army service and that Sally was his only widow. Throughout these records he is called George Guess.

The year after his discharge he and Sally were married according to tribal custom. The next year, 1816, Sequoyah is found at the Chickasaw council house, and there, under his English name of George Guess, on September 14, joined with fourteen other Cherokees in agreeing to a so-called treaty with Andrew Jackson and others, by which they were induced to yield to the United States a large part of their country. Sequoyah's associates on this occasion do not seem to have been important representatives of the Nation and their acts were subsequently ratified by a larger Cherokee council at Turkeytown.

Different versions of the labors that brought forth Sequoyah's Cherokee alphabet have been written, but they nearly all agree on the main facts. At an early age Guess realized that there was a magic in the written word that set apart from others those who could read and write it. Inspired by a desire to discover a

4

set of characters that could be used by his people to express the sense and sound of the Cherokee language, about 1809 he began his work.

Years of more or less aimless experimenting eventually led to the definite conception of his great objective. This was a slow and laborious undertaking, not only wanting encouragement from any source, but faced by ridicule and even menace. Finally, after twelve years of labor and discouragement he completed his syllabary. Its simplicity and adaptability to the speech and thought of the Cherokees enabled the people to master it in a few days, and soon a large part of the tribe employed the new invention in uses never known to them before. Its first appeal was to the most benighted members of the tribe, who learned the use and value of this novel instrument before those possessing any education or knowledge of English could be interested in it.

The Cherokee treaty of 1817 provided for the emigration to Arkansas of such members of the tribe as desired to remove west and join a thousand of their countrymen who had previously located there. Among the signers of the treaty was the chief John Jolly, who had removed to Arkansas several years before. Jolly recruited a large party to return with him to the west, including members of the tribe who were beginning to take an interest in education. Among these was Sequoyah. In February, 1818, the Cherokee agent started nineteen flatboats down the Tennessee River loaded with Cherokee emigrants bound for the unknown country on the Arkansas River.

Thirteen of these boats and four keel boats constituted the flotilla under the command of John Jolly. There were 331 persons in his party, of whom 108 were warriors, each armed with a new rifle; they carried their household goods and other personal property, and provisions for seventy days, the estimated length of their journey based on the experiences of other emigrants.

On the eve of their departure Chief Jolly wrote to Secretary of War Calhoun: "Father you must not think that by removing we shall return to the savage life; you have learned us to be herdsmen & cultivators, and to spin and weave. Our women will raise the cotton & the Indigo & spin and weave cloth to cloath our children. By means of schools here, numbers of our young people can read and write; they can read what we call the Preacher's Book sent to us from the great spirit to all people. It is the wish of our people that you will send us a branch of the missionary schools, or some other teachers. We shall settle more compactly on our new lands than we were here; this will be of advantage to teaching our children." Many of the children in this party recently had been taken from the mission schools to accompany their parents to the west.

The sentiments expressed by Jolly indicate an atmosphere congenial to Sequoyah, interested in promoting the education of his people. On the long days lazily drifting down the waters of the Tennessee, Ohio and Mississippi rivers and toiling up the Arkansas, or around the camp fires on the river banks, it is easy to imagine Sequoyah studying, planning making strange characters on boards, bark and rocks, improving the opportunity to discuss his alphabet with his companions. The destination of this company of Cherokee emigrants was the country on the north side of the Arkansas River, near the Illinois, in the pres-

6

ent Pope County, Arkansas. Here they settled and began their new life. And here Sequoyah also remained, where he continued his studies and contriving, and sought to interest his people in his great dream of a means for them to put their thoughts on paper as the white people did.

He had succeeded so far toward the completion of his work that before 1821 he again returned to the Cherokee Nation, taking to his people messages from their western friends in the characters thus far completed. After remaining in the east long enough to complete his work and witness its adoption by his tribesmen there, Sequoyah again, in 1822, departed for Arkansas to carry to his people in that remote country messages from their friends written in the characters which he soon taught them to read. And thus he bound together the widely separated divisions of his tribe by ties that were novel to them, demonstrated the great utility of his work, and awakened a general interest in and appreciation of it.

The American Board of Commissioners for Foreign Missions reported in September, 1825, that correspondence in Sequoyah's syllabary was being maintained between the Cherokees east and those west; and that "The Cherokees have for some time been very desirous to have a press of their own, that a newspaper may be published in their own language." Some months before, David Brown, a Cherokee, with the help of some of his countrymen, commenced the translation of the New Testament into Cherokee. "Already the four Gospels are translated and fairly copied; and if types and a press were ready, they could be immediately revised and printed and read. Extracts are now transcribed and perused by a few."

After Sequoyah's invention came into general use the Cherokee people were appreciative of the great service rendered by their tribesman and manifested their gratitude in a manner explained by Chief John Ross, written at his home: "Head of Coosa, Cherokee Nation, January 12, 1832. Mr. George Gist: My Friend: The legislative Council of the Cherokee Nation in the year 1824 voted a medal to be presented to you, as a token of respect & admiration for your ingenuity in the invention of the Cherokee alphabetical characters; and in pursuance thereof the late venerable Chiefs, Path Killer & Charles R. Hicks, instructed a delegation of this nation, composed of Messrs. George Lowrey, Senior, Elijah Hicks & myself to have one struck, which was completed in 1825. In the anticipation of your visit to this country it was reserved for the purpose of honoring you with its presentment by the chiefs in General Council; but having so long been disappointed in this pleasing hope, I have thought it my duty no longer to delay, and therefore take upon myself the pleasure of delivering it through our friend Mr. Charles H. Vann who intends visiting his relatives in the country where you dwell; . . . ."

The medal, wrote John Howard Payne in 1836, "was made at Washington & of silver to the value of Twenty Dollars. On one side was thus inscribed: 'Presented to George Gist by the General Council of the Cherokee Nation, for his ingenuity in The Invention of the Cherokee Alphabet, 1825.' Under the inscription were two pipes crossed and an abridgement of the above on the reverse of the medal encircled a head meant to represent George Gist himself."

The year the medal was struck the government officially

took notice of Sequoyah's gift to his tribe. On March 29, 1825, Thomas L. McKenney of the office of Indian affairs addressed the Cherokee, Charles Hicks:

"I thank you for the enclosure of Guess's extraordinary discovery. It is doubtless an invention of no ordinary genius and entitles its author to the respect and distinction of all men, but especially of those to whom he has given such an invulnerable instrument for the interchange of mind with mind; and who, but for this gift must have been doomed (I refer to the old Indians) to that limited intercourse that is carried on when friend meets friend face to face

"I was glad to see the Delegation had honored this man by having a medal struck for him. He should be noticed; and his life for the future made comfortable, and free from the embarassments which sometimes overtake the best of us. I have had a copy of the alphabet you sent me engraved, and expect to see it in print in a few days, accompanied by some remarks, and illustrations which I sent with it, to the printers."

The Moravians who established a mission in the Cherokee Nation in 1802 were the first in that field. For years they labored under the difficulty of translating their thoughts and teachings through a medium that could be understood by the Cherokees. Charles Hicks, an intelligent Cherokee, and the first convert from that tribe, gave the missionaries considerable information on the construction and inflection of the language. He said it could not be learned by writing it down as the pronunciation was different. He tried to show them how words and syllables were expressed partly through the nose and partly in the throat. The sounds were so peculiar, he said, that no com-

9

bination of English vowels and consonants could fully express them. After much patient labor Hicks translated the Lord's Prayer into Cherokee, expressing the sound of the syllables as best he could with English vowels and consonants.

Daniel S. Butrick, a missionary at Brainerd Mission, was commissioned by the American Board to learn the language and devoted several years to that purpose, with the result that "he found nine modes, fifteen tenses and three numbers, singular, dual and plural. No prepositions or auxiliary verbs were employed, these adjuncts being in the verbs themselves. Pronouns were seldom used; instead, the nouns were repeated. With the study of years Butrick was not able to express himself so as to be understood by the Cherokees."

And then came Sequoyah who, to their infinite relief, furnished them the desired medium. A Moravian chronicler wrote: "In the year 1821 a remarkable man, mixed-blood Cherokee, named Sik-wa-yi, commonly called Sequoya, came forward with a Cherokee alphabet which he had invented and which was destined to bring the Nation forward by leaps and bounds, making the Cherokee a literary Nation. Sequoyah had never attended school and in all his life never learned to speak, read or write the English language. Of a contemplative disposition, he observed, while on a trip to a neighboring village, that whitemen had a method of conveying thoughts on paper by a series of signs or marks, and he conceived the idea of inventing characters intelligible to the red man. He took up a stone and began to scratch figures on it with a pin, remarking that he could teach the Cherokee to talk on paper like the white man. He was heartily laughed at and his attempts ridiculed, but this seemed only to make him more earnest and he worked on until he had invented 86 characters, a complete Cherokee alphabet, by a system in which characters represented sounds out of which the words could be compounded—a system in which single letters would stand for syllables.

"In 1821, he submitted this Cherokee syllabary to a public test by the leading men of the Nation. It is said that the leading men assembled, placed Sequoyah and one of his sons at some distance from each other, had them write sentences dictated to them, and, having carried them by trusty messengers, had the writing of each read by the other, and in that manner tested the correctness of his claims.

"The alphabet was soon recognized as an invaluable invention for the elevation of the tribe, and in a little over a year, thousands of hitherto illiterate Cherokees were able to read and write their own language, teaching each other in cabins or by the roadside. The whole nation became an academy for the study of the system. Letters were written back and forth between the Cherokees in the east and those who had emigrated to the lands in Arkansas.

"In 1824 a young native convert in the Moravian mission named Atsi, made a manuscript translation of a portion of St. John's Gospel, which was copied hundreds of times and distributed widely through the Nation. In September, 1825, David Brown, a Cherokee preacher, completed a translation of the New Testament in the new syllabary, and this work was handed about in manuscript."

Sequoyah's alphabet was soon established as a practical instrumentality and became very popular with the people. After his removal west this great gift continued to enrich the lives of the Cherokees, but its larger use was greatly due to the young missionary Samuel A. Worcester, who arrived with his bride in the Cherokee Nation in October, 1825. Learning of Guess's alphabet, which he found in general use among the Cherokees, Worcester was quick to realize its potential value in the field of mission work and education. He brought the possibilities of printing in the Sequoyah characters to the attention of the Prudential Committee, who reported to the American Board of Commissioners for Foreign Missions:

"A form of alphabet writing invented by a Cherokee named George Guess, who does not speak English, and was never taught to read English books, is attracting great notice among the people generally. Having become acquainted with the principles of the alphabet, viz: that marks can be made of the symbols of sound, this uninstructed man conceived the notion that he could express all the syllables in the Cherokee language by separate marks, or characters. On collecting all the syllables which, after long study and trial, he could recall to his memory, he found the number to be eighty-two. In order to express these he took the letters of our alphabet for a part of them and various modifications of our letters, with some characters of his own invention for the rest. With these symbols he set about writing letters, and very soon a correspondence was actually maintained between the Cherokees in Wills Valley and their countrymen beyond the Mississippi, five hundred miles apart. This was done by individuals who could not speak English, and who had never learned any alphabet, except this syllabic one, which Guess invented, taught to others, and introduced into practice. The interest in this matter has been increasing for the last two years, till, at length, young Cherokees travel a great distance to be instructed in this easy method of writing and reading. In three days they are able to commence letter-writing and return home to their villages prepared to teach others. It is the opinion of some of the missionaries that if the Bible were translated and printed according to the plan here described, hundreds of adult Cherokees who will never learn English, would be able to read it in a single month."

Dr. Worcester repeatedly urged that steps be taken to provide facilities for printing in the Sequoyah characters, and it was largely through his efforts that the enterprise finally materialized. He was instrumental in securing the approval of leading Cherokees for the casting of type in Boston in the Cherokee characters.

Finally after many delays the American Board reported early in 1827: "The establishment of a printing press at the expense and under the direction of the Cherokees themselves has been delayed by various causes; but seems likely to take place soon. The Committee have been requested to execute this business and have cheerfully undertaken it for their Cherokee friends. Punches have been cut and types cast, after the model of Guess's alphabet at the foundry of Messrs. Baker and Greene, Boston. A fount of English type has also been procured, and a press of a very superior kind. It is hoped that printing will be commenced in Cherokee and English early in the coming year. Mr. Boudinot has been engaged by the Cherokee Council to superintend the publication of a newspaper, and of such other works, in the department of school-books, translations, &c., as

13

the exigency of the times may call for." The equipment was finally ready for shipment in November, 1827.

The American Board paid for the press and type and other equipment of the printing office, for which the Cherokee Nation fully reimbursed it. In the meantime the Cherokees had constructed a building for a printing office at New Echota, the capitol of the Nation, in Georgia. But it was not until late in January, 1828, that the press and type, shipped by water from Boston, completed the last leg of their journey by wagon 200 miles from Augusta, Georgia.

In the meantime a prospectus was issued for their first newspaper, which was called the *Cherokee Phoenix*. Management of the newspaper was under the direct control of the Cherokees. Elias Boudinot, a young school teacher of that tribe, who had been educated at Cornwall, Connecticut, was editor-in-chief at a salary of $300 a year.

Before the press and equipment were received Dr. Worcester made a translation of the first five verses of the book of Genesis. Its publication in the *Missionary Herald* in December, 1827, made it the first printing in the characters invented by Sequoyah. Preparations completed on the twenty-first of February appeared the first issue of the *Cherokee Phoenix,* a four-page newspaper, part in English and part in the characters invented by Sequoyah. In the fourth number, the March 13 issue, began the publication of the Cherokee laws enacted as far back as 1808. Elias Boudinot was succeeded as editor August 1, 1832, by Elijah Hicks, whom Chief John Ross appointed. The most nearly complete file of this newspaper in existence is one of the prized possessions of the British Museum, in London.

14

In the issue of February 11, 1829, the name of the paper was changed to read "Cherokee Phoenix and Indians' Advocate." This paper appeared regularly until its seizure in 1832 by Stand Watie and the authorities of Georgia, when it was run in the interest of Cherokee emigration. From that time it appeared more or less irregularly, with sometimes four issues in a month, sometimes three, two and one. After February 9, 1833, there was an interval of nine weeks before the paper appeared, and between April 17 and July 20 of that year only two issues. There were about thirty issues of the paper during the next ten months when it ceased altogether.

Subsequent employment of their printing press was explained by John Ross, Joseph Vann and a number of other prominent Cherokees in a communication of April 22, 1836 to the secretary of war in which they sought to recover it: "The Cherokee Council, held in the spring of 1835, resolved to remove the Nation's printing press to Red Clay (in Tennessee) and to issue a paper at that place, in as much as the Cherokees were prohibited from holding their councils at New Echota within the limits of Georgia, and Mr. Richard Fields was appointed editor. It became the duty of the Principal Chief to carry this resolution into effect. The Press and materials were at New Echota, and he sent a wagon for them.

"The messenger returned with information that before he arrived at that place, the whole had been seized by the Georgia guard, under orders from" Rev. John F. Schermerhorn and the Cherokee agent with the assistance of Stand Watie. From that time the Cherokees were not only denied the use of their press, but it was "used by the agents of the United States in the publication of slanderous communications against the constituted authorities of the Cherokee Nation."

Sequoyah in his western home became identified with the interests and problems of the Arkansas Cherokees and in December, 1827, he was named one of a delegation to go to Washington. The Cherokees were harassed and alarmed by the intrusion on their land of white people who stole their horses and cattle; and the credentials to the delegates directed them to solicit from the government a compliance with certain unfulfilled promises in their treaties; particularly in the matter of the survey of their lands so the whites could be warned just at what point they became intruders. Tobacco Will, John Rogers, Black Fox and three others were named members of the delegation; but Tobacco Will declining to go was supplanted by another. In Washington the Cherokee delegation stayed at Williamson's Hotel.

The principal result of their visit to Washington was the execution of a new treaty in May, 1828, by which the Cherokees agreed to exchange their lands in Arkansas for the extensive tract in what is now Oklahoma that became the permanent home of the tribe.

Writers frequently say that this delegation was sent to Washington for the purpose of making the treaty of 1828. This is not true. In May, 1825, they had passed a law threatening with death any person proposing the sale or exchange of their lands. This exchange may have been in their minds when they set out from home December 28, 1827, but the treaty was largely the work of white people who wished to get possession of their lands and improvements. However, it proved in the end a happy solution of the difficulties of the Indians and a most advantageous exchange. Guess and three other members of the delegation, signers of the treaty, wrote their names with the characters invented by the Cherokee Cadmus.

The treaty promised Guess $500 in recognition of the benefits he had conferred on the tribe by the invention of the alphabet, and $1000 to the Cherokees with which to set up a printing press in the west for use by them in printing in the Sequoyah characters. A salt spring on Lees Creek in the Indian Territory was given Sequoyah by the treaty in the place of one he would have to abandon in Arkansas.

These promises were redeemed by the government in a niggardly fashion; after nearly six years Sequoyah had received only $150 in cash, 22 salt kettles of the value of $150, three saddles and a small quantity of merchandise, in all amounting to $389.75. The printing establishment in the west never materialized. What the Indians later achieved with a printing press was with their own money.

How the government redeemed other promises to Sequoyah is indicated by a letter written June 16, 1838, to the commissioner of Indian affairs by the Cherokee, William Shorey Coodey, then in Washington on business for the tribe. This letter contains other information about Sequoyah.

"Washington City,
June 16, 1838

"C. A. Harris, Esqr.
Com'sr. Ind Offs

"Sir—George Guess a very worthy Indian, and inventor of

the Cherokee alphabet, has a claim upon the U. States, and desired I should give some attention to it.

"From the inclosed certificate of Genl. Smith it will be seen that he enrolled for emigration in 1818 under the provisions of the treaty of 1817, and was promised by the U.S. agent that his improvements [abandoned by him in the East] should be valued and the money paid at the Western Agency. He had two improvements and by the 6th Art. of the treaty of 1817 the Govt. stipulated a full valuation to all *emigrants* 'whose improvements are a real value to their lands.'

"By the treaty of 1819 however, the Cherokee boundary was so established that both improvements were included in the lands reserved to the Nation; still this did not alter his determination to emigrate. I do not now recollect the exact time of his removal. In 1828 we find him in this city, one of the Delegation from the Western Cherokees, and who formed the treaty of that year. He complied with all that was required of him by the terms of enrollment—abandoned his native country, his valuable improvements, and sought the future home of his people in the wilds of the west; and he took with him the *promise* of your agent. Many years have passed away and he has yet to receive the first dollar of this compensation.

"I have no testimony with me to offer as to the amount of Guess' claim, and merely state these facts for your consideration with the hope that you will instruct some of your agents in the Cherokee country to investigate the matter and report to the Department."

Sequoyah's fame had preceded him to Washington, where he was the object of much curiosity and attention. Interest in the visiting genius was increased by the simultaneous appearance of the first issue of the *Cherokee Phoenix,* the first Indian newspaper in history, which was the direct result of Sequoyah's contribution to Cherokee culture. It was only natural that during this visit to Washington Sequoyah should have been asked to sit for a portrait by Charles Bird King, the artist celebrated for his many Indian paintings, who painted the only picture of Sequoyah now extant.

Among the scholars and investigators of that day who studied and marvelled at Sequoyah in Washington was the distinguished essayist, editor and author, Samuel Lorenzo Knapp, who interviewed the Cherokee through the medium of the interpreters Capt. John Rogers and John Maw. He made Sequoyah the subject of one of his lectures on American literature, which he delivered in Washington the following winter. Extracts from this lecture were later published in *Niles' Weekly Register,* the *Cherokee Phoenix,* and other papers, and were incorporated in an article written in 1832 by Elias Boudinot for *Annals of Education,* reprinted years later in the *Cherokee Advocate,* reading in part as follows:

"No stoick could have been more grave in his demeanor than was See-quah-yah; he pondered, according to the Indian custom, for a considerable time after each question was put, before he made his reply, and often took a whiff of his calumet while reflecting on an answer . . . . Early in life he was gay, talkative, and although he never attempted to speak in council but once, yet was often from the strength of his memory, his easy coloquial powers, and ready command of his vernacular, a story teller of the convivial party."

In some of their deliberations on the subject of the written page or "the talking leaf" as they called it, the question arose among them whether this mysterious power was the gift of the Great Spirit to the white man, or a discovery of the white man himself? Most of his companions were of the former opinion, while Sequoyah as strenuously maintained the latter. "This frequently became the subject of contemplation with him afterwards, as well as many other things which he knew, or had heard, that the white man could do; but he never sat down seriously to reflect on the subject, until a swelling on his knee confined him to his cabin, and which at length, made him a cripple for life, by shortening the diseased leg.

"Deprived of the excitements of war and the pleasures of the chase, in the long nights of his confinement, his mind was again directed to the mystery of the power of *speaking by letters,* the very name of which, of course, was not to be found in his language."

Sequoyah was led to think on the subject of writing the Cherokee language by a conversation which took place at the Cherokee town of Sauta. Some young men were remarking on the wonderful and superior talents of the white people. One of the company said that white men could put a talk on a piece of paper and send it any distance, and it would be perfectly understood by those who would receive it.

All admitted that this was indeed an art far beyond the reach of the Indian, and they were utterly at a loss to conceive in what way it was done. Sequoyah, after listening awhile in silence to the conversation, observed, "you are all fools; why the thing is very easy; I can do it myself." And taking up a flat stone which lay near him, he began making words on it with a pen. After a few minutes he told them what he had written, by making a mark for each word. This produced a laugh and the conversation on that subject ended. This was enough however, to start the inventive Sequoyah to serious speculation on the subject.

He had to contend with the prejudices of the Cherokees who tried to convince him that God had made a great distinction between the white and the red man by relating to him the following tradition: In the beginning God created the Indian, the real or genuine man, and the white man. The Indian was the elder and in his hands the Creator placed a book; in the hands of the other he placed a bow and arrow, with a command that they should both make good use of them. The Indian was very slow in receiving the book, and appeared so indifferent about it that the white man came and stole it from him when his attention was directed another way. He was then compelled to take the bow and arrow, and gain his subsistence by pursuing the chase. He had thus forfeited the book which his Creator had placed in his hands and which now of right belonged to his white brother.

The narration of this story however, was not sufficient to convince Sequoyah, and to divert him from his great purpose. After the interview at Sauta, he went home, procured materials, and in earnest began to paint the Cherokee language on paper. His labors were further described by Mr. Knapp:

"From the cries of wild beasts, from the talents of the mocking-bird, from the voices of his children and his companions, he knew that feelings and passions were conveyed by different sounds, from one intelligent being to another. The thought struck him to ascertain all the sounds in the Cherokee language. His own ear was not remarkably discriminating, and he called to his aid the more acute ears of his wife and children. He found great assistance from them. When he thought that he had distinguished all the different sounds in their language, he attempted to use his pictorial signs, images of birds and beasts, to convey these sounds to others or to mark them in his own mind. He soon dropped this method, as difficult or impossible, and tried arbitrary signs, without any regard to appearances, except such as might assist him in recollecting them, and distinguishing them from each other."

Sequoyah at first thought of no way but to make a character for each word. He pursued this plan for about a year, in which time he had put down several thousand characters. He was then convinced that the object was not to be obtained in that way. But he was not to be discouraged. He firmly believed there was some way in which the Cherokee language could be expressed on paper, and after trying several other methods, he at length hit upon the idea of dividing the words into parts or syllables. He had not proceeded far on this plan, when he found to his great satisfaction, that the same characters would apply in different words, and that the number would be comparatively few.

After putting down and learning all the syllables that he could think of, he would listen to speeches, and the conversation of strangers, and whenever a word occurred which had a part or a syllable in it, which he had not before thought of, he "would recollect it until he had made a character for it." In this way he soon discovered all the syllables in the language. After commencing upon the last plan, it is believed he completed his system in about a month. He adopted a number of English letters which he took from the spelling book then in his possession. "At first these symbols were very numerous; and when he got so far as to think his invention was nearly accomplished he had about 200 characters in his alphabet. By the aid of his daughter, who seemed to enter into the genius of his labors, he reduced them at last, to 86, the number he now uses.

"He then set to work to make these characters more comely to the eye, and succeeded. As yet he had not the knowledge of the pen as an instrument, but made his characters on a piece of bark with a knife or nail. At this time he sent to the Indian agent, or some trader in the nation, for paper and pen. His ink was easily made from some of the bark of the forest trees, whose coloring preperties he had previously known; and after seeing the construction of the pen, he soon learned to make one; but at first he made it without a slit; this inconvenience was, however, quickly removed by his sagacity."

During the time he was occupied in inventing the alphabet, he was strenuously opposed by all his friends and neighbors. He was frequently told that he was throwing away his time and labor, and that none but a delirious person or an idiot would do as he did. But this did not discourage him. He would listen to the expostulations of his friends, and then deliberately light his pipe, pull his spectacles over his eyes, and sit down to his work, without attempting to vindicate his conduct.

"After completing his system, he found much difficulty in persuading the people to learn it. Nor could he succeed until he

23

went to the Cherokees in Arkansas and taught a few persons there, one of whom wrote a letter to some of his friends in the Cherokee Nation east of the Mississippi and sent it by Mr. Guess, who read it to the people on his return.

"This letter excited much curiosity: here was talk in the Cherokee language, which had come all the way from the Arkansas sealed up in paper, and yet it was very plain. This convinced many that Mr. Guess' mode of writing would be of some use. Several persons immediately determined to try to learn. They succeeded in a few days, and from this it spread all over the nation, and the Cherokees (who as a people had always been illiterate) were, in the course of a few months, without school, or expense of time, or money, able to read and write in their own language.

"This astonishing discovery certainly entitles Mr. Guess to the warmest gratitude of his country; and, should the Cherokee language continue to be spoken, his fame will be handed down to the latest posterity." The Knapp lecture incorporated the substance of a long article about Sequoyah that appeared in the *Cherokee Phoenix* in August, 1828, while he and his alphabet were live subjects of inquiry and discussion by his contemporaries, and the quotations in the last three paragraphs above are taken by this writer direct from that paper seen in the British Museum.

"His next difficulty," said Mr. Knapp, "was to make his invention known to his countrymen; for by this time he had become so abstracted from his tribe and their usual pursuits, that he was viewed with an eye of suspicion. His former companions passed his home without entering it, and mentioned his name as one who was practicing improper spells, for notoriety or mischievous purposes; and he seems to think that he should have been hardly dealt with, if his docile and unambitious disposition had not been so generally acknowledged by his tribe. At length he summoned some of the most distinguished of his nation in order to make his communication to them, and—after giving them the best explanation of his discovery that he could, stripping it of all supernatural influence, he proceeded to demonstrate to them in good earnest that he had made a discovery. His daughter, who was now his only pupil, was ordered to go out of hearing, while he requested his friends to name a word or sentiment which he put down, and then she was called in and read it to them; then the father retired and the daughter wrote; the Indians were wonder struck; but not entirely satisfied.

"See-quah-yah then proposed that the tribe should select several youths from among the brightest young men, that he might communicate the mystery to them. This was at length agreed to, although there was some lurking suspicion of necromancy in the whole business. John Maw (his Indian name I have forgotten), a full blood, with several others, were selected for this purpose. The tribe watched the youths for several months with anxiety, and when they offered themselves for examination, the feelings of all were wrought up to the highest pitch. The youths were separated from their master and from each other, and watched with great care. The uninitiated directed what master and pupil should write to each other, and these tests were varied in such a manner as not only to destroy their infidelity but most firmly to fix their faith. The Indians on this ordered a great feast and made See-quah-yah conspicuous at it. . . . . See-quah-yah became at once school master, professor, philosopher and a chief.

". . . . He did not stop here, but carried his discoveries to numbers. He of course knew nothing of the Arabic digits, nor of the power of Roman letters in the science. The Cherokees had mental numerals up to one hundred, and had words for all the numbers up to that, but they had no signs or characters to assist them in enumerating, adding, subtracting, multiplying or dividing. He reflected upon that until he had created their elemental principle in his mind, but he was at first obliged to make words to express his meaning, and then signs to explain it. By this process he soon had a clear conception of numbers up to a million. His great difficulty was at the threshhold to fix the powers of his signs according to their places. When this was overcome, his next step was in order to put down the fraction of the decimal and give the whole number to his next place—but when I knew him, he had overcome all these difficulties and was quite a ready arithmetician in the fundamental rules.

"I can safely say," continued Mr. Knapp, "that I have seldom met a man of more shrewdness than See-quah-yah. He adhered to all the customs of his country; and when his associate chiefs on the mission, assumed our costume, he was dressed in all respects like an Indian. See-quah-yah is a man of diversified talents; he passes from metaphysical and philosophical investigation to mechanical occupations with the greatest ease. The only practical mechanics he was acquainted with, were a few bungling blacksmith, who could make a rough tomahawk, or tinker with the lock of a rifle; yet he became a white and silversmith without any instruction, and made spurs and silver spoons with neatness and skill, to the great admiration of people of the Cherokee Nation.

"Sequoyah has also a great taste for painting. He mixes his colors with skill; taking all the arts and sciences of the tribe upon the subject, he added to it many chemical experiments of his own, and some of them were very successful, and would be worth being known to our painters. For his drawings he had no model but what nature furnished, and he often copied them with astonishing faithfulness. His resemblances to the human form, it is true, are coarse, but often spirited and correct, but he gave action and sometimes grace to his representations of animals. He had never seen a camel hair pencil when he made use of the hair of wild animals for his brushes.

"The manners of the American Cadmus are the most easy, and his habits those of the most assiduous scholar, and his disposition is more lively than that of any Indian I ever saw. He understood and felt the advantages the white man had long enjoyed, of having the accumulations of every branch of knowledge from generation to generation, by means of a written language, while the red man could only commit his thoughts to uncertain tradition. He reasoned correctly when he urged this to his friends as the cause why the red man had made so few advances in knowledge in comparison with us; and to remedy this was one of his great aims and one which he has accomplished beyond that of any other man living, or perhaps, any other who ever existed in a rude state of nature."

Another man who interviewed Sequoyah in Washington and marveled at his genius was Jeremiah Evarts, who asked the

Cherokee why and how he invented the alphabet. This is the shrewd answer of the Indian:

"He had observed, that many things were found out by men, and known in the world, but that this knowledge escaped and was lost, for want of some way to preserve it. He had also observed white people write things on paper, and he had seen books; and he knew that what was written down remained and was not forgotten. He had attempted, therefore, to fix certain marks for sounds, and thought that if he could make things fast on paper, it would be like catching a wild animal and taming it. He had found great difficulty in proceeding with this alphabet, as he forgot the sounds, which he had assigned to marks, and he was much puzzled about a character of the hissing sound; but when this point was settled, he proceeded easily and rapidly. This alphabet cost him much study. He afterwards made an alphabet for the pen (that is for speedy writing), the characters of which he wrote under the corresponding characters of the other.

"Sequoyah is about fifty years old, modest in appearance, and was, at the interview mentioned dressed in the costume of his country. He speaks only the Cherokee language."

Another observer quoted in the *Advocate,* said that "when I travelled through the Cherokee nation during the months of January and February, 1828, before the press was set up, or any printing had been executed in the alphabet of Guess, I was informed in many parts of the nation that almost all the young and middle aged men could read in the alphabet, with many of the old men, and of the women, and of the children. . . . . I frequently saw as I rode from place to place, Cherokee letters

28

painted or cut on the trees by the roadside, on fences, houses, and often on pieces of bark or board, lying about the houses.

"The alphabet of Guess has never been taught in schools. The people have learned it from one another; and that too without books, or paper, or any of the common facilities for writing or teaching. They cut the letters, or drew them with a piece of coal, or with paint. Bark, trees, fences, the walls of houses, &c., answered the purpose of slates.

"That the mass of a people, without schools or books, should by mutual assistance, without extraneous impulse or aid, acquire the art of reading, and that in a character wholly original, is, I believe, a phenomenon unexampled in modern times."

Elias Boudinot related that the first he ever heard of Sequoyah and his labors was in the winter of 1822–23 when he was traveling in company with John Ross along the road past the cabin of Sequoyah. Ross told him that in this place lived George Guess, who for a year had been so intensely absorbed in his foolish undertaking that he had neglected to do other labor, and permitted his farm to be overrun with weeds and briars.

"We rode on," said Boudinot, "and I thought no more of Sequoyah and his alphabet, until a portion of the Cherokees had actually become a reading people. The first evidence I received of the existence of the alphabet, was at a General Council held at New Echota in 1824, when I saw a number of Cherokees reading and writing in their own language, and in the new characters invented by one of their untutored citizens."

The 2500 Cherokees removed from Arkansas in 1829 up the Arkansas River to their new home and Sequoyah located on the west side of Skin Bayou. His residence was in the present Sequoyah County about twelve miles northeast of where is now Sallisaw.

Here Guess tended his little farm and looked after his few head of live stock that found pasturage on the rich bottom of Skin Bayou and adjacent upland. And at intervals when the larder ran low or inquiries from customers accumulated, he yoked up the oxen to his old cart, into which he loaded tools, camping equipment and a supply of food and started north through the woods for his salt lick near Lees Creek. Here, ten or twelve miles from home, Sally and the children, he would remain for days and weeks at a time making salt. The kettles had to be filled with water from the salt springs. Cords and cords of wood were needed to feed the furnace fires under the kettles. He cut what he could but purchased the most from others in exchange for salt. The kettles required attention and when the water was evaporated the salt remaining must be scooped out and replaced by fresh water.

But he was never too busy to stop and explain the characters of his alphabet to all who came to his salt lick on business or out of curiosity to see the much talked about Cherokee philosopher, or, seriously seeking information about the alphabet, listen to his interesting conversation. Taking a charred stick from the fire and a piece of smooth bark from his wood pile, he would sit down on a log and patiently explain to his listeners gathered round, the principles of his alphabet, simultaneously making sounds of Cherokee syllables and marks on the bark that represented them.

It was the same thing at home where he encouraged friend and stranger alike to call and listen to him talk of his great obsession, his alphabet that was to revolutionize his tribe. These activities were varied by excursions through the Cherokee settlements where he spent weeks teaching the alphabet to all who would learn; regaling grateful hosts and other listeners with absorbing tales of Indian lore—and above all, the alphabet, the marvel of the age.

And thus he lived for the next ten years a useful life with the western Cherokees, who grew in numbers with accessions from the east until there were five or six thousand of them.

Sequoyah was a frequent visitor at Dwight Mission. Every week or two he would saddle his pony and ride up the military road a few miles to Dwight to get the latest issue of the *Cherokee Phoenix* that was regularly sent him from Georgia. The miracle of reading in this paper the news of his people in the East, and happenings among the white people, in characters of his own invention never grew stale. And to see other uneducated Indians enjoying the same privilege as a result of his own industry and genius was a source of never-ending gratification to him.

The bicameral legislative body of the western Cherokees, called "The Committee and Council," in the summer of 1832 took steps to establish the school system which the Government agreed to finance with the annuity of $2,000, now belated since the treaty of 1828. The Cherokees provided for a school in each of the districts and an "extra" school for the whole nation where Sequoyah would teach his alphabet to the Cherokee people, for $400 annually.

Three years later another marvelous realization came into Sequoyah's life. In 1835 Dr. S. A. Worcester established a printing press in the western Cherokee country, which was to be employed in printing in his characters. At first set up at Union Mission, it was removed in December, 1836, to Park Hill where Mr. Worcester superintended the publication for years of a remarkable output of literature for the Indians, much of which was in the syllabary of Sequoyah. Before 1861 this press printed 13,980,000 pages of books, tracts, pamphlets, passages from the Bible, much appearing as originals or as translations into the alphabet of Sequoyah.

In the spring of 1839 came the remainder of the tribe, about 13,000, the survivors of that ghastly tragedy of Cherokee removal. Then opportunity for service in a great national emergency beckoned to Sequoyah.

The recent arrival of the Cherokees was attended with perplexing and serious problems. Constituting two-thirds of the tribe, the threatened dominance of the government by this majority was bitterly assailed by the remaining third who had previously come to the Indian Territory and who were in possession of the local government. When asked by the newcomers to meet them in council and help organize a new government under which the tribe could unite and in which all could participate, they arrogantly replied that they could submit to the old government and that no further concessions would be made them.

The differences between them were deep-seated and well nigh irreconcilable. The minority faction was composed of what became known as "Old Settlers"—those who had come from Arkansas in 1829 and others who had emigrated from time to time from their eastern home; and members of the

"Treaty Party," the adherents of the Ridges, Boudinots, Stand Waties, Starrs and others, an insignificant number of unauthorized persons who had signed in 1835 what became known as the "false treaty" of removal. Against the protest of 90 per cent of the tribe this spurious document was ratified by the senate and the emigration of the Indians demanded by the government. The great majority, unwilling to abandon their beloved native land, refused to remove and were driven from their homes by thousands of soldiers. After months of suffering and misery over what became known as the Trail of Tears, and the loss of nearly 4,000, mostly children and aged, from privation, strange diet and hardship, the remainder, something over 13,000 arrived in their new home.

They were bitter at the minority who had signed the "false treaty," whom they regarded as the authors of their wrongs and sufferings. John Ross, chief of the newcomers, the great majority of the tribe, with other leaders planned a meeting of all factions at Takatokah, or Double Springs, seven miles northwest of Tahlequah. After several weeks of futile negotiation the overtures of the majority of the tribe were rejected by the resident minority and the meeting broke up on June 20.

It was then that Sequoyah brought his name and influence to bear on the critical situation. Disavowing the action of other Old Settler leaders, he immediately joined with Rev. Jesse Bushyhead, one of the recent immigrants, in reassembling the Indians present in a meeting, where a resolution was adopted calling another meeting of the tribe to adopt a new government.

The adjourned meeting began July 1 at Illinois Camp Ground, nine miles from Takatokah, one mile from Illinois

River, and a mile and a half down the creek from Tahlequah. Two thousand Cherokees camped in the beautiful little shut-in valley with its fine springs, to participate in the proceedings and listen to the talks of their leading men. Two of them, Sequoyah who acted as one of the presidents of the conference representing the Old Settlers, or "Western Cherokees," as they then called themselves, John Ross, and other leaders, on July 2 addressed a communication to other Old Settler leaders urging them to attend the conference.

As this invitation was rejected, Sequoyah individually tried again and wrote a letter, in his syllabary, of course, to his friends of the Old Settler faction:

"We, the old settlers, are here in council with the late emigrants, and we want you to come up without delay, that we may talk matters over like friends and brothers. These people are here in great multitudes, and they are perfectly friendly towards us. They have said, over and over again that they will be glad to see you and we have full confidence that they will receive you with all friendship. There is no drinking here to disturb the peace though there are upward of two thousand people on the ground. We send you these few lines as friends and we want you to come on without delay; and we have no doubt but we can have all things amicably and satisfactorily settled."

The conference was conducted in the face of active opposition of non-attending leaders of the Western Cherokees and the Treaty Party, who were bitterly opposed to surrendering their leadership to the men representing the great majority of the tribe, and particularly to Chief John Ross, the idol of more

34

than two-thirds of the Cherokee people, whose leadership provoked their bitter jealousy and hatred.

The constructive efforts of John Ross, Sequoyah and other leaders were successful in spite of the active opposition of Gen. Matthew Arbuckle and leaders of the Old Settlers and Treaty Party. An act of union was adopted on July 12, 1839, by which the two parties were declared "one body politic, under the style and title of 'The Cherokee Nation'."

This document was written by William Shorey Coodey and after its adoption by the Cherokees it was signed by George Lowrey as "President of the Eastern Cherokees" and by George Guess, "President of the Western Cherokees." These signatures were followed by those of numerous other leading men representing the two factions.

The convention at Illinois Camp Ground continued in session for several weeks, then adjourned and met at Tahlequah, where, on September 6, the Cherokees adopted the constitution which was preserved throughout the tribal existence of that nation as a basis of government and laws.

Sequoyah had an abiding and ardent interest in the welfare of his people. And when the Cherokees of Texas were attacked by Lamar and his troops in July, 1839, with the loss of 100 men headed by their brave chiefs The Bowle and Hard Mush, Sequoyah was deeply moved by their misfortune. With their homes destroyed and their little farms ravaged, 1500 survivors fled across the Red River into the Choctaw Nation where they found a temporary refuge. Here they nursed their grievances and planned reprisals against the whites of Texas. The wise Sequoyah however, sent them a friendly letter counselling prudence, advised them not to return to Texas but to join their tribesmen in the Cherokee Nation. This the majority of them did to their great and permanent benefit.

Contemporary descriptions and accounts of Sequoyah are all too meager, but it is possible to present a few here, thus enabling the reader to see this remarkable man as some of his visitors did, and to possess some of the most authentic accounts of his work. One of the most interesting contributions was made by Capt. John Stuart of the Seventh Infantry, who saw much service in the Indian Territory. He was so greatly interested in the Indians that in the winter of 1837–38 he published a little book entitled *A Sketch of the Cherokee and Choctaw Indians*. Sequoyah's home was near the military road running from Fort Smith to Fort Gibson and it was an easy matter for passing army officers and other travelers to stop for a visit with this remarkable Indian. At the time Stuart's little book made its appearance about a year before his death at Fort Wayne, he was in command of Fort Coffee. The Author has never been able to find a copy of this book and all he knows of it is a few contemporary references to it, an advertisement of the book by the *Arkansas Gazette* that printed and offered it for sale at 37½ cents, and the following extract in the *Gazette:*

"George Guess, the inventor of the Cherokee alphabet, is a man of about sixty years of age. He is of middle stature, and of rather a slender form, and is slightly lame in one leg, from disease when young. His features are remarkably regular, and his face well formed, and rather handsome. His eyes are animated and piercing, showing indications of a brilliancy of intellect far superior to the ordinary portion of his fellow men.

36

His manner is agreeable, and his deportment gentlemanly. He possesses a mild disposition, and is patient, but is energetic and extremely persevering and determined in the pursuit or accomplishment of any object on which he may fix his mind. He is inquisitive, and appears to be exceedingly desirous of acquiring information on all subjects. His mind seems to soar high and wide; and if he could have had the advantages of an enlightened education, he would no doubt have brought himself to rank high among the acknowledged great men of the age in which he lives. He has been in the habit, ever since he could apply his language in that way, of keeping a journal of all the passing events which he considered worthy of record: and has, at this time (it is said), quite a volume of such matter.

"His connection in blood with the whites, is on the side of his father. His mother was a full-blood Cherokee; and he was raised entirely among the uncultivated portion of the Cherokees, and never received much, if any, advantage from an intercourse with the whites. He does not speak one word of the English language. From a very early age, he has possessed a natural talent for drawing, and very far surpasses any man in his nation in that art; but he never received any kind of instruction from any practical artist. He can draw a horse, hog, deer, &c., remarkably well; and no man in the United States can surpass him in drawing a buffalo. He can also draw rough portraits, a circumstance which, connected with his fondness for drawing, contributed very much toward inducing him to attempt the formation of a type for his language.

"Mr. Guess, when engaged in the very laudable purpose of inventing his alphabet, had to encounter many very serious obstacles, and which but few men would have surmounted. No one had the least confidence in the success of his project, and thought him to be laboring under a species of mental derangement on that subject. He was laughed at by all who knew him, and was earnestly besought by every member of his own family to abandon a project which was occupying and diverting so much of his time from the important and essential duties which he owed to his family—they being, in some measure, dependent on his daily labor for their subsistence. But no argument or solicitation could induce him to change his determination. And although he was under the necessity of working much at night, by lights made from burning pine, he persisted until he accomplished fully the object of his desire. Even after he had completed the alphabet, and the art of applying it to writing, and when he was fully able to write anything that he might wish, and when he had made records in books, and kept a running book account of his monied transactions, &c.—even then, it was with great difficulty that he could induce the members of his own family to believe that it was anything more than a wild delusion.

"At length, however, he prevailed upon one of his young daughters to learn of him his newly invented alphabet, and its arrangement, she being the only one of his family, and in fact the only person, he could prevail on to undertake the supposed useless task. She made rapid progress in learning, and soon became able to write and read with ease and fluency any thing the father would write. This began to open the eyes of the family and some of the neighbors, but did not prove to be entirely satisfactory. A meeting, therefore, was held, of the people, on

38

the subject, and by separating the father and daughter, and requiring them to write, as dictated to, by the company, and to read, while separated, the writing of each as dictated to them by others, and that being accordingly done in every instance, led the persons present into a full conviction of the truth, as well as the utility, of the *invention*. And several of the most influential men in the nation immediately learned it, and discovering all its practical advantages, recommended it in high terms to the people. From that time it spread into general use; and the people of the nation are at this day in the full enjoyment of its great benefits.

"George Guess, in forming an alphabet for the Cherokee language, found that eighty-six distinct characters would be necessary. To make so many distinct figures differing so much in their shape, as to be easily distinguished from each other, and, at the same time, to be easily and quickly made with a pen on paper, was a matter of much difficulty. But, being one day on a public road, he found a piece of a newspaper, which had been thrown aside by a traveler, which he took up, and, on examining it, found characters on it that would be more easily made than his own, and consequently picked out for that pur-, pose the largest of them, which happened to be the Roman letters, and adopted in lieu of so many of his own characters—and that, too, without knowing the English name or meaning of a single one of them. This is to show the cause and manner of the Roman letters being adopted."

Following the great service of Sequoyah to his people in the national crisis of 1839 the next known sketch of him is furnished by a visiting merchant. His alphabet had excited the interest and wonder of learned men throughout the land and even in foreign countries. Travelers coming to the Indian Territory made a point of visiting Sequoyah to observe a remarkable man whose fame was known over the country and abroad. John Alexander, a merchant of Philadelphia on a business trip, in January, 1840, while traveling the military road from Fort Gibson to Fort Smith, stopped along the way to visit Guess. After leaving Dwight Mission, with Martin Benge for interpreter, he reached Sequoyah's home. His diary, now in a California museum, yields the following about the famous Cherokee:

". . . I found the old gentleman's farm to consist of 10 acres cleared land and 3 small cabins clustered together; his stock is 2 mules, 3 yoke oxen, a wagon with a small stock of cattle and hoggs. He has had five wives and 20 children; his present wife has 5 children, the youngest 2 years old; 10 dead and 10 alive; his son Jos 8 years old. He is apparently above 60 years of age, rather low in stature & crippled since his youth. He is of a pleasant countenance & indicates a good deal of jenius. He conversed very freely on various topics, becoming very animated when my answers & questions pleased him.

"His alphabet was the main topic & appeared to be a pleasing one to him. He informed me that at a certain time in company with several others he was engaged in drawing the figure of a horse and the thought struck him that an alphabet might be invented so as to wright their talks by the use of characters. He sujested this to his companions who laughed at him and called him a fool; he nevertheless thought of it a great deal asking others if somebody could not be found in the nation who could make such characters; they said no; he said he thought it could

CHEROKEE ALPHABET.

CHARACTERS AS ARRANGED BY THE INVENTOR.

R D W Ⴠ G Ꝙ Ꮽ Ꮲ Ꭺ Ꮴ y Ꭷ Ꮬ Ꮁ Ᏽ ꝑ M ꭰ Ꮿ Ꮜ

Ꮃ Ꮃ B ꝗ Ꭰ Ꭶ ꮀ ꭲ Ꮹ J Ꮍ Ꮞ Ꮖ G Ꝥ Ꮼ ꝓ Ꮓ Ꮓ Ꮓ

Ꮐ Ꮢ Ꮀ ꮏ Ꮼ Ꭺ ꮃ ꭼ Ꮎ Ꮏ Ꮖ Ꮥ ꭷ ꭶ ꭱ Ꮢ J Ꮶ ꭳ ꭰ Ᏽ Ꮎ

Ꮐ Ꮖ J ꭲ Ꮎ Ꮥ Ꮤ Ꮜ Ꭶ ꭱ Ꮥ ꮉ Ꮥ ꮎ Ꮖ Ꮬ Ꭶ ꮃ P Ꮎ ꭷ Ꭲ Ꮿ

Ꮮ ꮃ ꭴ ꭰ Ꭺ ꮃ Ꮞ

CHARACTERS SYSTEMATICALLY ARRANGED WITH THE SOUNDS.

D a	R e	T i	ꭰ o	ꝑ u	i v
s ga ꮒ ka	ꮁ ge	y gi	Ꭺ go	J gu	E gv
ꮫ ha	Ꮓ he	ꭱ hi	Ꮓ ho	Ꮁ hu	ꭴ hv
W la	ꭰ le	ꮅ li	G lo	M lu	ꭹ lv
ꮿ ma	ꭳ me	ꮑ mi	ꮽ mo	ꝩ mu	
ꭱ na ꮂ hna ꮐ nah ꭰ ne	Ꮒ ni	Z no	ꝺ nu	ꭳ nv	
ꭲ qua	ꮽ que	ꮗ qui	ꮈ quo	ꝗ quu	Ꮛ quv
ꭰ s Ꝫ sa	4 se	Ꮜ si	ꝑ so	ꝑ su	R sv
ꮃ da w ta	ꮞ de ꮞ te	ꮧ di ꮣ tih Ꭺ do	s du	ꮯ dv	
ꭰ dla ꮅ tla	Ꮮ tle	G tli	ꮣ tlo	ꝵ tlu	P tlv
G tsa	Ꮵ tse	ꮅ tsi	Ꮶ tso	J tsu	ꮯ tsv
ꭰ wa	ꮼ we	ꮼ wi	ꮼ wo	ꮄ wu	e wv
ꭰ ya	ꭹ ye	ꮓ yi	ꮒ yo	Ꮿ yu	B yv

SOUNDS REPRESENTED BY VOWELS.

a   as *a* in *father*,   or short as *a* in *rival*,
e   as *a* in *hate*,   or short as *e* in *met*,
i   as *i* in *pique*,   or short as *i* in *pit*,
o   as *aw* in *law*,   or short as *o* in *not*,
u   as *oo* in *fool*,   or short as *u* in *pull*,
v   as *u* in *but* nasalized.

CONSONANT SOUNDS.

g nearly as in English, but approaching to k. d nearly as in English, but approaching to t. h, k, l, m, n, q, s, t, w, y, as in English.
Syllables beginning with g, except ꮞ, have sometimes the power of k; Ꭺ, s, ꮯ, are sometimes sounded to, tu, tv; and syllables written with tl, except Ꮮ, sometimes vary to dl.

FROM THE COLOPHON

The Cherokee Alphabet

GWY

ᏣᎳᎩ

CHEROKEE PHOENIX.

PHOENIX.

VOL. I.   NEW ECHOTA, WEDNESDAY JULY 9, 1828.   **NO. 20.**

EDITED BY ELIAS BOUDINOTT.

PRINTED WEEKLY BY

ISAAC H. HARRIS,

FOR THE CHEROKEE NATION.

At $2.50 if paid in advance, $3 in six months, or $3.50 if paid at the end of the year.

To subscribers who can read only the Cherokee language the price will be $2.00 in advance, or $2.50 to be paid within the year.

Every subscription will be considered as continued unless subscribers give notice to the contrary before the commencement of a new year.

Any person procuring six subscribers, and becoming responsible for the payment, shall receive a seventh gratis.

Advertisements will be inserted at seventy-five cents per square for the first insertion, and thirty-seven and a half cents for each continuance; longer ones in proportion.

☞ All letters addressed to the Editor, post paid, will receive due attention.

Resolved by the National Committee and Council, That no person shall be allowed to erect or establish a billiard table in the Cherokee Nation, without first obtaining a license from the Treasurer of the Nation, and paying into the Treasury the sum of two hundred dollars as a tax pr. annum, and such license shall not be given for a longer period than one year at a time: and any person or persons, who shall erect or establish a billiard table without first obtaining a license as herein required, shall, upon conviction, pay a fine of four hundred dollars, for the benefit of the Cherokee Nation.

New Echota, Nov. 16, 1826.

JNO. ROSS, Prest N. Com.
MAJOR RIDGE, Speaker.
his
Approved—PATH × KILLER.
mark

CHARLES HICKS.
A. McCOY, Clerk of the N. Com.
E. BOUDINOTT, CH. N. Coun.

Resolved by the National Committee and Council, That the resolution passed Oct. 15th 1825, suspending the poll tax law, and the law imposing a tax on citizen merchants of the Cherokee Nation, be, and the same are

TKA, 16, ᎧᏬᏘ 1836.

[Cherokee syllabary text]

TKA, 16 ᎧᏬᏘ, 1836.

[Cherokee syllabary text]

be done; he then threw his horse aside and quit his nonsense and went to work at it & in one month he invented and learned the alphabet so that he could wright & read by the use of it.

"His little Daughter who was not more than 6 years old was much with him and learned to read from observing him without any effort to teach her; all his effort to teach others was ridiculed & he was thought to be crazy; he then came to Arkansas to the Cherokee Settlement & told them of his invention; they laughed at him and said he was a liar; he told them they would find some day that it was true; he wrote many alphabets for them & returned to the East again, and wrote many letters to his friends & when they came to him he would take up the letters and read the contents to them; they thought he was crazy. On one occasion he was engaged with some of his people endeavoring to convince them; Turtle Fields was present and he had wrote the name of Turtle Fields on his book. At the same time his little daughter above named was standing at the window observing and on seeing her father write, she immediately red out what was written & when Fields heard her read his name he was surprised & began to believe.

"In the meantime the people in Arkansas began to write to him letters announcing that they had learned the alphabet and believed in it. This at once convinced the people of the East and he was called upon from all quarters for the alphabet. He wrote them off for all who called on him without charge. They offered to pay him but he said there was many who could not afford to pay anything and therefore he would not charge any one any thing. I told him I thought he had done a more valuable service to the Cherokees than if he had given each of the Nation a Bagg of Gold. He smiled and said that Governor Houston had told him it was worth more than a double handful of gold to each of the Nation. I told him I hoped he felt happy in knowing that his people were deriving great advantage from his invention; his Countenance as well as tongue answered in the affirmative."

When John Howard Payne was in Georgia in 1835 collecting material with which he planned to write a history of the Cherokees he recorded what he had heard of Sequoyah, whom he had not met but knew of as George Gist: "Gist still resides in Arkansas . . . . is lame—was so, I believe, from infancy . . . . he was troubled with a wife whose capacity was very limited and who did not enter into his ambitions. He built him a cabin apart from his family & there would study and contrive. His habits were always silent & contemplative . . . . to this cabin he confined himself for a year, the whole charge of his farm and family devolving on his wife. When all his friends had remonstrated in vain, his wife went in and flung his whole apparatus of papers & books into the fire, & thus he lost his first labor . . . . after two more years of application completed his work. All speak highly of his drawing & of his silver work . . . ."

Five years later, a few months after the visit described by Alexander, Mr. Payne, then visiting in the Indian Territory, was afforded the long desired opportunity to meet Sequoyah, with whom he had an interesting visit at the home of Chief John Ross. He wrote a long account of his impressions of the man, which is to be seen in manuscript in the Library of Congress. The following are some of the passages written by Payne:

"George Guess, the inventor of the Cherokee Alphabet, came

here on a visit to me. I got a brief notice of his life, by the help of an Interpreter; and then he told me there were some ancient memories of the past which I ought, by all means, to gather. I begged him to communicate them and he said he would. The Cherokee who interpreted was a short, thin, long visaged, deep voiced personage, covered with what had once been a 'whity-brown' overcoat, with vast bone buttons, of which some remained, while the fragments of the coat draped him on every side in varied fantastic shapes innumerable. He was equally anxious with myself to hear (for the Cherokees know very little about their own annals), and Mr. Ross came and remained with us.

"We were all in the cockloft of Mr. Ross's story and a half log house, where the light and wind enter through thousands of chinks. Guess sat in one corner of the fireplace and I on the opposite side at a desk; the other two between. Guess had a turban of roses and posies upon a white ground girding his venerable grey hairs;—a long dark blue robe, bordered around the lower edge and the cuffs, with black;—a blue and white minutely checked calico tunic under it, confined with an Indian beaded belt, which sustained a large wooden handled knife, in a rough leathern sheath;—the tunic open on the breast and its collar apart, with a twisted handkerchief flung around his neck & gathered within the bosom of the tunic. He wore plain buckskin leggings; and one of a deeper chocolate hue than the other. One of his legs are [*sic*] lame and shrunken. His moccasins were unornamented buckskin. He had a long dusky white bag of sumac with him, and a long Indian pipe, and smoked incessantly, replenishing his pipe from his bag. His air was al-

43

together what we picture to ourselves of an old Greek philosopher. He talked and gesticulated very gracefully;—his voice alternately swelling,—and then sinking to a whisper,—and his eye firing up and then its wild flashes subsiding into a gentle & most benignant smile. Before long, poor I seemed entirely forgotten by the rest of the audience. First, one quarter of an hour,—then another,—and then another went over, and no translation came."

After interminable conversation between Guess and the interpreter altogether in Cherokee, Payne was told that the old man was not interrupted for fear of breaking the thread of his recollections. The evening was thus spent without yielding to Mr. Payne any of the historical material he hoped to secure; so in the morning the visitor asked to have the conversation of the night before repeated slowly and "linkistered" or interpreted so that Mr. Payne could write it down; but he had no sooner placed himself for the task than Guess said that he had not remembered the whole tradition right "but if he could have his old friend Tobacco Will, and another man now at Red River, with him, they could make out to recall, among them, enough to do the story proper credit; but, unless he could manage thus, he would rather not expose himself to be criticized by the old people, who might say he had not reported the truth"; and thus the modesty or diffidence of Guess deprived posterity of his interesting recollections.

Within a year after Payne's visit, General Ethan Allen Hitchcock, a distinguished army officer, came to the Cherokee Nation on a tour of investigation. Here he met and observed Sequoyah, Guess, or Gist, as he called him. In his diary and in a letter to the secretary of war he wrote his impressions and information imparted to him by Chief John Ross and other Cherokees:

"Guess, Guest, Gist, who invented the Cherokee alphabet . . . . Mr. Ross told me last night that he is of mixed blood. That General Taylor of Cincinnati told him in Washington City some years ago that a Virginian, a Mr. Gist, had been sent among the Cherokees on some mission where he remained for some time and expressed his belief that the Cherokee Guess was the son of Mr. Gist. That Mr. Gist was the father of the present Mrs. [Francis Preston] Blair, wife of the editor of the [Washington Daily] Globe. Mr. Ross seemed to have no doubt of this.

"I have just been talking with Mr. Payne, a young man of mixed blood living at the mouth of the Sallisaw. Payne was educated at the Dwight Mission as he says by Asa Hitchcock, who is a cousin of mine from Brimfield, Massachusetts, now residing in Illinois. Payne speaks English and Cherokee and writes both languages. He says that Gist came to this country with the Chief Jolly in 1818 and used to live down in Illinois Bayou in Arkansas. That when he set about inventing letters he was not only ridiculed but very much abused and that very many ignorant Cherokees feared that he was engaged in a league with dark powers for the discovery of something that would become a great injury to the nation. Says that Gist had great difficulty in satisfying the Cherokees. That on one occasion being distant from the council then in session he wrote a message to one of his pupils at the Council and sent the written paper declaring first its contents and requiring the messenger after hearing it read to bear testimony to it. He did so, certifying to the correspondence between the reading of the message at the Council and Gist's account of it at the time he sent it. This he says had a great effect in relieving the fears of the people.

"Mr. Payne says that Gist's grandfather on the mother's side was part Shawnee and his father a white man, so that he had very little Cherokee blood in him. He tells me he is precisely in the same situation. It pleased him to praise Gist who he says has a very good head, 'can express a great idea in a few words,' adding that he is now and has been for a long time engaged in writing a history of the Cherokees.

It is generally known that the Cherokee has become a written language, through the invention of signs by 'the philosopher Guess.' This man . . . . has an extremely interesting, intelligent countenance, full of cheerful animation with an evident vein of good humor—may be 55 or 60 years of age—habitually wears a shawl turban and dresses rudely, as if not caring for the outward man. His walk has been impaired by a rheumatic affection which has contracted one of his limbs. He has been a kind of Silver Smith among the natives and was early fond of exercising a talent for drawing pictures of men and horses and other animals. He invented the Syllabic signs in the 'Old Country' and emigrated to this country in 1818. It is a remarkable fact that while engaged in inventing the signs for writing Cherokee he was ridiculed by some for his temerity, while many of the common people took alarm and became apprehensive that he was in league with the powers of darkness for the discovery of something that was to work great mischief to the nation; and nothing was wanting but the power, to make him renounce his discovery and desist from his labor.

"I have not introduced this detail to add truisms; but to state that by means of the invention of Guess the Cherokees have been furnished with considerable reading in their native language, including translations of portions of scripture. The entire gospel of Matthew and John and several of Paul's Epistles; and they have a neat little volume of hymns in Cherokee, which they sing with remarkable skill and taste. It is known that in the Old Country (as they call their former country east of the Mississippi) they had a newspaper issued among them printed one half in English and one half in Cherokee. I am informed that a Cherokee can learn to write his language in three days or even a less time."

Sequoyah's son, who served as interpreter during the Cherokee emigration 1838–39, told one of the doctors attending the emigrants many interesting things about his father. He said the thoughts of Guess were first directed to the making of an alphabet by observing his nephew who had just returned from a distant school, spelling some words, whereupon he immediately exclaimed that he could effect the same in his vernacular tongue. He constructed a hut in a retired location where he could carry on his studies in private. Constantly engaged in making queer marks on stones and bark and scraps of paper, and from morning to night making unaccountable and unintelligible articulations as he practiced all the sound forms of the Cherokee language, it is small wonder that his superstitious fellow countrymen became suspicious of him. Believing that he was engaged in some diabolical plan to destroy the nation they succeeded in drawing him from his hermitage, when they burned up his cabin, hieroglyphics and all. But nothing daunted, he returned to his supposed black art until he had accomplished his object.

47

In the summer of 1842, a few months after Colonel Hitchcock saw him, Guess departed from the Cherokee Nation. He spent some time in the vicinity of Park Hill, making his preparations and assembling a company he had induced to travel with him, whom he pledged to secrecy concerning his mission. The companion on whom he seemed to rely principally was the Cherokee named The Worm, who afterwards related their experiences to the editor of the *Cherokee Advocate* in which they were published.

They spent some days at the home of Archibald Campbell and purchased supplies and equipment from Lewis Ross in the same neighborhood. When they got under way there were nine mounted men in the party with three pack horses: George Guess, his son Tessee Guess, The Worm, and six others. They crossed the Arkansas river a short distance below Fort Gibson, passed Edwards's settlement on Little River near the present Holdenville, and took Leavenworth's road to Red River, where they arrived fifteen days later. While Guess remained here in camp to rest, he dispatched The Worm and two of the young men in the party to the Wichita village on the south side of Red River near the mouth of Cache Creek. Their mission there was to inquire whether there were living in the vicinity any Cherokee Indians who had come from Mexico. They were informed that there were no Cherokees living among the Wichitas but that there were some on the Washita River.

After twelve days they returned and found Guess very sick. He had been unable to find suitable food and though they offered him honey and venison, of which they found an abundance, he was unable to eat of them and said he desired bread, of which there was none. The Worm then found some wild plums of which Guess ate freely and he became better.

The Worm then planned to depart again next morning, four days travel to the Wichita village to procure bread and other food that the old man could eat.

"Observing me make ready," related The Worm, "he enquired if I were going back to the village? and when informed of my determination to do so, approved the plan and requested that I should go and return in my former route; as he and the rest of the company would follow on, if he should be able to ride, and we should thus meet some sooner again. While sick, and at other times, when not traveling, he was constantly writing. On the morning of the fifth day after leaving Sequoyah, the second time, myself and company arrived at the Wichetaw village, where we bought about three bushels of corn at three dollars per bushel, packed it on our horses and immediately started back. On the evening of the third day of our return, my horse gave out, but fortunately, we met Sequoyah and party. It was then determined to encamp, and hunting up a shady place with good water, a fire was immediately made and the men began to prepare some food, which he was very impatient to obtain. He ate freely of bread, honey, and a kind of hommony. After eating he felt much refreshed, requested a pipe and some tobacco; smoked, expressed himself much better and then requested to lie down, that he might stretch his weary limbs for rest. I took a seat close by him and inquired what was his complaint. He replied, that he had been taken with a pain in his breast, which extended to different parts of his body, but that he felt so much refreshed from eating, he thought he should now

49

soon get well, by the aid of diet. Feeling so well that evening, and wishing to continue on to the village, as some of the company were anxious to buy horses, he proposed to rest the next day at his camp, and on the following, go forward to some water course, where we should spend a couple of days—thinking by this time he would be able to travel. It was his purpose not to remain long among the Wichetaws, but to return to the timbered country, where we could hunt.

"After the expiration of the time allowed above for rest, he hurried on, that he might soon return, to the hunting grounds —his health continued to improve. On the second morning after the meeting noticed above, the company left the camp, travelled part of a day—came to a water course, where we encamped two nights and a day, and then set out for the village, at which we arrived, after travelling nearly three days. We came to the village of the Echasi, in the neighborhood of the other villages. Soon after arriving and encamping, the head man of the Echasi, called by the Cherokees, Oo-till-ka, or the man who has a feather in his head, came to the camp, met us as his friends, said that he was very sorry to find the old man so sick, and that he would take him to his lodge, where he could take care of him. He would not talk much to him, for fear of wearying him while sick, but busied himself in providing such nourishing food as he could eat. This chief is very kind to all strangers.

"The next morning after breakfast, the Chief told the company to visit any of the villages, as if at home, without ceremony, and to buy such things as they wished. This they did, visited all the villages and did not return until late in the evening. The following morning after breakfast awhile, a messenger arrived from the Chief of the most remote village, that of the Wichetaws, 4 miles off, inviting the company to his lodge, as he should have something for them to eat. His invitation was accepted and the company, excepting myself and young Guess, who stayed with the old man, accompanied back the messenger, and spent the day with the Wichetaws.

"About noon of this day, Sequoyah became much better and requested that the Chief with whom he was staying, might come into the lodge set apart for him. Oo-till-ka did so, took a seat near by where Sequoyah was seated, and said to him: 'I am glad to see you in my lodge. I am friendly with all of the tribes north of me, and meet them always as friends. I am glad to inform you that, though all these tribes were once at war against each other, they have made treaties of peace and now hold each other so firmly by the hand that nothing can separate them.' He said further, that, on the day previous, he and the principal men of the six neighboring villages, had met together and he was glad to have an opportunity, now, to converse a little with him upon those things about which they had met in council—which were concerning the peace and friendship existing between the different tribes; but as they had no good interpreter, what had already passed was as much as they could expect. Sequoyah seemed to be very weak, he proposed that he should lie down again and rest, which he did.

"Then a messenger came to Oo-till-ka, to inform him of the arrival, at a neighboring village, of a Texan runner, inviting them to meet the Texans in council, near the Waco old-village. —The Chief then told Sequoyah that he would talk more with him in the morning, when he was stronger, but would now go to see the Texan. He left. Sequoyah continued laying until evening, (the chief not having yet returned), when he again set up.

"Sequoyah then inquired of me whether I did not think it would be better for the young men of our company, to return, as they might become sick by remaining in the village? I replied that I should agree in his opinions.

"The next morning Sequoyah said to our company, 'My friends, we are a long way from our homes; I am very sick, and may long remain so before I recover. Tomorrow therefore, I wish you all to return home, but my son and Worm, who will journey on with me. I wish you to consent to my proposal; for should we all continue on and some of you be taken sick, it will not be within our power to give such proper attention.' To this request they acceded, and took leave.

"Sequoyah, his son and myself, then prepared to resume our journey, which we did after Sequoyah had talked a little with the Chief, Oo-till-ka, and made him some presents of tobacco and other small articles.

"At the instance of Sequoyah, we took our former route, on the sixth day arrived at the place selected by him as a camping ground, where we spent four days in hunting and then went on until we came to a water course, at which Sequoyah wished to rest some days for the purpose of bathing himself and that a supply of honey might be obtained. He said, at this place, that his health was improving, but he was afflicted still with pains, and a cough, which had the effect to weaken him. After four days' rest, we made ready to start; He then said to me, 'My friend, we are here, in the wilderness; do not get tired of me, I desire to reach the Mexican country. You know the course.'

Being assured of my willingness to go with him, he requested me to take the course—which I did. Travelling on five days more, he again said to us, 'You will not get tired of me, altho' sick? If I die you can do what seems best, but while alive be guided by me.' Continuing on for ten days, we came to a water course, where we rested four days. A few days after, while encamped on a river, the report of guns was heard and then a drum. In descending the river to discover who were so near us, we came upon a road along which some persons had just passed. When appraised of this, Sequoyah determined to follow on the next morning, and overtake them.

"We then took the road and when we overtook them, found them to be Shawnees, and with whom we encamped that night. The next morning the Shawnees inquired of Sequoyah, where he was going? He replied, that he had a great anxiety to visit the country of the Mexicans, but should return in a short time. The Shawnees stated that they were on a hunting expedition, that he could proceed on his way and, if he found any thing interesting, they would be glad to hear it on his return. He then inquired of them the direction of the nearest Mexican towns, or villages? which they pointed out in the same course, Sequoyah remarked, that I had been pointing. We then started and traveled six days in succession, when we stopped—with the intention of hunting a few days, but the old man determined to proceed directly on until we came to a large water course. We proceeded on until a while after sun up, and having crossed a mountain, we came to a small branch but passed on, till we reached a very beautiful, bubbling spring, where the company halted. While still mounted, a number of bees came to the spring, when Sequoyah said, 'As we are neither runaways nor in such a hurry, but that we can stop and look for some honey;' and requested me to hand him some water.

"We encamped at the spring—soon after pulling the saddles off our horses, Young Guess walked away a short distance, and found a bee tree. We spent two nights at this spring. The second night that we encamped there, some Tewockenee Indians came upon us, and stole all our horses; we pursued some distance and could probably have overtaken them, but were afraid to leave the old man long alone, and so returned to the camp. The next morning he requested us to take him to some safe hiding place; to secrete our effects in the tops of trees, and proceed straight to the village of the Tewockenees. After complying with the first part of his request, he altered his determination, and told us not to go in search of our horses which might be some time or other recovered, but to proceed directly to the Mexican settlements, where probably we could obtain other horses.

"We set out on foot in the evening, leaving the old man alone. Travelling on some four miles, Young Guess and myself came to a river called Mauluke, which could not be crossed. We ascended it some distance, until late in the evening and then encamped for the night: in the morning made a raft, crossed the river, proceeded that day a short distance, and again encamped. About noon, the day following, while eating, the reports of many guns were heard in the direction of our route. We immediately proceeded on at a rapid rate till we cleared the mountains and, coming to a prairie, saw the tracks of a wagon.—Here we halted and spent some time, I having advised my companion that we had perhaps, better not proceed to the town until towards night.

"I felt convinced that we were lost, but was unwilling to express an indisposition to proceed on, lest my companion should consider me cowardly. We however, pushed on until we came within about one hundred yards of the town, when hearing a good deal of talking, we stopped and, listening, heard none but the Spanish language. Having turned around and walked back a short distance, we encamped for the night, determined not to go into the Fort until morning. This night we did not sleep much as the firing of guns was kept up throughout the night. The place was San Antonio. In the morning, proceeding into Town, we were not perceived by any one until we got in some distance, when we met with two soldiers, who came up, shook our hands friendly and requested us to follow them. We did so, until met by an officer who, inviting the soldiers and ourselves to follow him, conducted us around a considerable portion of San Antonio to a store, where the people were drinking. The officer having entered the store for a few seconds, told us to follow him to the quarters of the commanding officer, and informed us that we were then in a situation that we could do nothing, intimating that we were prisoners.

"Upon entering the quarters of the commanding officer, he seated himself upon the opposite side of the room from that occupied by ourselves and the soldiers and others who crowded around us. Remaining silent for sometime, and then pacing the room to and fro, this officer at length, came to us and inquired, of what tribe we were, and when informed, declared that he did not at all like the Cherokees, because they had been, a short time previous warring against the Texans. When apprised, that we resided on the Arkansas, within the limits of the U.S., and that we wished to borrow horses, ours having been stolen by the Tewockenees, he repeated his dislike of the Cherokees, and said, he had no horses to lend, and that the Tewockenees and other tribes, some of whom were doubtless prowling about the neighborhood that day, had stolen many of their horses. He further inquired, whether we had any pass-ports? and when told none, said, they were necessary. To which it was replied, that we were ignorant of the fact, as we had frequently visited the towns and settlements of the whites in Arkansas, without ever having any demanded of us. We were also told by him that they would have fired upon and killed us had it not been for the *caps* on our heads, which alone saved us, as the neighboring tribes go with bare heads.

"Sometime was spent in conversation with the officer, who became quite friendly, and gave us tobacco, pass-ports, and a very good axe, that we might bring thereafter a quantity of honey. He also admonished us to be on our guard, in going about the country, as there were many hostile persons among the wild tribes. We then parted.

"In going through the town some of the women called and invited us to take something to eat, but we told them we could not, being in a great hurry—soon after leaving the town, met three or four soldiers, riding very sorry ponies, who also told us to be on the lookout, as there were many Comanches about. After leaving them we began to travel pretty fast, and kept increasing our speed until we got into a run, and throwing away the borrowed axe—travelled a great distance that day,

"Se-Quo-Yah Teaching Ah-Yo-Keh the Alphabet," by Miss C. S. Robbins.
From George E. Foster, Se-Quo-Yah, the American Cadmus and Modern
Moses (*Philadelphia, 1885*)

Sequoyah's cabin in Indian Territory

for fear that the Texans might intend to entrap or take some advantage of us.

"The day after leaving San Antonio, we arrived at the camp of Sequoyah, who was well and fast gaining strength. He then requested we should procure him a good supply of provisions, find a secure retreat and set out again, for the Mexican settlements to get horses. A safe retreat was found some three miles from the encampment; he was placed in it and a supply of honey and venison sufficient to last him twenty days procured. The secure retreat was in a cave, which seemed to be above high water; but in case that it should not be, there was a log which he could climb up easily to a more elevated place. Having placed him in this cave, we set out, and travelled on two days; on the third day, which was windy, just as we were approaching a cedar thicket, I happened to look behind, and saw three men coming upon us at full speed. We fell back upon a small patch of timber and threw down our packs for the purpose of defending ourselves; as they came near, I hailed them, and enquired in the Comanche language, if they were friends? They said they were, and immediately threw down their lances and arrows, and came up and shook hands with us, and said as we are friends we will sit down and smoke the pipe.

"The Comanches then said, that when they first saw us they supposed us to be Texans by having on caps, but when they got nearer and saw feathers in them, they took us to be Shawnees or Delawares, and that had it not been for the feathers in our caps, they would have fired upon us. This was the second time that feathers in our caps had probably saved our lives—and they had just been placed there by young Guess, who had killed a turkey. After smoking, one of the Comanches returned for their women whom they had left, upon discovering our tracks. They then inquired where we were going, and when informed, said that our route would be very rough and mountainous; but as they were going there themselves, if well, we would all travel together, as they would be able to show us a nearer and better route. This we consented to and travelled with them three days; we then separated, and travelled fourteen consecutive days before reaching the frontier settlements of Mexico. Before reaching the town we came to a river that we could not cross and had to encamp. Not being aware whether we were near any habitations or not, it caused us so much anxiety that we could not sleep—when some time in the night we heard a drum.

"In the morning we rose early, and there happening to be a turkey seated on a tree near by, young Guess shot it. This we hastily prepared and ate. Soon as this was over we attempted to cross the river, but could not; we then set about making a raft, but just as we had a couple of logs, a mounted Mexican appeared on the opposite bank—inquired who we were, and informed us that there was a ferry lower down. On arriving at the ferry we found the boat ready and a company of armed men in attendance. After crossing, an officer informed us that he would go with us to the principal man of the town, which was about six miles distant; on reaching the town we observed many women washing, who as well as men and boys, immediately gathered around us, being entire strangers, and conducted us into the town. The officer stated the crowd was attracted by curiosity to see us as we were strangers; but had no intention to harm us. He conducted us to the head man of the place. We were led into the house of this man—the crowd that followed us and one that came meeting us, having stopped, at what we supposed to be the limits allowed them.

"The town was small—the houses made of large brick—the people dressed in different kinds of costumes. The houses looked odd, being low with flat roofs. Many of the women were very pretty. Thirteen officers were present. Much time was spent in looking up an Interpreter, who was a Spaniard, that spoke English. Soon as the Interpreter came, the Officer enquired who we were? And being informed, said he was glad to see us, and asked our notions and what object we had in view in visiting Mexico, and also if there were any news of importance from the Texans, whom, *he said* the Mexicans had a short time before defeated in battle, and taken some three hundred of them prisoners. Having satisfied him on these points, and given him to understand that we had not been despatched to his town on any special business of a public nature, he expressed the pleasure it gave him and the other officers to see us, and insisted on our remaining that night in the town, as the day was too far gone for us to reach the Cherokee village, which he informed us, was some thirty miles distant. He then had us conducted to a lodging place in the quarters of some soldiers, telling us to call before leaving in the morning, to receive passports.

"We remained some time in the house assigned us, and then took seats outside it, to observe the people and the soldiery, and sentinels on duty. While thus passing away the time, a Mexican approached me silently and touched my back in order to attract my attention towards him. I looked around, and beheld, pierced through with a stick that he had in his hands, a couple

59

of human ears, taken from one of four persons they had killed a short time before. An officer then came and requested us to walk about the town with him; we complied and followed him about for some time.—He conducted us, amongst other places, into a bake shop and into two or three houses, in each of which he gave us to drink of ardent spirits, which he called whisky, but which tasted very different from any we had ever before drunk. Before we had wandered much about the town, I felt lost, owing to the striking resemblance between its different parts. It being after the hour of twelve o'clock, there was but little business doing, as nearly all of the shops were closed. While yet rambling about the place, a soldier came, to request us to go back to our lodgings, upon reaching which we found the soldiers on parade, ready to march off a short distance. By invitation we joined them and kept along with them, until we came to a kind of public square, where there were a number of large kettles containing bread, beef and soup.

"From these large pots the waiters served the officers, ourselves, and the soldiers in order, by taking up pieces of meat with a fork and giving it to us in our hands. What was given me I ate through politeness, but with some difficulty, so highly seasoned was it with pepper, some of which I was so unfortunate as to get into my eyes. Early the next morning we met with a man who spoke English, and who conducted us to a place where we obtained a breakfast that an Indian could eat without cost, for the man who gave it to us said that he could not be behind the Cherokees; he had been much among them without any expense, he could not therefore charge us; but hoped that we would take our meals with him while we remained there.

"This day, we remained in town, but having passports, left the following morning, in company with a Mexican, who went with us to a town called by the Mexicans, 'San Cranto,' some thirty miles distant. Upon arriving at San Cranto, we were informed that there were a couple of Cherokees in the place, but thinking it would be difficult to find them, we went with our Mexican companion to the house of his brother where we spent the night and by good luck met with our countryman. It gave us great pleasure to see this man, whose name is Standing Rock. He answered a great many questions, and assured us that it would give the Cherokees in Mexico great joy to see their brothers among them, and proposed to accompany us forthwith to their village, about ten miles distant. About seven miles from San Cranto we passed through a small settlement of runaway negroes, some two or three of whom I met with spoke the Cherokee language. Three miles further we arrived at the Cherokee village, situated within a large prairie, in a grove of timber, half a mile wide, and some three miles long, and watered by means of a ditch, from a large spring, some two miles distant.

"Our brothers were very glad to see us, and gave us a warm welcome to their little village. Being soon apprised that we came to obtain assistance, to convey in the aged Sequoyah, who was very anxious to visit them, they declared their readiness to afford us company, but could not furnish any horses, as all of their's, save those that were very poor, had died, since they went into Mexico. They, however, promised to borrow some of the horses belonging to the Mexican army, at a neighboring town. But there being none, the commanding officer referred us back to San Cranto, to which place we returned, after two days' rest-ing with the Cherokees. The officer there could lend us but one horse, the others having been taken off a few days before, to some other post, but supplied us, without solicitation, with bread, meat, salt, sugar and coffee, for the journey. The company then, consisting of nine persons, immediately set off with the borrowed horse—crossed the river again at the ferry, and after constant travelling, on the seventeenth night, camped within a few miles of Sequoyah's cave. Much solicitude was felt by us, for the safety of the old man, as we saw much 'sign' of the wild Indians on our way. Three men were accordingly sent on in advance, to the Cave, with provisions to relieve his wants, if still alive, and in need.

"Mau-luke, we crossed on a raft. Shortly after passing over a very rocky country, we came upon a trail made by wild cattle and horses through a cedar thicket, and along which we discovered the tracks of a man, going in a different direction from ours. These tracks we soon discovered to be those of Sequoyah, from the fact of his being lame. This caused myself and another of the company to hasten to the cave, and gave us no little anxiety, as we discovered that several persons had been but recently along our way.

"Arriving at the cave, we met with our advance company, and discovered a log of wood leaning against a tree, and a letter bound to one of its limbs. The Letter was written by Sequoyah in his own native language, and informed us that, after being left alone, he had met with misfortune—the water having rose very high, drove him from his retreat and swept away his store of provisions and almost everything else; that, under these circumstances he had determined to pursue his journey; that if not too long absent we would be able to find him, as he would fire the grass along his way and the smoke would arise, and that he hoped, although out of provisions, to be able to support life until overtaken by us, as he had cut off meat from the heads of some deer skins. He had no gun, although persuaded to take one when setting out, but relied upon our rifles. We had now great hopes of soon overtaking him, as he had been gone but four days. After reading the letter, we immediately started in pursuit, tracked him to the Mauluke, which he had crossed on a raft.

"We left this camp and returned to our companions—tracked him to the river, saw where he had sat down, followed down the river and came to a raft he had crossed on; we crossed at the same place, came to one of his former camping grounds, and saw where a horse had been tied; feeling confident that he must have obtained a horse by some means or other, we followed on very fast to another camping ground, where we saw bones, which assured us that he had obtained food likewise. There were many speculations, how he had come by the horse and provisions, some surmising one thing and some another.— From the constant rapidity with which we pushed on, and our long journey, the Mexican horse as well as myself began to get tired; I then selected two men, and sent them ahead, while the rest encamped for the night. The two men kept on until night coming on, they lost his track near a creek, but did not stop, hoping to discover a light. They however passed by his camp, as they supposed from the appearance of the sign late in the evening, and returned. In passing near the river, they heard a horse neigh, and then penetrating into the centre of a thicket

63

in the forks of the river, found him seated by a lonely fire. He was greatly rejoiced to meet them. One of the men remained with him while the other returned, and conducted us next evening to his camp. He expressed the great happiness our return gave him; and said that his mind was relieved of much anxiety, as he had suffered much from sickness, and his lonely situation —fearing that his son and myself had either met with some accident or been killed.

"Again expressing the happiness our return gave him, he observed, that for two days past, he had as much provision as desired, and that we must have remarked his mode of travelling, which was brought about under the following circumstances. While engaged, he said, in making a raft to cross the Mauluke, that he might continue on towards Mexico, he suddenly took a notion that he would walk to the summit of a neighboring hill. Throwing down his tomahawk, he started up the hill, and just as the top was gained, to his great surprise, he came close upon three men, who quickly halting, one of them declared themselves to be 'Delawares,' and to which he replied, 'I am a Cherokee.' They camped with him that night, and gave him some of their victuals and partook of his honey. In the morning, the Delawares said to him, 'Come, let us now return to our own villages, we will take you to your door,' He replied, 'No, I have sent forward two young men to the Mexican country, whom I shortly expect back; I am anxious to visit that country. Go with me there. We will shortly return to our own country.' Finding that they could not agree, the Delawares said, that they would remain with him until they killed for him some meat, which they did. While they were hunting, he wrote a letter for them

64

to convey home. Being aged and crippled, the Delawares, when about to part with him, generously gave him a horse to ride.

" 'Such,' said Sequoyah, 'was the way he came by the horse' —and that he would now tell us what happened to him at the cave.

"The twelfth night after we left, the rain poured down and the water came into his cave. He placed all his effects upon a rock in the cave which the water soon surrounded and forced him on a large log. This in turn being moved by the water, he climbed the log, which his son and myself had leaned against the side of the cave and sought refuge in the ledge of the rock— having abandoned everything but a couple of blankets he tied around him; his flint, steel, and spunk and a few small articles that he could get into his pockets. From the ledge of rocks he succeeded in making his way out of the cave and ascending to the top of the hill, where he spent the night under a tree and in unceasing rain. In the morning, finding a dry place, he kindled a fire, by which he warmed himself and dried his clothing, and then went to look at his former home, but found it still covered with water.

"Two days after, he again returned and found that everything had been swept away. But following down the branch he found his saddle bags, around a little tree, from which he recovered all his papers and other things, and also a tent and three blankets; and on the day following a brass kettle. After this he made no further search—giving up all for lost; but even felt glad to escape as well as he did, especially with his life which he said was far more precious than aught else. The water having swept away his supply of food, he was now left entirely without, and when he could get nothing else, lived on what little flesh he could shave off from the skins of deer killed by us before leaving. During the greater part of the time however, he ate nothing but wild honey, which he obtained from a couple of large trees, that he fortunately discovered and felled at the expense of repeated efforts, with a small tomahawk. His health had not been good, but such he said, as would have confined almost any one to his bed. For each day that we were absent, before leaving his cave, he cut a notch in a large oak tree.

"We remained four or five days at the camp, where we found Sequoyah and in the vicinity, until a stock of provision was killed, and then resumed our journey, and after travelling sixteen days forded the river mentioned before, near the Mexican village. In a few days more, halting along for a short time at the different towns, where Sequoyah received the kindest hospitality from the Mexicans, the company arrived at the Cherokee village.

"The Worm spent some time with the Cherokees and then returned at the solicitation of Sequoyah, with a party of Caddoes, to the Wichitaw town to recover, if possible, the horses that had been stolen from them. He was unable to get them, and not meeting with any person going to Mexico, could not return early as expected. At length several Caddoes arrived from Mexico and brought tidings that Sequoyah was no more, which was soon confirmed by a party of Cherokees. The complaint that terminated his life, was the cough which had long afflicted him, combined perhaps with some disease common in that country. His death was sudden—having been long confined to the house, he requested one day some food, and while it was preparing breathed his last."

The next year after Sequoyah's departure from home, the Cherokee National Council, on October 25, 1843, passed an act authorizing the publication of a national newspaper to be called the *Cherokee Advocate*. It had for its object the diffusion of important news among the Cherokee people, the advancement of their general interest, and defense of Indian rights. It was to be published both in English and in the Cherokee language in the characters of Sequoyah's invention. The editor was to be selected by the national council, and he was to publish all laws and treaties affecting the Indians.

Five days after the enactment of the measure establishing the *Cherokee Advocate* an act was passed declaring all the salt springs in the Cherokee Nation to be the property of the Nation to which a rental or royalty thereafter would have to be paid for their use. However, with a continued sense of obligation to the long absent Sequoyah, it was expressly provided that his salt spring was excepted from the operation of this law, so that he could continue to make salt there rent free.

The first issue of the *Cherokee Advocate* appeared September 26, 1844. The paper contained four pages of six columns each. It was a useful organ of the Cherokee people, who found in it all the laws currently enacted by their national council and much other valuable information, besides the news of the day. Publication of the *Advocate* was suspended for lack of funds September 28, 1853, and was not resumed until April 26, 1870. With slight interruptions it was published from that time until 1906.

Preceding the *Advocate* by a few weeks was the *Cherokee Messenger,* printed on the Baptist Mission press a few miles north of where is now Westville, Oklahoma. Twelve numbers in English and the Cherokee characters of Sequoyah appeared from August, 1844, to May, 1846. The first number contained much information about Sequoyah's alphabet and instructions concerning the principles involved, to facilitate the study of it.

About two weeks after the first issue of the *Cherokee Advocate* members of the Cherokee National Council met in regular session in October, 1844. Proud of their national newspaper, their thoughts naturally turned to Sequoyah, more than any other man responsible for their progress on the road to literacy. He had been gone more than two years.

"But what," their anxiety was expressed in the columns of the *Advocate,* "has become of this remarkable man, whose native genius has struck light from darkness—conferred inconceivable blessings upon his people and achieved for his own name an enviable distinction among those few truly great names, with which are connected imperishible honor? is he still alive? or does his venerable head repose beneath some unknown clod of the Grand Prairie? These are questions that we cannot now, satisfactorily answer.

"The Council of this Nation," continued the *Advocate,* "out of respect for his character and in consideration of his great invention, have allowed him, for many years, an annual pension." When this pension was inaugurated is not stated, but December 29, more than a year after Sequoyah departed from the Cherokee Nation the national council passed an act providing that "in lieu of the sum allowed to George Guess, in consideration of his invention of the Cherokee alphabet, passed December 10th, 1841, and which is hereby repealed, the sum of three hundred dollars to be paid to the said George Guess out of the National Treasury, annually, during his natural life." It provided also that in the event of the death of Guess the pension should be paid to his wife Sally Guess annually as long as she should live. Annual appropriations were accordingly made thereafter to meet the payments of the pension, and in 1853 when financial difficulties had greatly depreciated the value of Cherokee warrants, the council, with a strict sense of obligation, passed an act directing the treasurer of the nation to pay Sally Guess cash for the warrant issued to her December 16, 1852. This was probably the first literary pension in American history, and certainly the first and only one ever granted by an Indian tribe.

Continued the *Advocate's* account of Sequoyah's wanderings: "Several reports concerning him, have reached his friends in this country. That which seems to be most probable, when the hardships to which in his wanderings, he has been necessarily exposed are remembered in addition to his decrepit form, and the weight of many years, is that this truly great man full of years and of honors, sleeps the sleep *of Death,* in some wild and unknown spot, far from his wife, his country, and his people."

Anxious to discover the whereabouts of their long absent countryman, the Cherokees applied to Indian Agent Pierce M. Butler for funds with which to finance a search for him. Butler, on November 23, presented the matter to the secretary of war, who, on January 17, 1845, authorized the expenditure of $200 of tribal funds in the effort to discover Sequoyah and bring him home.

The Cherokees were delighted, said the *Advocate,* with the provisions "for tracing up the venerable wanderer and restoring him to his family and country. Governor Butler feels the liveliest interest in the destiny of George Guess, whose name shall be forever enshrined in the affections of his whole people. He will take immediate measures to carry out the designs of the War Department, which receive our sincere acknowledgements and which we ardently hope may be crowned with entire success. There is no event, we are persuaded, that would afford more heartfelt joy to the Cherokees at large, than to have their distinguished countryman among them once more."

Apparently the messengers who were to look for Sequoyah had not departed on their errand March 6, 1845, for on that day the *Advocate* carried the following information: "George Guess. —Recent intelligence has been received which renders it highly probable that the inventor of the Cherokee alphabet has not, as is generally supposed, been gathered to his fathers, but is still among the living. If the intelligence be correct, he is now with some of his countrymen, who are living near Matamoros, Mexico. Some Cherokees are supposed to leave this country, in the course of a short time for Matamoros, for the purpose of restoring him to his country, if still alive."

Further information touching the fate of Sequoyah and the search for him is disclosed by the following statement of some of his companions on their route home, to Cherokee Agent Pierce M. Butler: "Warren's Trading House, Red River, April 21st, 1845. We, the undersigned Cherokees, direct from the

Spanish dominions, do hereby certify, that George Guess, of the Cherokee Nation, Arkansas, departed this life in the town of Sanfernando in the month of August, 1843, and his son (Chusaleta) is at this time on the Brasas River, Texas, about 30 miles above the falls, and intends returning home this fall.

"Given under our hands day and date above written. Standing Rock [by mark], Standing Bowles [by mark], Watch Justice [by mark], Witness: Daniel G. Watson, Jesse Chisholm."

There is also the later report in the characters of Sequoyah's invention to Agent Butler by Oo-no-leh, one of the messengers sent to search for him. The report, as translated into English reads as follows: "P. M. Butler Cherokee Agent, Sir; After reaching Red River on my way, I met with the following Cherokees from Mexico:—Jesse, the leader of the party, The Worm, Gah-na-nes-kee, The Standing Man and The Standing Rock. The last named, The Standing Rock, attended Sequoyah during his last sickness and also witnessed his death and burial. Isse-sa-de-tah, the son of Sequoyah, remains on Red River. He is very sorry that the remains of his father are buried so far from his own country, and remains where he is on this account.

"As Sequoyah was the object for which I had started in search, and having learned the fact of his death which I am communicating to those who sent me, it will be useless for me to proceed further. I will return toward home. He is dead without a doubt. His remaining family, widow, two daughters and a young man live somewhere in Skin Bayou District.

"Bayou District, 15th May, 1845.   Oo-no-leh."

The personality, occupation and environment of this remarkable Indian are elusive, particularly before 1821 when he completed his invention. He was obviously possessed of a strong sense of public concern and duty which with an active and brilliant mind brought forth his great work. No writer about Sequoyah has ever before mentioned his military service, which introduces a new phase of character. This occupation, his wedding to Sally, participation in the treaty council of 1816, his journey to Arkansas in 1818, are meager hints of some of the other things that engaged the attention and energies of Guess during the nine years he was working on his alphabet.

And what about his lameness? Observers and writers have said that he was lame from disease since childhood. But it is hard to believe a cripple would have been accepted in the army; this suggests the thought that he was wounded in the service, but the records in the war department contradict that supposition. The picture of this Indian philosopher limping along with his company into battle from a strong sense of public duty is an intriguing one at least.

The late W. J. Weaver of Fort Smith said he knew Sequoyah and his family well. When they lived about fifteen miles from Fort Smith on Skin Bayou in Sequoyah district, Cherokee Nation, from 1839 to 1842 he often enjoyed the hospitality of their cabin home in his rides in the vicinity, and traded with them in his store in Fort Smith for their products, "such as honey, butter, eggs, chickens, deer and coon skins which they exchanged for family supplies; but they never bought any whiskey, and I think they were strictly temperate."

Mr. Weaver wrote of Sequoyah at some length for his paper, the Fort Smith *Elevator,* retailing much that was already in print or set forth here. Unfortunately he did not tell much of his impressions of the Indian. He did say, however, that he would have been taken for a full-blood. Differing with other observers, he said "he was quiet and morose in manner and would not talk English, but he understood it; in this respect he was like many other Indians, who would speak to you in their language and understand you in English. His wife was different. She was affable, pleasant, talkative, and spoke the English language fluently, and it was from her that I learned much of George's history." She lived in the neighborhood many years after the death of her husband. "She was a good housekeeper; she was always dressed in homespun wear, and had a loom. In fact at that time many of the Cherokees were expert in spinning, weaving and coloring, and seldom bought any clothing but 'ontnowo yunago' (white domestic) for underwear. George always wore the conventional homespun hunting shirt trimmed with red fringe, with a red shawl twisted around his head as a turban. Tessee, his son, was grown to manhood, and his daughter was about seventeen, both unmarried, when their father went to Mexico. The family lived comfortably on their farm and had ponies, cattle and hogs on the range." After his return from Mexico Tessee related to Mr. Weaver interesting accounts of their wanderings, which unfortunately were not preserved.

Heroic and pathetic was the figure of this man groping in the dark for something he had never seen; an objective only vaguely conceived, but something he very definitely believed he could bring into being for the great good of his people. Toiling, striving patiently alone, with no human being to bear him company, none to understand or encourage, none with whom he could communicate or ask counsel; unable to read in any language and therefore unable to call to his aid any of the accumulated wisdom and experience of the white man. By his industry and perseverance incurring the misunderstanding, ridicule and hostility of those he was trying to serve.

Ignorant of the writings and teachings of white philosophers, Sequoyah hit upon the great truth, and what to him was an original discovery, that enlightenment and civilization of a people would progress and develop in proportion as they were able to express themselves and preserve their ideas upon the written and printed page, and exchange these ideas, one with another by this medium.

For the instruction and enlightenment of the people many temperance and other tracts, primers, spelling books, arithmetics, annual almanacs, passages from the Scriptures, catechisms, hymn books, and other publications were printed in whole or in part with the type of Sequoyah on the Mission press at Park Hill. The same characters were used in the printing of the constitution and laws of the Cherokee Nation in various editions, resolutions of the national council, messages of the chiefs, on the national press at Tahlequah, the capital, from which issued the *Cherokee Advocate*. Even the current acts of the legislative council were printed in this same medium and promptly circulated among all the people who read them with interest and profit.

As a result, the Cherokees became better informed of their laws and the actions of their public servants than members of any other Indian tribe. Published in fairly limited editions, in the main nearly one hundred years ago, few of these prints are to be seen outside occasional libraries of collectors and great public institutions, where they are reserved among the rare books. A quantity of the Cherokee type used on the national Press is now deposited in the United States National Museum at Washington.

Thinking of Sequoyah and his achievements the mind is bewildered in trying to conceive the background that produced this miracle. While it is agreed that his mother was an Indian woman of the Cherokee tribe, conflicting theories of the paternity of Sequoyah have flowed from the pens of many writers. After weighing all the evidence the account given here is believed to be authentic and plausible.

The most convincing testimony on the point made contemporaneously with the living Sequoyah was the previously quoted statement by Gen. Ethan Allen Hitchcock while he was in the Cherokee Nation in 1841, where he met and observed Sequoyah. Like many others he was curious about the parentage of this remarkable man. He wrote in his diary what he heard on the point from the lips of Chief John Ross.

Some writers have subscribed to the wholly improbable and unauthenticated theory that Sequoyah's father was a vagabond itinerant German named George Gist, whose rovings brought him in the Cherokee Nation. That the amazing genius of this remarkable Indian must have been sired by a man of vastly superior qualifications is obvious.

Such a man was Nathaniel Gist, a friend of George Washington, who spent many years among the Cherokees in the capacity of hunter, explorer, and soldier. Their attachment to Gist had induced them to give him Long Island, a valuable holding in the Little Tennessee River. So intimate was he with

75

the Indians that his loyalty to the whites came under suspicion and it required an official inquiry by the governor and general assembly of Virginia to clear him of the charge of aiding the Cherokees in their hostilities against the whites. The council made its findings December 17, 1776, vindicating Gist and in less than a month he was commissioned colonel of a regiment in the Continental Army. Washington then sent him to the Cherokees to secure recruits for the army and he brought seventeen warriors to Virginia to fight for the Colonies against Great Britain.

The arguments that have been adduced relating to this subject are much too extended to be set out here but they are sufficient in the mind of the Author to establish that the father of Sequoyah could not have been the German clod whose existence even is not established, but must have been Nathaniel Gist, progenitor of many other distinguished Americans.

Nathaniel Gist was married in 1783 to Judith Cary Bell and by this union were born several daughters who married prominent men: One, Sarah Howard Gist, married Jesse Bledsoe, United States senator from Kentucky; Anne Cary Gist married Dr. Joseph Boswell; Eliza Gist married Francis Preston Blair, distinguished journalist, publicist and editor of the Washington *Globe;* they were the parents of Montgomery Blair, a member of Lincoln's cabinet, and Francis Preston Blair, Jr., United States senator from Missouri and a brigadier-general in the Civil War; Maria C. Gist, a fourth daughter of Nathaniel Gist, married Benjamin Gratz, a wealthy citizen of Lexington.

Francis P. Blair, Jr., was the Democratic candidate for vice president with Seymour in 1868; and B. Gratz Brown was the

76

Democratic candidate for the same office on the ticket with Horace Greeley in 1872. Major Gist Blair, son of Lincoln's postmaster general, owns and occupies the historic and interesting old Blair home on Pennsylvania Avenue in Washington. He cherishes many authentic family traditions of kinship to Sequoyah, with which he has generously aided the Author.

In the Bureau of American Ethnology in Washington is a letter written by John Mason Brown of the Louisville bar, a descendant of Nathaniel Gist, who stated that Sequoyah had visited the Gist descendants in Kentucky, probably on his way to or from Washington in 1828; on this occasion he was looking up his white kin. Maj. Gist Blair told the Author that when he was a youth about 1878, he went to Kentucky to see some of the Gratz relatives and there learned of the accepted fact that Sequoyah was the son of Nathaniel Gist.

Major Blair hopes to discover the names and records of the seventeen Cherokees who enlisted with Nathaniel Gist and aid in enrolling their male descendants in the Sons of the American Revolution, of which he is an active and prominent member.

The witnesses quoted in this sketch not only strongly support the Nathaniel Gist theory of the paternity of Sequoyah, but make his birthday nearer the birth of our country than 1760 or thereabouts, a date frequently ascribed to Sequoyah. The latter date would make him 53 years old when in 1813, he enlisted for service in the Creek War. It is much easier to believe he was then under 40, as he would have been if he had been born in 1773 or later, than to believe that on the waning side of middle age he went to war.

The name and fame of Sequoyah have been recorded in

honorable remembrance and still survive, long after his alphabet has passed into the realm of historic *curioso,* while its influence continues as a vital force in the civilization of Oklahoma. In 1851 the Cherokee Council changed the name of Skin Bayou District in which Sequoyah lived to Sequoyah District. Substantially the same area became Sequoyah County of the new state of Oklahoma. For this great Indian was named the giant redwood tree of California, and in 1902 the Sequoya League, with headquarters in California, designed to improve the conditions of all Indians.

During the summer of 1905 a convention of representative citizens of the Indian Territory, Indians and whites, at Muskogee wrote a constitution for a proposed state of the Union which they named Sequoyah. This document, signalizing the first political co-operation of the Indians and whites was submitted for popular vote of the people of the Indian Territory and adopted by a majority of more than 47,000. However, it was rejected by the national administration in favor of a plan for a state to be composed of the union of Indian Territory and Oklahoma Territory two years later.

In 1911 when Oklahoma was four years old, the legislature provided for the placing of a statue of Sequoyah in Statuary Hall in the National Capitol. A contract for the making of the statue was entered into with the sculptor Vinnie Ream. Protracted ill health prevented her from executing the commission, and after her death in 1916 her husband, General Hoxie, requested the Washington sculptor George Julian Zolnay to take over the contract. Given a free hand in planning the work, he undertook it enthusiastically. The garb worn by the Sequoyah

78

of Statuary Hall is not that of the Sequoyah of history, but the reason is explained by Mr. Zolnay in a letter to the Author: "It might also interest you to know that one of the determining factors of success, both artistically and historically, was my determination to use the blanket which is highly characteristic and invests the statue with a dignity no other treatment could have given it." In making the statue Mr. Zolnay used as a model Miss Ann Ross, a Cherokee of Oklahoma, great granddaughter of Chief John Ross, who helped him, he said, in catching the racial characteristics of the subject. This classic statue was unveiled and presented by Oklahoma to the United States on June 6, 1917, with appropriate addresses and other proceedings in Statuary Hall, in the Senate and in the House.

When Sequoyah departed for Mexico in 1843 the home in which he left his family was a log cabin. A set of house logs cut by him, with which he planned to build another room, lay near by. In 1855, the year she presented her bounty claim to the Indian Office, Guess's widow sold the property to another Cherokee named George Blair, who constructed the additional room so that his home became a double log house with a huge stack chimney between the two rooms. Mr. Blair died in 1887 at the age of ninety-eight years and his remains lie in the little family cemetery near by. Among his survivors was a son Thomas, who was born in 1844 and died in 1932.

In 1930 the Author of this sketch visited the Sequoyah-Blair home and secured pictures and a statement concerning its history from Mr. Thomas Blair. He was eleven years old when his father bought it and not only recalled the transaction, Mrs. Guess, and her children, but remembered the things his father told him touching the history of the place. He recalled that after the sale Mrs. Guess and her two children removed to another home a few miles southwest and the Blair family occupied the Sequoyah improvements. These things the Author reduced to writing which was signed by Mr. Blair and filed in the archives of the Oklahoma Historical Society. This statement, with the result of other investigations and study, was employed by him in the press of Oklahoma and other quarters in promoting a movement for the preservation of the Sequoyah home.

In 1936 Judge R. L. Williams, Hon. W. W. Hastings and the Author took steps to this end. Title to ten acres of land, including the Sequoyah home, was secured in the name of the State of Oklahoma for the use and benefit of the Oklahoma Historical Society. Approval of a Federal Works Progress Administration project was secured, under which was performed all the work of construction now in evidence at the Sequoyah shrine. The north room, constructed by Mr. Blair after Sequoyah left the country, was torn down and the original log cabin enclosed in a handsome stone structure. The logs of the north room were employed in the construction of a custodian's lodge near the entrance. Water works, a toilet and lighting system have been installed and the whole ten acres enclosed by a handsome stone wall. For the purchase of the material that went into this shrine, donations amounting to more than $4,000 were made by a number of Creek, Seminole, Choctaw, Osage, Quapaw and Cherokee Indians. To the perseverance and industry of Judge Williams much credit is due for the success of this enterprise. The corner stone of the stone building was laid June 13, 1936, with appropriate ceremonies in the presence of thousands of interested citizens, Indians and whites.

At the northern limits of the town of Calhoun, Georgia, stands a monument to Sequoyah, surmounted by a large figure intended to represent the American Cadmus. This was designed and constructed in 1927 by W. L. Hillhouse of Calhoun, and paid for by the Calhoun Woman's Club. Two miles east of this monument on the Chatsworth road is the site of New Echota, the former capitol of the Cherokee Nation, where stood the printing office of the *Cherokee Phoenix*. On this spot is a Cherokee Indian memorial designed and constructed by Mr. Hillhouse, paid for by an act of Congress, and dedicated in 1931. On two faces of the monument are bronze tablets containing information about the Cherokee people; one of these refers to the alphabet invented by Sequoyah and the Cherokee newspaper published there. Through the influence of Robert Sparks Walker of Chattanooga, the old Crutchfield Spring eight miles south of that city, and at the foot of Lookout Mountain, was recently formally re-christened "Sequoyah Spring," by the Cumberlands Hiking Club. He is also heading a movement with promise of success, to change the name of Monroe County, Tennessee, to "Sequoyah County."

Most significant and lasting memorial to the immortal Sequoyah is the learning and culture of a fine body of Americans, the Cherokee people. Their advanced position in society directly traceable to Sequoyah's works, exercised a beneficent influence on other tribes of Indians and contributed substantially to the civilization of the new state of which they are a part.

INDEX

UNIVERSITY OF OKLAHOMA PRESS : NORMAN